Let the Lions Roar!

THE EVOLUTION OF BROOKFIELD ZOO

Let the Lions

Chicago Zoological Society 1997

Roar!

THE EVOLUTION OF BROOKFIELD ZOO

Andrea Friederici Ross

First Edition

Library of Congress Catalog Card Number 97-66395

ISBN 0-913934-24-0

Brookfield Zoo is owned by the Forest Preserve District of Cook County and managed by the Chicago Zoological Society.

Chicago Zoological Society, Brookfield, Illinois 60513

Printing: Worzalla   Design: Quick+Faust   Editorial contributions: Chris Howes   Printed in the United States of America on recycled paper.

Contents

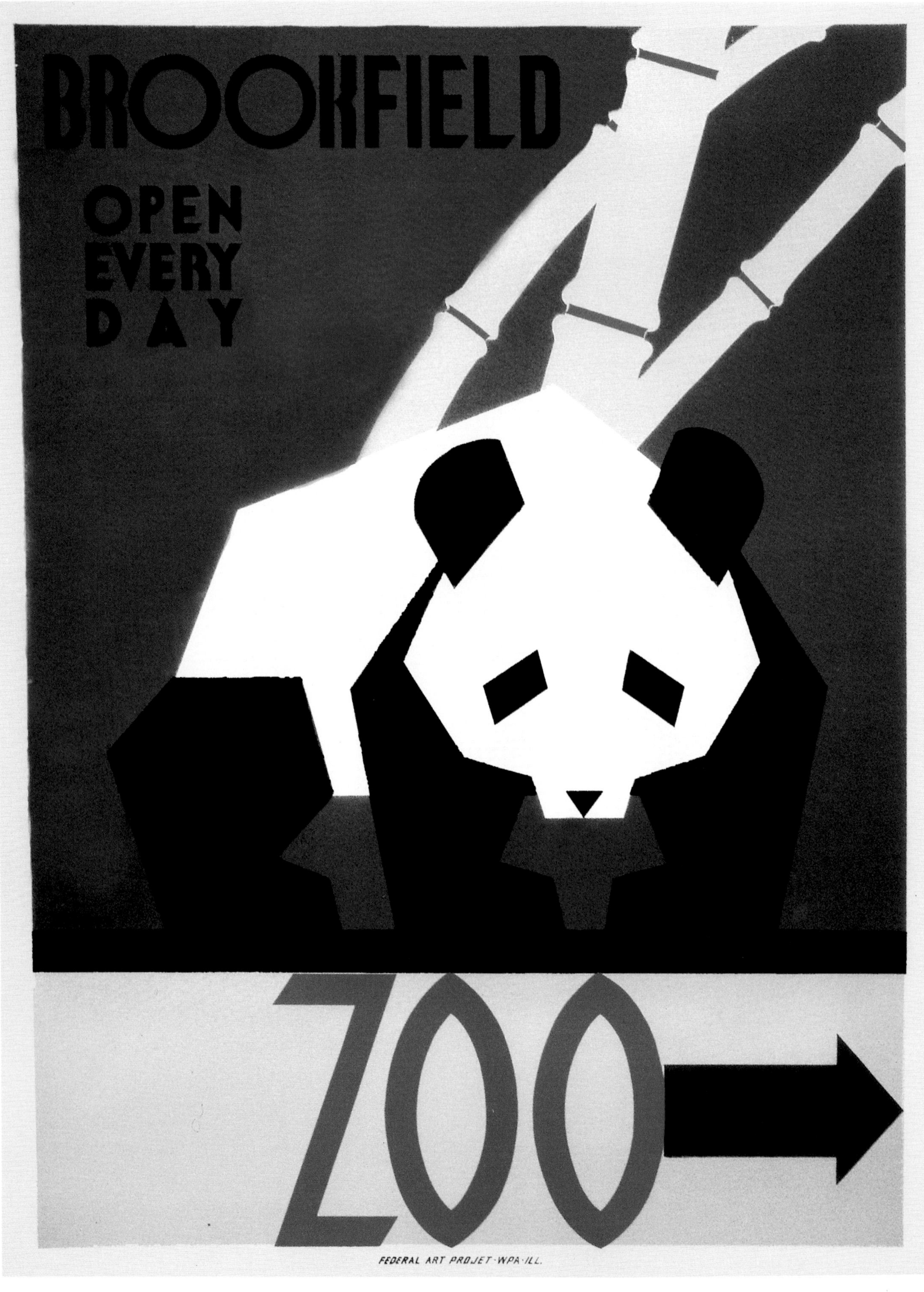

BROOKFIELD

OPEN EVERY DAY

ZOO →

FEDERAL ART PROJET·WPA·ILL.

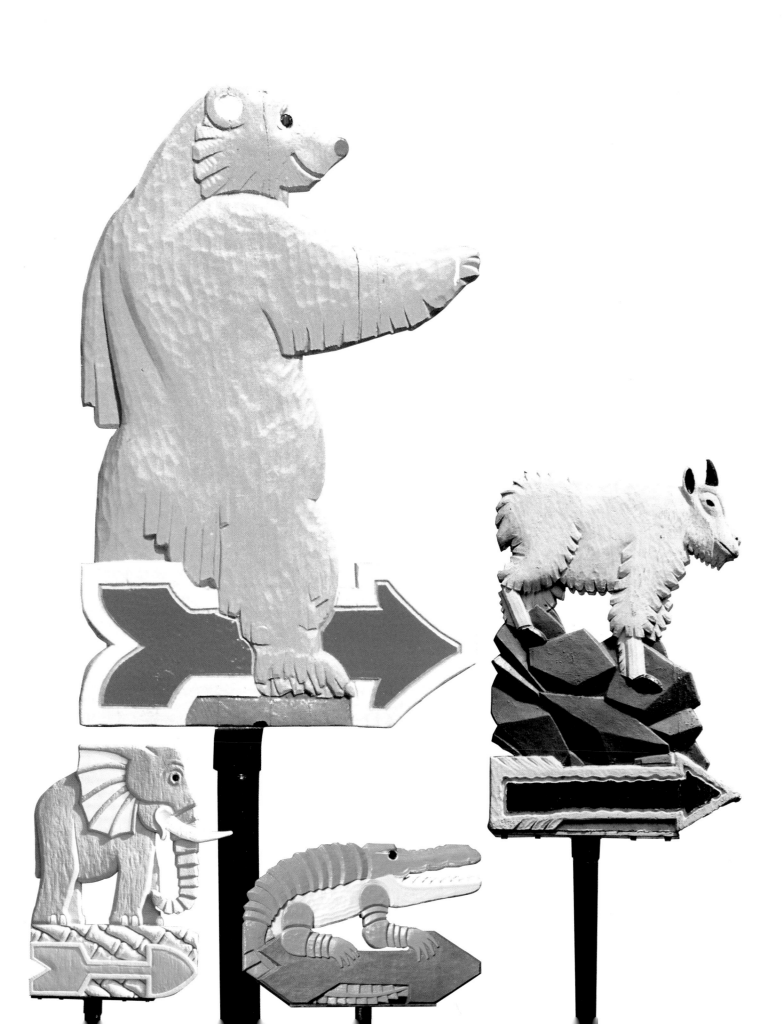

Writing a history of Brookfield Zoo is a bit like shooting at a moving target: it never stands still. A trademark of the zoo throughout its history has been that even at its proudest moments, even while celebrating new exhibits, the institution looks forward to the next challenge, the even bigger hurdle. Perhaps this is what keeps it changing so rapidly—and what makes its history so riveting.

The ways in which Brookfield Zoo has changed over the years are many and varied. The budget expanded from an estimated $50,000 in 1926 (approximately $400,000 in today's dollars) to $38 million in 1996. The staff began as a few dozen keepers and a handful of administrators. Today, that number reaches nearly 1,000 employees on a summer day. The scope of operations has grown tremendously, and it now includes school and subscription programs, gift shops, special events such as Holiday Magic and Zoo Run Run, the travel program, lecture series, conservation efforts in Australia and Florida, behavioral research, animal nutrition and genetic programs, and a half-dozen in-house publications.

A quick look at one building neatly illustrates exactly how much the zoo has evolved. When it was built in 1933, Primate House was a typical indoor exhibit. It enjoyed a central location on the zoo's formal mall, and its architecture matched that of all other early buildings: Italian Renaissance, with cream-colored brick walls, red tile roofs, and impressive stone columns. Inside, it featured unembellished cages side by side, with mammoth skylights flooding the building with natural light.

The zoo's Board of Trustees felt that primates, as a vital and engaging part of the animal kingdom, should be displayed in their own building. The architect was told to design a building for primates, and he did so, with appropriate cage sizes, ventilation, and heating and cooling systems. Aside from the animals in their cages, signs identifying species, and lush plantings that grew around the tall gibbon cages under the central skylights, there wasn't much in the building.

When Brookfield Zoo decided to renovate the building in the 1990s, the staff team responsible for the project was given a much different charge than the one the architect had received 60 years earlier. They were told to design an exhibit that illustrates the many benefits humans derive from natural systems and that motivates people to actively protect the environment. They had the freedom to choose the best animals, habitats, and educational techniques for getting the message across. In March 1996, the building reopened as The Swamp.

Prologue

Opposite and this page: The changes to Primate House have been as important as the animals that have lived in the building throughout Brookfield Zoo's history. The outside has not changed much, although the exterior cages that once held peering orangutans have been turned into a greenhouse. Inside, an alligator glimpsed through the swamp mist thrills visitors where a mother and her children regarded gibbons from the other side of a grill of iron.

In the 60 years between the two projects, not only did exhibit design advance tremendously, the zoo changed its reason for existence. Displaying a variety of animals for visitor recreation and education is no longer sufficient. Today, the zoo aims to inspire each and every visitor to live more in harmony with the natural world. All new exhibits are designed with this challenge.

The differences between the two exhibits are indicative of the old philosophy of zoo design versus the new one. The first time, a lone architect was responsible for designing the facility, a task he accomplished in only a few weeks. The second time, an assortment of specially trained individuals argued long and hard—for several years, in fact—until they agreed on what habitat best conveys their assigned message.

In the early years, the role of a primate keeper was merely to care for the animals. Today, the responsibilities of a Swamp keeper include visitor education and research along with animal management.

Initially, the building housed only primates, displaying them taxonomically and as the only interpretive approach. The Swamp now features a complete ecosystem, including reptiles, birds, amphibians, mammals, insects, fish, and plants. It incorporates murals, mist, plantings, boardwalks, and over 100 signs, many interactive, to help create a mood and, more importantly, to convey a message.

Finally, the cost of erecting Primate House was $175,000, while The Swamp required $5 million before it was completed.

It is a remarkable tale of evolution. As you read through this history, you will no doubt notice the changes. At the same time, though, don't lose sight of what hasn't changed: the unmistakable delight of a child seeing an elephant for the first time, a parent teaching a child about the natural world, a family picnicking on the mall, a young couple walking hand in hand, grandparents pushing babies in strollers.

And while animal management has been through a revolution all its own, the pictures of giraffes, polar bears, lions, penguins, and snakes in this book are essentially timeless. One thing in particular has remained the same: there is no such thing as an "ordinary" day at the zoo.

Please let me conclude with one note about how this book is arranged. The chapters are sequenced chronologically, but each chapter follows a specific theme. Occasionally, an event described within a chapter appears out of sequence because, thematically, it finds a better fit in that chapter. This is not meant to confuse you but rather to help organize this tale of evolution.

Andrea Friederici Ross
March 1997

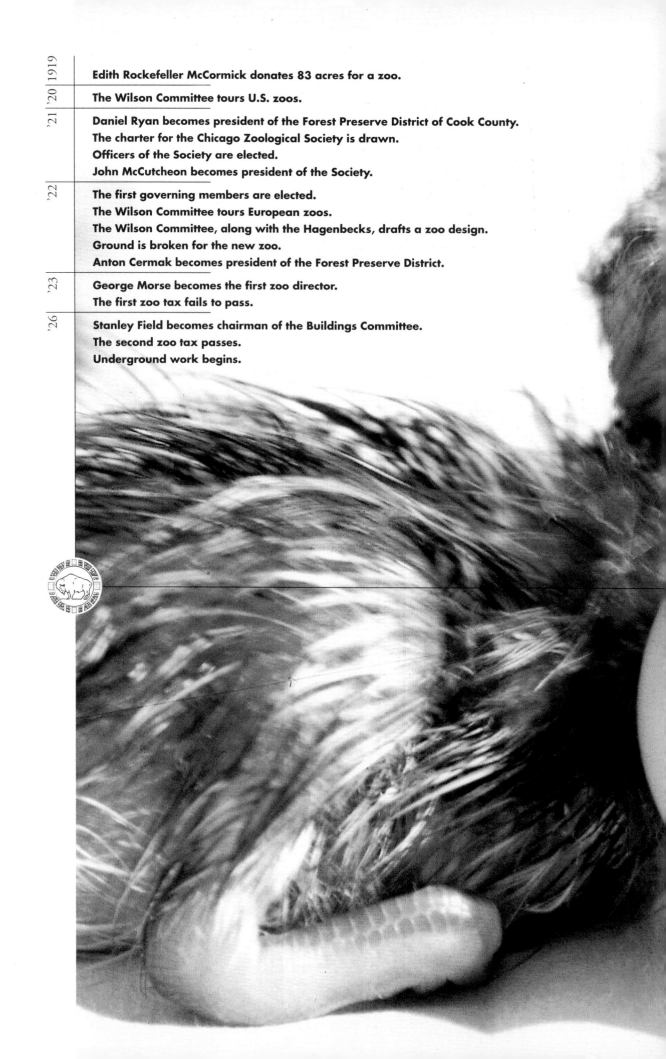

1919 Edith Rockefeller McCormick donates 83 acres for a zoo.

'20 The Wilson Committee tours U.S. zoos.

'21 Daniel Ryan becomes president of the Forest Preserve District of Cook County.
The charter for the Chicago Zoological Society is drawn.
Officers of the Society are elected.
John McCutcheon becomes president of the Society.

'22 The first governing members are elected.
The Wilson Committee tours European zoos.
The Wilson Committee, along with the Hagenbecks, drafts a zoo design.
Ground is broken for the new zoo.
Anton Cermak becomes president of the Forest Preserve District.

'23 George Morse becomes the first zoo director.
The first zoo tax fails to pass.

'26 Stanley Field becomes chairman of the Buildings Committee.
The second zoo tax passes.
Underground work begins.

CHAPTER ONE

Getting Started

(1919-1926)

Edith Rockefeller McCormick

Edith Rockefeller McCormick

An unusual woman made Brookfield Zoo possible. In December 1919, Edith Rockefeller McCormick offered to donate 83 acres of land near the town of Riverside to the Forest Preserve District of Cook County for the express purpose of creating a large, modern zoo. Daughter of wealthy industrialist John D. Rockefeller and wife of agricultural machinery manufacturer Harold F. McCormick, Edith Rockefeller McCormick was an enormously rich woman and the grande dame of Chicago in the years preceding and during the 1920s.

Some of her interests were quite odd. She believed strongly in reincarnation and would pay $25,000 for her horoscope, in those days a considerable fortune worth over $200,000 in today's dollars. She studied philosophy ("My object in the world," she once said, "is to think new thoughts") and considered herself the reincarnation of Ankn-es-en-pa-Aten, Tutankhamen's child bride. These unconventional interests led, in a roundabout way, to the donation of land that was to become Brookfield Zoo.

McCormick was drawn to a new school of thought led by doctors Sigmund Freud and Carl Jung: psychoanalysis. Bored with her lot in Chicago and embarrassed by talk of unfaithfulness in her marriage, she decided to see firsthand what Dr. Jung's philosophy was about, so she left for Switzerland, presumably for a few months. In the end, her stay lasted eight years.

During her residence in Switzerland, McCormick visited several large "barless" zoos in European countries. These zoos, modeled on the naturalistic designs of Carl Hagenbeck of the Hagenbeck Zoo in Stellingen, Germany, featured spacious enclosures surrounded by moats instead of bars and incorporated extensive landscaping to make the exhibits look natural. They inspired her to create something similar in Chicago.

McCormick decided she wanted Chicago to have a zoo with more space than the existing Lincoln Park Zoo could offer, one that would promote the kind of scientific research on animals that might contribute to knowledge about "the human soul," in her words. It was an opportunity to create something new, unique, and lasting, and it fit right in with her self-appointed mission to "think new thoughts." After several years of psychotherapy and searching for her own soul, here was a chance for a scientific look at what lay within the human soul.

REACHING THE HUMAN SOUL

On January 26, 1923, two Chicago papers, the *Daily News* and the *Chicago Daily Tribune*, ran stories on a speech Edith Rockefeller McCormick had given the day before at the city's Union League Club. During her talk, McCormick discussed her reasons for her gift of land as the foundation of a zoo.

It is interesting to note how the two reporters heard some of the same words, yet printed different quotes.

From the *Daily News*:

"My fundamental idea in giving Chicago this opportunity for establishing a zoological garden of sufficient size to afford a duplication of the native haunts of animals was born not from my personal love of animals, but from my devotion to human beings. It is important that we have opportunity for scientific study of the processes in animals that we may better understand the processes in ourselves and thus be of material aid to those whom we call neurotics. The gardens will supply a practical laboratory to the children, who, in time, will be taught the theoretical side of zoology in the schools. At present little is known of the science of psychology of animals. When we can make scientific deductions of the actions and reactions of animals, we will find ourselves in a position to reach the human soul."

From the *Chicago Daily Tribune*:

"I want to tell you the real reason for my foundation of the zoo. I am considered the mother of the zoo and I want to give to the public for the first time my innermost motive. It is for the study of the psychology of animals. This is a science of which little is known. When we can make scientific deductions of the actions and reactions of animals we will find ourselves in a position to reach the human being. We must get nearer animals to reach the human soul."

Aside from McCormick's noble plans, there were other, perhaps less altruistic, reasons for the gift. The land was part of a larger tract given to her by her father, and she had been selling lots for development. Some had sold, but interest was simply not what she had hoped. It began to look like a rather poor, time-consuming, energy-intensive investment.

Later, zoo leader John McCutcheon summed it up. "This Zoological project," he said, "is the child of a real estate failure. Mrs. Edith Rockefeller McCormick had a large tract of land out near Riverside. It was laid out as a subdivision. A few folks bought lots, but the customers weren't standing in line. Each year the tax bill came in, and they kept coming in during Mrs. McCormick's eight years in Switzerland. All in all, things could have been better from her point of view. And as a solution of this situation, she offered her land to the Cook County Commissioners with the condition that it be used as a great modern zoo such as she had seen abroad. Also the Commissioners were to assume the back taxes. So it was an ill wind that blew us good. It blew a first-class zoo into the lap of Chicagoland."

Strangely, once the land donation was finalized, McCormick's involvement was minimal. She attended a few planning meetings, but emotionally she was never fully invested. With her fortune, she might have endowed the zoo for life or donated enough funds to get it off the ground, but her financial donations went to other projects.

Edith Rockefeller McCormick's story does not end happily. In the late 1920s, she went to work on a new project: Edithton, her own city. She spent millions of dollars buying up land, excavating, and developing plans for a posh city on Chicago's lakefront. Her idea was to create a Palm Beach-type neighborhood just south of Kenosha, Wisconsin, a place for the grandly affluent to live and mingle. It was, after all, the extravagant '20s.

When the stock market crash of 1929 hit, McCormick's finances were depleted. Here was a woman whose possessions had been the envy of Chicago, who had owned single pieces of jewelry worth over $2 million—virtually penniless. Edithton was not to be. Her brother, John D. Rockefeller, Jr., came to her rescue by installing her with a strict, though abundant, daily allowance of $1,000. The knock-out punch came about the same time as her financial ruin: McCormick discovered she had cancer. She bravely tried to cure herself by psychology, but in vain. She died in 1932, at the age of 60.

But the gift of land in 1919 was enough to start a zoo. Certainly the Forest Preserve District commissioners realized what they were getting when McCormick donated the land: a fine tract with considerable potential, few strings attached, and little long-term oversight or involvement by the benefactor. While representing a certain amount of work and cost on their own part, it was a good deal.

Public announcement of Edith Rockefeller McCormick's gift was made by the Forest Preserve District Board on December 30, 1919. The next day, the *Chicago Tribune* made the following editorial comment under the headline "The New Zoo."

"Although Chicago has had an excellent zoo, of its kind, in Lincoln Park for years, other great cities are far ahead of us in this field. The modern type of zoological garden, evolved by Hagenbeck, is superior to the older type represented at Lincoln Park because it allows us to see wild animals virtually at large; not penned up in a small cage, but free and natural in action and habit. The great park at Hamburg which Hagenbeck created is one of the wonders of the world.... Mrs. McCormick deserves public thanks for her interesting gift."

A decade earlier, the Chicago Plan Commission, a committee planning the overall development of the city, had stated that Chicago needed a new zoo, a great zoo, one much larger than Lincoln Park Zoo could ever be. And so it was only natural that McCormick's gift be received with delight.

There was at first some confusion among the public about how much land had been donated. Some reports told of up to 300 acres. The deed actually covered 83.13 acres. With adjacent lands already in public hands for use as streets, the total came to just over 100 acres. Later, the Forest Preserve District threw in an additional 98 acres, land that had been bought from McCormick two years earlier, bringing the total to nearly 200 acres.

The Forest Preserve District spent the next three years planning and organizing. President Peter Reinberg quickly convened a committee of commissioners, led by Frank Wilson and including William Maclean and George Miller, to study the idea. Reinberg also organized a Special Citizens Committee to help investigate whether the project had civic support. The Citizens Committee, no shabby assemblage, included Art Institute of Chicago president Charles Hutchinson; Chicago Plan Commission head Charles Wacker; *Chicago Tribune* publisher Colonel Robert McCormick; Judson Stone, manager of the McCormick real-estate interests; and Chicago Telephone Company chairman Bernard Sunny.

Right: On November 30, 1920, many important men met to launch the Chicago Zoological Society. Standing from left to right are William Huebsch, Judson F. Stone, George A. Miller, A. D. Weiner, Henry Zender, and Joseph Dillabough. Seated from left to right are Frank J. Wilson, Charles H. Wacker, Peter Reinberg, and Charles L. Hutchinson.

Charles L. Hutchinson

The Chicago Zoological Society

The Chicago Zoological Society was chartered on February 7, 1921. Four days later, at the first regular meeting of the trustees of the Society, Charles Hutchinson set forth the following mission for the institution: "The foundation, maintenance and control of Zoological Parks and Gardens and other collections; the promotion of Zoology and kindred subjects; the instruction and recreation of the people; the collection, holding and expenditure of funds for zoological research and publication; the protection of wild life; and kindred purposes."

Bylaws were modeled after those of The Art Institute of Chicago and the New York Zoological Society. From the very beginning, Peter Reinberg had declared that the Society was to be led by "a nonpolitical board of most suitable members.... Politics, which though many of its phases are admirable, has others that, when its functions are misused, are very undesirable, must not be allowed to dictate in this. In that event, I am confident that we shall create an enterprise which will invite the peoples of all the world to marvel and praise."

Sadly, Forest Preserve District president Reinberg, whose support was largely responsible for getting the project off the ground, died in February 1921, robbing the zoo of one of its greatest and most influential advocates. It was fortunate that Reinberg's successor, Daniel Ryan, also became a strong zoo advocate.

Enthusiasm was high in those early days, and much was accomplished quickly. The Wilson Committee of Forest Preserve District commissioners had already gone on a whirlwind tour of some of the nation's largest zoos at the time—in New York, Washington, D.C., Philadelphia, Buffalo, St. Louis, and Cincinnati—to gather ideas and learn. The land outside of Riverside was examined for its appropriateness as a zoo, not just by local officials, but also by national and international zoological authorities, such as Heinrich and Lorenz Hagenbeck, sons of Carl Hagenbeck and leaders in the barless zoo concept; William Hornaday of the New York Zoo; and Henry Muskopf of the St. Louis Zoo.

Excitement began to build in neighboring communities, such as Brookfield and Riverside, with each laying claim to the zoo. Some angry articles were written in local papers. "How come all this talk of the zoo being at Riverside?" a Brookfield resident was quoted as saying to a *Suburban Magnet* reporter. "We have stood a whole lot from places nearby which try to claim everything within miles, and it's about time they quit that game." But most local citizens were simply excited at the big happenings and hopeful that events would mean more business and more money for their town.

John Tinney McCutcheon

At the December 13, 1921, trustee meeting of the Society, officers were elected and an Executive Committee was formed. Charles Hutchinson was a natural choice for the first president of the Society, but he expressly stated he would not consider the position as he was too involved in other projects. Instead, via letter, he contacted *Chicago Tribune* cartoonist John Tinney McCutcheon on the island in the Bahamas the artist owned and frequented several months each year.

In his autobiography, McCutcheon recalls, "As I was sitting unsuspectingly under a palm tree down on the Island...there came a letter from Charles L. Hutchinson, long president of the Art Institute and one of Chicago's most valuable citizens. He explained the formation of the Chicago Zoological Society and asked me to accept the presidency. As I look back, I am quite aware that I had few of the qualifications necessary for the executive management of a project involving millions of dollars. While I do not now recall the process of reasoning which led to my acceptance, I suspect two motives, one above criticism, the other natural but not so noble. This latter reason was doubtless the gratification of my vanity; the more virtuous one was the feeling that men who benefit from their citizenship should be willing to serve in civic affairs. Here seemed a chance to do something for the city which had done so much for me."

Perhaps a cartoonist wouldn't be the first person many people would consider for running a zoo, but in this case it was a match made in heaven. McCutcheon was the *Tribune* cartoonist for over 40 years, and his work often graced the front page of the paper residents read over breakfast. He brought smiles and chuckles to millions of readers. His story "Injun Summer," about an imaginative Indiana boy daydreaming haystacks into tepees, became a Chicago classic to be reprinted every autumn.

An admirer of McCutcheon's once wrote him a letter praising a recent cartoon. "Welcome back to Chicago, which, as far as I can tell, belongs to you anyway," went the opening statement. McCutcheon was an inspired choice for president of the Society because his stature as cartoonist gave him entry to any and all Chicago institutions and organizations. He was a welcome guest anywhere and counted such influential men as former President Teddy Roosevelt among his friends. In the early days of the zoo, which proved to be quite controversial, this characteristic was invaluable.

John T. McCutcheon

The Society Gains Steam

Along with election of officers, the December 1921 meeting provided an opportunity to posthumously enroll Peter Reinberg as the Society's first member, in tribute to the man who had gotten the zoo off the ground.

Twenty-five trustees were selected, and the Society began to assemble governing members. The Commercial Club of Chicago, whose members were influential movers in the city's affairs, agreed to sponsor the zoo and helped considerably by identifying suitable people.

The first 49 governing members were elected on January 18, 1922. The list reads like a *Who's Who in Chicago* for the period: John Borden, Thomas E. Donnelley, Charles G. Dawes, Samuell Insull, Robert P. Lamont, John T. Pirie, Martin A. Ryerson, Howard Van Doren Shaw, John G. Shedd, James Simpson, and Charles H. Thorne, among others. The McCormick clan had ample representation, with Edith and her former husband, Harold, on the governing member list, as well as cousin and *Tribune* publisher Colonel Robert McCormick. Other McCormicks would join the Society in later years.

In the summer of 1922, the members of the Forest Preserve District's Wilson Committee and chief engineer Emmett Flavin continued their education on a tour of European zoos. (While the three commissioners from the Committee were so committed to the project that each paid his own way, Flavin's expenses were covered by the Forest Preserve District, a fact that later irritated various members of the media and public, as the zoo project had yet to be publicly approved.) The group toured zoos in London, Rotterdam, Amsterdam, Hamburg, Berlin, Frankfurt, and Munich, among others. Flavin remained in Hamburg with the Hagenbeck brothers to draw up a design for the new zoo, not returning to Chicago until October.

Also in 1922, William Hornaday, head of the New York Zoo and a nationally recognized expert on zoos, gave a speech to the Society (at a substantial $500 cost to the Forest Preserve District) urging it to proceed with the project and reaffirming the Society's belief in the worth of the endeavor.

Above: In 1922, the Wilson Committee visited the Hagenbecks' park in Germany to help in drafting a design for their new zoo. Pictured from left to right are F. Mehrmann, Emmett Flavin, Heinrich Hagenbeck, Emmett Whealan, Lorenz Hagenbeck, Frank J. Wilson, Fritz Wegner, and Bartley Burg.

GLOSSARY

The Chicago Zoological Society: The nonprofit organization managing the operations of Brookfield Zoo and other endeavors related to the Chicago Zoological Society's mission.

Brookfield Zoo: The 216-acre zoological park located in Brookfield and Riverside, Illinois, as well as all of the zoo's animals, research, and programs.

The Forest Preserve District of Cook County: The official owner of Brookfield Zoo that sets admission and parking rates and oversees allocation of tax revenues to the Chicago Zoological Society.

Governing Membership: The volunteer body of local leaders who oversee the business of the Chicago Zoological Society.

Board of Trustees: The elected subset of the governing membership of about 30 people that meets several times annually to set policy, make decisions, and develop recommendations for the full governing membership.

Executive Committee: The subset of the Board of Trustees responsible for making decisions between Board meetings and for making recommendations to the full Board.

Annual Meeting: The annual event in which the governing membership comes together to listen to trustees' reports on Society business.

President: The volunteer head of the Board of Trustees. (The title has been changed to chairman.)

Director: The paid staff member hired to direct the day-to-day operations of Brookfield Zoo; the chief executive officer.

Said Hornaday, who never lacked in vocabulary or opinion, "Mr. Chairman and gentlemen: I have had my ear to the ground for several years, listening for the rumble of this event. I call it an event because I look upon it, as I think the most of you do, as the beginning of a great, new scientific and popular institution for the city of Chicago. I felt sure that the time would come when the best and the strongest men of Chicago would get together around a luncheon table and decide that the time had come to establish in Chicago a zoological park commensurate with the intelligence and wealth of the population of this, the second greatest city in the United States. Now, that hour seems to have arrived.

"In these days of turmoil, unrest, vanity and cussedness all over the world, really it is delightful to find men who are willing to leave their mirth and their enjoyment and to devote their time, their money, and their hard labor to the creation of a new institution for the betterment of mankind. You have it easily in your power, gentlemen, with the foundation of real estate and forest and waters, which we inspected yesterday, to develop without loss of time in the city of Chicago an institution that will immediately become famous, and that will be of immense educational and recreational benefit to the three million people of Chicago; and that also will be one of the great show places of Chicago for people coming to Chicago from without."

October 1922 found the work of the Society well along, and it was decided that a groundbreaking was in order. Accordingly, a special ceremony marking the turning of the first shovel of soil was scheduled for Friday, October 27, chosen because it was the birthday of former President Teddy Roosevelt, widely considered the country's leading naturalist. The ceremony was held at 2:00 p.m. at a special speaker's stand erected just south of today's South Gate. John McCutcheon, Charles Wacker, and Daniel Ryan, among others, addressed several hundred attendees.

Wacker, as head of the Chicago Plan Commission, expressed his excitement at the opportunities this new zoo afforded. "So we are present at the beginning of an enterprise for the people of Cook County, the advantages of which I venture to say none of us can appreciate today in their full magnitude. Think of the benefits, educational, recreational, and financial, which a zoological garden, ideally located and wisely developed as this one will be, will bring. What a source of delight and instruction such a place will be to persons of all ages; from the children who can barely toddle to the grandparents who will take them!

"All alike will be fascinated to watch, in an environment that is appropriate, the movements of animals and birds that otherwise would be as unreal to them as the goblins that they can only read about. We miss half the joy of life if we do not know nature, and this Zoological Garden will help our people to that knowledge.

"So hopefully, happily, as we look into the future and picture all it will mean, we turn the first earth in what we confidently believe will be the finest zoological garden in the world, and a boon to the people of Chicago."

By 1923, the governing membership had grown substantially and included Colonel George Buckingham, John Eastman, Samuel and Wallace Evans, Marshall Field, Cyrus McCormick, Joy Morton, Honore and Potter Palmer, Charles Schweppe, and William Wrigley, Jr. Governing member Robert McCormick had even approached his publishing colleague, William Randolph Hearst, about joining the Society, but the New York-based Hearst had declined.

George Frederick Morse, Jr.

January 1923 brought another new figure to the zoo. The Board decided it needed a salaried manager to run the affairs of the Society and, eventually, the zoo. For advice, McCutcheon turned to William Hornaday, who recommended two men: Emerson Brown, director of the Philadelphia Zoo, and George Frederick Morse, Jr., director of the Boston Zoological Garden.

Hornaday summed up Morse and his job situation as only he could...and with emphasis on certain characteristics not usually mentioned in more modern descriptions of individuals. "A sudden turn of fortune's wheel has injected outrageous politics into the Boston Zoological Garden, utterly destroying the morale of the force, and rendering it necessary for its director [George Morse] to resign in order to maintain his own self-respect. A disreputable keeper was, after many offenses, finally reported to the Park Board and was dismissed by that body. Mayor Curley decided that the German keeper should be reinstated in order to have the German vote, which he was seeking.... The offensive German keeper has been reinstated. The force of keepers is now thoroughly demoralized, and Mr. Morse intends to resign immediately. This renders him available for another position, and it gives me the greatest pleasure to nominate him to you as a candidate for the position of director for the Chicago Zoological Park.

"His full name is George Frederick Morse, Jr.; age 38 years; married, with two children. He was born in Philadelphia, but has lived 37 years in Massachusetts. Physically he is a man of fine presence and a most agreeable personality; his height is six feet; his weight is 178 pounds, and he is physically perfect. His dignified bearing immediately impresses those who become acquainted with him.... It may interest you to know further that Mr. Morse comes of pure native American stock. His great, great-grandfather, on his mother's side, was commander in chief of the American army after Washington, and his great, great-grandfather on his father's side, John Craft, once owned a considerable portion of the city of Chicago."

With this glowing recommendation, the Executive Committee decided on Morse, and he was hired effective January 1, 1923, at an annual salary of $5,000.

George F. Morse, Jr.

Left: In October 1922, ground for the new zoo was broken by Forest Preserve District president Daniel Ryan (with the spade). Also present were William Maclean, Henry Zender, John T. McCutcheon, James Simpson, William Busse, Charles H. Wacker, George A. Miller, Mrs. Daniel Ryan, Bartley Burg, Mrs. Peter Reinberg, and Frank J. Wilson.

Preparing for the Vote

Despite this flurry of activity, things began to go sour in 1923. The contract between the Chicago Zoological Society and the Forest Preserve District of Cook County spelled out that the Forest Preserve District would own the land and pay for construction and maintenance of buildings out of tax revenues, with the Society responsible for the purchase and care of the animals.

Illinois House Bill 817 was passed June 8, 1923, allowing for this contract and enabling countywide tax collection to support the project. All fine and good, but the contract would not take effect until voters approved the zoo tax. This was slated for the November 6, 1923, election.

The zoo tax was to provide $500,000 a year for five years of construction and approximately $250,000 a year thereafter for building maintenance. For a homeowner paying $100 per year in taxes—most people paid less than that at the time—it would increase the taxes by 40 cents for each of the first five years and 13 cents for each year thereafter.

Zoo supporters maintained that taxpayers would barely feel the tax and that it was certainly a good investment. After all, they argued, a new zoo would make Chicago a more desirable place to live, increasing tourism. Just look at the New York Zoo, they said, with one million visitors each year, hundreds of thousands of them prolonging their stay to visit the zoo. They maintained that the revenue of the merchants and hotels of New York City was increased by several million dollars each year—because of the city's zoo.

It's important to note that from the outset, the Society's trustees had no intention of building just another zoo. Every speech, every article, every mention made of the zoo refers to it as the world's greatest zoo. Here was a chance for the city of Chicago to leap ahead and create a modern park on a large tract of land and attract notice from around the world. While the New York Zoo was considered forward-thinking and the zoos in Philadelphia, St. Louis, and Washington, D.C. were quite appealing as well, the opportunity to build a new zoo entirely from scratch on such a large property was unique in the United States. And while Chicago already had Lincoln Park Zoo, this was to be one on an entirely different scale than Chicagoans had ever imagined.

THE DETAILS OF THE DEAL

On January 26, 1920, during a meeting of the Forest Preserve District commissioners, President Peter Reinberg offered a resolution that set the building of the zoo into motion.

Peter Reinberg

"Whereas, Mrs. Edith Rockefeller McCormick has generously offered to transfer forever to the Forest Preserve District of Cook County, a valuable Tract of Land for the establishment of a Zoological Garden, and

"Whereas, In order to stabilize and perpetuate this enterprise, it becomes necessary to take certain preliminary steps in the premises,

"Therefore, Be it Resolved:

"First: The Board of Forest Preserve Commissioners of Cook County, deeply appreciate the noble generosity and public spirit that moved Mrs. Edith Rockefeller McCormick to offer as a gift such valuable land for the benefit of the people.

"Second: The Board of Forest Preserve Commissioners herewith accepts the gift on behalf of the District and expresses its heartfelt thanks on behalf of the District and behalf of the people to the donor.

"Third: The property donated shall be maintained in perpetuity as a zoological garden.

"Fourth: The said Zoological Gardens shall be developed annually and in units and be fully completed as a zoological garden within five years.

"Fifth: An amount no less than Five Thousand Dollars shall be appropriated in the next Annual Budget for the purpose of beginning actual work on the establishment of the garden, and additional adequate amounts shall be appropriated from year to year, for the purpose of establishing and maintaining such garden.

"Sixth: All lots within the limits of the tract shall be acquired by the District, either by purchase or condemnation and become a part of the Zoological Garden and be maintained in perpetuity for this purpose.

"Seventh: All unpaid taxes and special assessments shall be paid by the District.

"Eighth: All streets within the limits of the tracks shall be vacated; except if necessary, Golf and Forbes Roads.

"Ninth: The officers of the District are hereby authorized to take all legal steps necessary to receive said gift, and to obtain title to said land for the District and to have all of above conditions inserted in the Deed of Gift to be obtained."

John McCutcheon and others went out stumping, bringing people up-to-date on developments, drumming up interest, and generating support. They spoke at clubs and gatherings and wrote editorials for the newspapers. McCutcheon, with his unique angle at influencing the public, featured the zoo in several of his front-page cartoons.

The proposed zoo had many well-placed supporters, but it had vocal and powerful opposition as well. The City Club, a rival of the Commercial Club in terms of Chicago leadership, came out strongly against the zoo. The Chicago Federation of Labor, the Chicago Bureau of Public Efficiency, the Cook County real-estate board, and the Chicago Civic Federation, among others, all urged their constituents to vote against the zoo. McCutcheon and Colonel McCormick's paper, the *Tribune*, was in favor, as was its chief competitor, the *Herald Examiner*, but many less prestigious papers, such as the *Daily Journal*, were relentless in their opposition.

It wasn't that people didn't want this state-of-the-art zoo. Rather, they objected to the way the zoo was to be obtained, constructed, and managed. Most Chicagoans didn't believe that Edith Rockefeller McCormick donated the land for philanthropic reasons, and much attention was paid to the back taxes on the land, as well as to the other conditions of her gift.

McCormick's gift did have restrictions: that the tract be used and maintained as a zoological garden to be known as the Chicago Zoological Garden of the Forest Preserve (although today the official name is the Chicago Zoological Park, it became known informally as Brookfield Zoo, a handier and catchier moniker); that the zoo be opened within five years; that taxes and assessments be assumed by the Forest Preserve District; that adjacent lands be acquired to complete the rectangle lying between the Des Plaines River and Salt Creek; and that the land revert back to her possession if it were no longer used as a zoo.

The value of the gift of land was put at $140,000. Taxes and assessments due on the land totaled $20,500. Much was made in the press of this $20,500, as many people intimated that losing this debt was the real reason for McCormick's gift.

Public Opposition to the Zoo

Some citizens felt that McCormick was to profit from the zoo in other ways. One of her conditions required acquisition of lots throughout the zoo, and people speculated that these were to be bought from her at a profit. In fact, Forest Preserve District records do show payments totaling approximately $23,000 over several years to McCormick for lots on zoo property, although it is hard to believe that the millionaire would be concerned over what would be to her such small amounts.

Other opponents believed that McCormick's condition that the land revert back to her estate if not used as a zoo was unfair. They reasoned that tax money was to be used to improve the land, so she would benefit from increased real-estate value.

While zoo supporters referred to the project as the "new zoo" or the "Riverside zoo"—the land was and remains half in Riverside, half in Brookfield—many detractors called the project the "McCormick zoo," insisting that it was to be a tribute to Edith Rockefeller McCormick. Although the trustees discussed various ways of honoring the benefactress, she had clearly stipulated up front that the zoo be called the Chicago Zoological Garden of the Forest Preserve.

With their high hopes for and serious concerns about this new undertaking, Riverside and Brookfield residents were unsure which way to vote. They had a mass meeting the Friday night prior to the election to hear arguments, both pro and con. Morse spoke in favor of the zoo, while Chicago alderman Wiley W. Mills took the opposition.

Director Morse tried to dispel some concerns. "If the zoo is established," he said, "curious strangers will not picnic on your front lawn, congest your streets nor parade your thoroughfares flying toy balloons and blowing horns. The park will be so big you will hardly notice the noise of the animals. An insurmountable wall that no animal save a monkey can climb will enclose the park insuring against animals escaping the enclosure. There will be no smell whatsoever. They are fed as good food as you have on your own table. This will be a model zoo—a thing that will attract attention to the whole world! Car lines will unload directly at the zoo gate. Although the automobile traffic will be enormous, none of it need traverse Riverside streets."

Alderman Mills also spoke his mind. "I am opposed to the McCormick Zoo because it is primarily a real estate speculation. I am also opposed because when the people have it all paid for they wake up to the sad knowledge that they don't own it and that the animals, paid for out of public funds, can be sold by the directors and the money converted to their use at the expiration of the 25-year contract period."

Mills then summed up the history of the zoo bill, concluding that "ordinarily legislation does not move so swiftly. At least it takes more than 19 days to get legislation through our state legislature. If the project has a true, unselfish motive and is as public spirited as advertised, why was the legislation so quietly and quickly executed? Since last spring the realty company handling the McCormick properties reports that its sales have amounted to more than $1,000,000. However, the greatest objection in my mind is the right the governing body has to dispose of the animals and other zoo accouterments upon the expiration of the 25-year contract."

The *Riverside News* reported that "as a direct contrast to the manner in which the auditors received the speech of Mr. Morse, Mr. Mills had no more than completed his address before the people from all over the hall began firing questions at him." Here are some excerpts:

"Mrs. McCormick has always acquiesced," declared Judge Fred J. McClory, "to anything that might benefit Riverside. In justice to the woman who has done more for Riverside than any other person I know, I believe that bringing her name into proceedings that might be construed as being questionable is entirely out of place."

"Mr. Mills," said Ferdinand Oudin, "if property values increase, which you infer they will, we may all profit instead of lose by the establishment of the zoo here."

"The zoo bill," said Elizabeth Gordin, "was not engineered through both houses as quietly as you say. We knew before the bill was presented that it was coming up and had every opportunity to be present if we wished. The reason the bill passed both houses so quickly was the fact that it carried no opposition."

It appears that the "pro" side prevailed during the mass meeting, as evidenced by A. H. Hein, president of Brookfield, who declared himself in favor of the zoo and said he would be delighted if thousands of visitors made weekly pilgrimages to Brookfield.

"I am for the zoo and don't care if anyone else is or not," he said. "I live two blocks from it and think it will be a great thing. Suppose Mrs. McCormick did make some money from the increase in adjacent land values. Don't we have the same privilege of profiting in the inflation that will come to our holding through Mrs. McCormick's gift? I own an acre of land near the zoo and I haven't witnessed with reluctance its steady increase in value. Mrs. McCormick's gift was a conscientious one and was given with no idea of profit. What are a few dollars to what Mrs. McCormick already has? The zoo will mean better streets, better transportation, better street lighting, and better police facilities. Let the lions roar."

The zoo might have withstood these smaller arguments, but in the end, two larger stumbling blocks brought the project down. First was the issue of the Chicago Zoological Society. Voters were being asked to pay taxes for an institution whereby their hard-earned money would be spent by a private society. This made many people nervous. They felt that some sort of public accountability was necessary if tax money was to be spent.

Many were careful to state that it wasn't that they didn't trust the Society members or the Board of Trustees, per se, but what sort of precedent was this setting? Who could predict what shady institutions might model themselves off this precedent and gain tax money for less noble purposes? And nobody knew who might succeed this highly esteemed Board of the zoo. All in all, it was a scary step to take.

The biggest objection, however, had little to do with the zoo itself. Also on the slate in the November 6 election was a tax increase for schools. The Chicago school system was in trouble: too many children, too few schools, too few seats. Some schools had taken to a double shift of classes: one group of students in the morning, another in the afternoon. Classes were overcrowded, and many educations were at stake. Although a defeat of the zoo bill would not add a single extra school building or additional seat, the two projects were perceived as mutually exclusive. "Schools, not monkeys" became the battle cry.

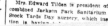

KIDS AND ANIMALS

[Copyright: 1923: By The Chicago Tribune]

Rain, Too, Lend: Share of Roma

BY JAMES O'DONNELL BENN

Great weather for hiking!

Not warm; not too chill, just as the saying is.

The Prairie club, membersh ...ze 15 years, took one of its hikes yesterday.

Nine miles over clean autum ...around spongy edges of swa ...through patches of silent wo...

Above: John McCutcheon's cartoons, which ran on the *Tribune*'s front cover, were an excellent opportunity to influence readers.

Newspaper articles in the *Daily Journal* were clear in their advice: vote against the zoo and for the schools. The November 1 edition of the *Journal* had a different antizoo headline on every page: "To Vote Against the Zoo is Not Enough; Tell Your Friends To Do So," "Higher Taxes Mean Higher Rents; Kill the Zoo Tax to Keep Rents Down," "A Zoo Is a Luxury, Schools Are a Necessity; Vote 'No' on the Zoo Nov. 6," and "Not a Cent for Animals in a Zoo Until Every Child Has a Seat in School." Page two of that issue carried a sample ballot (below) marked to demonstrate how to vote for the school tax and against the zoo.

McCutcheon and his Board members tried their best to counteract these editorial efforts. The front page of the Sunday, November 4, *Tribune* prominently displayed a very prozoo cartoon, and the *Tribune*'s sample ballot showed how to vote for both the zoo and the school tax.

On November 6, 1923, more people voted on the zoo issue than on any other item on the ballot. Residents of the western suburbs voted heavily in favor of the zoo. In Brookfield, 645 voted in favor of the zoo and 163 voted against. In Riverside, 423 voters supported the enterprise, while 322 were opposed. The neighboring communities of Lyons and Western Springs also reported a final tally in support of the zoo.

However, downtown opponents outnumbered zoo supporters as over 93,000 people voted against the zoo. The zoo tax referendum was defeated by a margin of over two to one.

SPECIMEN PROPOSITION BALLOT

PROPOSED ASSENT TO AND AUTHORIZATION OF INCREASE OF SCHOOL TAX LEVY ON ALL TAXABLE PROPERTY IN THE CITY OF CHICAGO FOR BUILDING PURPOSES AND THE PURCHASE OF SCHOOL GROUNDS TO ONE PER CENT UPON THE VALUATION TO BE ASCERTAINED FOR ASSESSMENT FOR STATE AND COUNTY TAXES.	YES	X
Shall assent and authority be given to levy on all taxable property in the City of Chicago a school tax for building purposes and the purchase of school grounds of one per cent upon the valuation of such property to be ascertained for the assessment for State and County taxes, and also assent and authority to the Board of Education of the City of Chicago (and any other necessary officers or public bodies) to cause, require, direct, demand or order such tax to be levied, assessed and collected.	NO	

How to Vote Against Zoo Tax

FOREST PRESERVE PROPOSITION BALLOT

For the adoption of an Act to authorize the commissioners of the Forest Preserve District of Cook County, Illinois, to establish and maintain a zoological park and to levy and collect a tax to pay the cost thereof.	YES	
	NO	X

Hanging On

It's remarkable that the project didn't just die at that point. In fact, things got worse rather than better. Former Forest Preserve District president Dan Ryan died in 1923, and Charles Hutchinson, who had been a leading figure in the project from the very first day, died in October 1924. Several governing members and trustees lost heart and backed out of the project. At that time, the chief source of income for the Society was membership dues from the governing members. In 1923, this brought in $14,900. In 1924, it dropped to $100.

The years 1924 and 1925 were rough for everyone involved with the zoo, primarily for the newly hired director, George Morse. What does the director of a nonexistent zoo do? He aided the Board, which struggled to reconfigure elements of the contract with the Forest Preserve District and convince Edith Rockefeller McCormick to relinquish some of the conditions of her gift. He also spoke before numerous clubs and maintained his contacts in the zoo world.

But as the unfriendly *Daily Journal* reported in one article, "Mr. Morse has busied himself as best he could. There being no zoo to direct; no ringtailed monkeys; no squatty rhinoceri; no giraffes; no chuckling hyenas—why, Mr. Morse felt compelled to turn to literature to earn his $5,000 a year." The paper went on to share Morse's account of what zoo animals eat. The article portrayed his activities as trivial and expressed extreme disapproval that a director had been appointed before the zoo was officially in business.

George Morse didn't last long. He began to itch for more demanding and fulfilling work—and perhaps questioned whether the Chicago Zoological Garden of the Forest Preserve would ever actually come to be. As early as 1923, he had begun helping out the new Shedd Aquarium with planning, and in 1926 he was offered the directorship there. Sorry to see him go, the trustees agreed that the opportunity was good for Morse and gave him their blessing. Certainly there were many zoo trustees who had an interest in the new aquarium; powerful trustee Stanley Field was head of the Shedd Aquarium at the time, and John Shedd was on the Chicago Zoological Society's Board as well.

Luckily, many trustees refused to give up hope, persevering with discussions with the Forest Preserve District and Edith Rockefeller McCormick.

On April 13, 1926, the zoo tax was again scheduled for referendum. Several changes had been made in the contract with the Forest Preserve District, chiefly with respect to the administrative powers of the Society, and McCormick had relaxed some of her early conditions of the gift. In fact, by the time of the second referendum, she had asked only that the property revert to her estate if the referendum failed or if the zoo was not completed by July 1934. But clearly the biggest item in the Society's favor was the fact that there was no school tax on the ballot.

Many prominent Chicagoans came out in support of the zoo project, among them Forest Preserve District president Anton Cermak, later to become a very influential mayor of Chicago, and city planner Charles Wacker.

April 13 was met with considerable anxiety by the Society. It was a case of "now or never." If county voters didn't endorse the project, the property would revert to McCormick ownership. The Society knew that if the project was voted down again, it would be many years before Chicago could realize its hopes for a new, world-class zoo.

But guarded optimism was the theme of the day. After all, the Society had met and dealt with many of the criticisms leveled at the 1923 campaign. In the end, its faith and hard work were rewarded. The zoo tax passed easily, with the majority vote very nearly two to one. Six years after the initial offer of land, the zoo was finally in business.

1926   **Stanley Field becomes chairman of the Buildings Committee.**
The second zoo tax passes.
Underground work begins.

'27   **The first tax money comes in.**
The first buildings are constructed.
Ed Bean becomes director and Robert Bean becomes assistant director.

'28   **Administrative offices are moved to the zoo.**
Norway maples are planted along the malls.

'30   **John Hurlimann begins rock work.**

'32   **Pachyderm House, Insect House, and Parakeet House are constructed.**
Edith Rockefeller McCormick dies.
**Work begins on Small Antelope House, Primate House,
Australia House, Aquatic Bird House, and the North Gate.**

'33   **Grace Olive Wiley arrives.**
George Getz's animal collection is transported from Michigan.

'34   **The Chicago Zoological Park opens.**

CHAPTER TWO

Breaking Ground

(1926-1934)

The Building Program Begins

For the Chicago Zoological Society, 1926 marked a joyful turning point. Once the zoo tax passed in April, the trustees were off and running. At a special April 27 meeting of the Board, called to initiate plans, Anton Cermak pointed out that tax funds would not be available for another year and approved a $75,000 loan to the Society to begin work.

At a May trustee meeting, Stanley Field was approved as a trustee and began a 36-year span as chairman of the Buildings Committee. As well, Edwin H. Clark was appointed as the Society's architect. The building program could finally begin.

Aside from the property owned by Edith Rockefeller McCormick, perhaps 30 families had purchased lots on the site prior to its designation as a zoo. Some properties were small and undeveloped, others were considerably larger and sported houses or summer cabins for Chicago residents seeking relief from the city. (At that time in Chicago's history, the western suburbs were quite undeveloped and considered to be "out in the sticks.")

The Forest Preserve District went to work buying private properties. The smaller, unimproved sites were purchased for a few hundred dollars. The larger lots were bought for $10,000 or $15,000, and usually an additional $1,000 compensated the owners for the houses they had built. While some owners readily complied, others were less willing and went to court to fight for a better price. Most of the houses were demolished, but a particularly nice one in the zoo's northwest quadrant was retained for use as a director's cottage.

Above: In the 1920s, Chicago's western suburbs were sparsely settled.

Left: The zoo director's cottage, one of some 30 homes on the land donated by Edith Rockefeller McCormick, was purchased for $11,000 by the Forest Preserve District. The plot itself fetched $6,500.

STANLEY FIELD

Society president John McCutcheon, with his usual charm and humility, once stated, "My most valuable quality as president, as I see it, was that I did not try to act like one all the time."

This is probably true. In many ways the guiding force and spiritual leader, McCutcheon wasn't the dictatorial type. Several prominent Chicagoans stepped up to become leaders at the zoo, and McCutcheon graciously gave them the spotlight. Chief among these was Stanley Field.

Stanley Field, nephew of famous merchant Marshall Field and president of Chicago's Field Museum of Natural History, gave tremendous time and energy to the zoo. He was largely responsible for construction of the zoo's original buildings.

More authoritarian than McCutcheon, Field took up the reins and, in many respects, presided over the zoo for decades. It is testimony to McCutcheon's gentle, innate leadership qualities that this never diminished his role. McCutcheon was the godfather, Field the workhorse.

Mae Rose Jana, who worked in the director's office for many years, was once asked to describe Field. "He was the boss," she said succinctly.

Field was chairman of the Buildings Committee of the Chicago Zoological Society. From 1927, when construction started in earnest, until he stepped down in 1962, Field awarded building contracts, monitored progress, and, ever eagle-eyed, watched each building rise from the ground.

His yearly reports at the annual governing member meetings were so comprehensive, including figures on building, finances, visitors, and other categories, that all other committee chairmen rising to report after him invariably stated, "As Mr. Field has so ably reported on the zoo's progress, I shall simply submit my report in written form for the record."

Field saw this new zoo as a park waiting to be shaped, a new project, and an opportunity to leave another mark, and he jumped in with both feet. He pushed, he prodded, and he saw to it that the park opened in 1934. During this period, in addition to his responsibilities at the new zoo and at the Field Museum, Field was also president of the Shedd Aquarium Society, overseeing planning and construction on the new aquarium. Without this able, aggressive, and energetic man, who knows when or how the park would have opened.

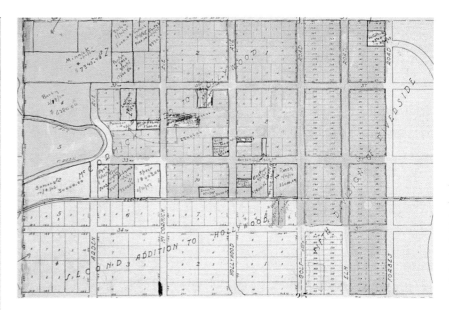

Above: An early map of the area donated by Edith Rockefeller McCormick included owners' names and purchase prices.

Designing a Zoo

As early as 1922, the Forest Preserve District's Wilson Committee had worked on a zoo design with Heinrich and Lorenz Hagenbeck. Not only had the Hagenbecks visited the proposed zoo site early on and pronounced it fit, but Forest Preserve District engineer Emmett Flavin had spent nearly six months in Europe, working with the Hagenbecks on plans for the zoo.

The Hagenbeck brothers received $5,000 for their work. Their plan received considerable scrutiny during the years of political indecision as the Board of Trustees had little else to do. Modeled after the Hagenbeck Zoo, their informal design featured a roadway encircling the entire zoo (a drive-by concept enabling visitors to see animals without leaving their cars) and a central restaurant from which people could view several exhibits.

The Society's 1927 yearbook noted objections to the design. "From the viewpoint of the European, who prefers to observe the Gardens in a leisurely manner, eating and drinking the while, this arrangement is ideal. It does not appeal to the more energetic American temperament.... Perhaps the greatest contribution of the Hagenbecks was dimensions for moats, rock formations, etc., which would give an artistic effect and yet afford ample protection against the escape of animals."

THE NEW WAY TO DISPLAY

This excerpt from *Zoo Book* by Linda Koebner details Carl Hagenbeck's new style of zoo design.

"In early zoological gardens, more often than not animals were kept caged alone, even animals that we now know live in social groups of families, like chimpanzees and gorillas. With many animals to care for and little time or money, keepers had to make care of the animals as simple as possible. The early cages often looked like bathrooms, made completely of tile and concrete that was easy to hose down. A zoo animal was kept in a bare cage with heavy iron bars separating it from the visitor. The animal had nowhere to hide, often no place to get up off the floor. There were no objects, or 'furniture,' in the cage. The big cats, lions or tigers, might have shelves to sleep on.

"Carl Hagenbeck decided to open his own zoo. It would not be an ordinary zoo, with animals in cage after cage. Rather, he wrote, 'I wished to exhibit them not as captives, confined to narrow spaces and looked at between bars, but as free to wander from place to place within as large limits as possible and with no bars to obstruct the view and serve as a reminder of captivity.'

"Hagenbeck introduced a new concept of building moats around the exhibits. The moats were not obvious to the visitors. They were camouflaged with plants and landscaping. But for the animals, these deep moats were intimidating obstacles not to be jumped over, into or out of. Hagenbeck was able to design the exhibits to look as if predator and prey, lion and zebra, were in the same exhibit. In reality, a concealed moat was keeping them apart."

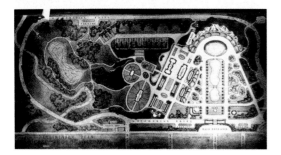

Above: Edwin Clark drew on the Hagenbeck brothers' ideas for an early zoo design.

Right: Lorenz Hagenbeck (with the pointer) explains his model to zoo and Forest Preserve District officials in 1923. Among those present are Anton Cermak, Emmett Whealan, Emmett Flavin, and Henry Zender.

While most of the Hagenbecks' plan for the Chicago Zoological Park did not come to pass, no one questioned that the zoo should be generally modeled after their Stellingen zoo, "with various wild animal families presented in surroundings reproducing as far as artificial and other means will permit the natural habitat of each." In fact, this decision, made as far back as 1922, would be one of the elements that set Brookfield Zoo apart from all other American zoos at the time.

Armed with the 1922 design by Flavin and the Hagenbecks, as well as a design drafted by a bored Director Morse, architect Edwin Clark went to work. He was familiar with the Society's goals and wishes, having been a governing member since 1923. (He resigned his membership after being appointed architect to avoid a conflict of interest). Clark attended the September 27, 1926, trustee meeting equipped with a model and general plans for the zoo, which were promptly approved. Clark was sent on his way to develop specifics so that construction could begin.

The zoo promptly contracted with Cyclone Fence to construct eight-foot fencing around the park. As well, a topographical survey was conducted, underground utility and sewer lines were installed, a well was dug, and a large lake at the west end of the property was excavated.

"We don't have much to show for the work, it's all underground," reported Stanley Field at the January 1927 annual meeting. But things were off and running. The Board hoped to have the park completed in time for the 1933 Century of Progress Exposition in Chicago, which would draw tourists from around the world.

Below: Edwin Clark drew up several plans for the new zoo. A later one (inset) was approved. (Left to right) Edwin Clark, F. Kriz, John Magill, James Simpson, Emmett Whealan, Frank Wilson, Mrs. E. W. Bemis, Lester Falk, John McCutcheon, and Anton Cermak discuss Clark's approved design in September 1926.

HOW TO BUILD A BARLESS CAGE

An excerpt from the 1936 *Brookfield Zoo Guide Book* explains how the zoo's barless exhibits were built.

"Barless cages have been extensively used in Europe since 1900. The creation of this type of construction is attributed to Ursus Eggenschwiler, a Swiss artist. On the side from which the visitors view the animals, empty or water-filled moats form intervening barriers preventing the animals' escape. Usually unscalable rock work is used to enclose the background. The rockwork formations are artificial; for most scenes pillaric basalt has been reproduced. A small scale model is prepared and from it the steel skeleton is shaped; it is made of round steel rods of various diameters. The skeleton is then covered with metal lath; a thin coat of cement and sand plaster is applied to the lath. A greater thickness of plaster is added by the cement gun.... While the cement is still 'green,' that is, before the mixture crystallizes, it is sculptured and tinted with fresco colors. In connection with the barless cages the visitor will observe the unusual spaciousness of the accommodations and the use of accessory planting of foreign plants."

In the September/October 1922 issue of *Parks & Recreation*, Washington Park Zoo director (and later Brookfield Zoo director) Ed Bean commented on the merits of the barless zoo concept.

"There is a new era on, in which a great many changes will be made in zoological parks, especially in the way that animal enclosures will be built. All must admit that animals should be exhibited in as near natural conditions as possible. The zoo today is mostly an incongruous conglomeration of bars, spikes, fences, rails, pickets, gratings and other equally as obscene and hideous signs of captivity and of the imprisonment of the animal. If we are to believe that all animals think in some degree, or are at least sensitive to confinement, surely the psychology of the continuous looking through bars day and night, year in and year out, will break the spirit of any highly organized animal.... It is with great pleasure and anticipation that I learn what will probably be the greatest zoological park in the world is to be built in the forest preserve of Chicago along this method of barless exhibition."

It is amusing to look back at a budget drafted in June 1926. It was meant only to tide over the institution until tax money could become available.

Architect	$ 12,000
Clerk	$ 5,000
Office rental	$ 1,000
Telephone, etc.	$ 500
Furniture	$ 1,000
Yearbook and other publicity	$ 5,000
Animal man	$ 7,500
Unforeseen costs	$ 18,000
Total	$ 50,000

*(about $400,000
by modern standards)*

By July, just one month later, the total had doubled to include $35,000 for fencing and $15,000 for road construction. The trustees were, after all, just shooting in the dark. There was little guidance to be found in terms of actual costs for creating a modern barless zoo in the northern United States. As time went on, the operating budget continued to expand.

Today, it's easy to overlook that a certain amount of visionary planning was necessary. Edwin Clark combined the open, barless elements of the Hagenbeck plan with a formal promenade design to create a park with magnificent malls and open vistas that would also allow for naturalistic animal exhibits.

With their yellow and white brick walls, red tile roofs, and stone columns, the buildings were considered "simple country Italian renaissance," and they complemented the formal malls without overwhelming the naturalistic animal areas. Old photos of the site before construction show Midwestern elements: flat terrain, with heavily wooded areas and a great collection of shrubs and prairie grasses.

It's important to note that fewer than two dozen living trees were removed from the zoo during construction. Many trees, including at least one 60-foot elm, were moved carefully and with considerable difficulty from one location to another within the park for the sake of preservation. It was, after all, Forest Preserve District land.

Below: Reptile House was built in 1927. As animal exhibits were constructed, energy from a powerhouse, seen behind the exhibit, became vital.

Above left: Many methods were used to excavate the lake on the zoo's west side.

Above: In 1927, the South Gate, seen from where Roosevelt Fountain later would be situated, was one of the first buildings to be constructed.

Constructing a large zoo in northern Illinois brought other challenges. Most large, outdoor barless zoos were in warmer climates. Even Hamburg, where the most northern of these zoos was located, was slightly warmer than Chicago.

This presented Clark with additional headaches: how to exhibit primates, giraffes, and other warm-weather animals in enclosures that were hardy enough for the cruelest Chicago winters while still presenting the illusion of natural habitats. It required creativity and cleverness. Clark scored points with skylights, murals, and plantings, but most of the indoor exhibits were the least visually interesting enclosures in the zoo. In some cases, such as Small Mammal House and Australia House, the barless notion was too difficult to manage, and Clark had to fall back on more traditional zoo exhibitry, with barred cages of more uniform appearance.

The first few zoo buildings arose in 1927: the South Gate complex, complete with administration building and restrooms; a powerhouse; and Reptile House, the first animal building. Stanley Field oversaw continued work on the lake excavation, the well and water-distribution system, sewers, underground heating, and plowing and disking of the main mall area.

Edward and Robert Bean

With the departure of Director George Morse and the acceleration of work, it was clearly time for a new administrator. The trustees found this person in Milwaukee: Ed Bean, director of the Washington Park Zoo. Bean was familiar with Chicago, having worked at Lincoln Park Zoo before moving to Milwaukee in 1906. Vice-president of the American Institute of Park Executives and a member of the Board of Directors of the American Association of Zoological Parks and Aquariums, which he helped launch, Bean was well-connected and well-respected in the zoo community.

Bean's comments about the new zoo in Brookfield included thoughts about conservation and education that were visionary at the time. "It is only a matter of a few years until all animals will have to be reared in captivity if we are to preserve the various species for scientific and educational purposes," he said. "It is a source of great satisfaction to me that the grounds and equipment here will be well adapted to animal raising. It is my purpose, with the approval and cooperation of the members of the Society, to make our animal collection an educational factor of considerable importance to Chicago and suburbs. It should take its place in this respect along with art institutes, museums and similar institutions."

Edward Bean   Robert Bean

EDUCATION

"The world is drifting more and more to visual education, and I think an institution like this zoological garden can be an important part of the school system of the country and city. We can show the marvels and the beauties and the goodness—and the badness of the animal kingdom in a supremely vivid way."

–Ed Bean

THE ROLE OF ZOOS

Ed Bean had a remarkably forward-thinking belief in the role of zoos in wildlife preservation, one that he talked about in the September/October 1922 issue of *Parks & Recreation*.

"Fundamentally...the object of a zoological garden is to help preserve wild life and first of all to preserve the wild life of this country. With the dwindling haunts, many species of native birds and animals are making their last stand. Already some have disappeared. There are too many hunt clubs and there are too many preserves. There is too much wild life considered as big game and game birds in this country. There are only two absolute refuges today, reservations under governmental control and the zoological garden. In America nearly every form of wild life can be found, but nearly every species has already been so desperately ravaged that some have lost the struggle and surely many others are going to. The little that is left must be saved, must be saved soon, and can best be saved in the American zoological park."

ROBERT BEAN

In Emily Hahn's book *Animal Gardens*, Robert Bean recalled his childhood.

"I was born in the Lincoln Park Zoo on May 27, 1902. My father was bird keeper there at the time. He stayed in the zoo business, of course; few people leave it once they're in. Well, soon after I was born, we moved from Chicago to Milwaukee; my father started the Washington Park Zoo there. I caddied for the keepers when I was a kid, fetching their cans of beer when they were off duty, helping to mix pheasant feed and taking care of setting pheasants—doing as many odd jobs as a boy can possibly squeeze in outside school hours. Then I spent a couple of summer vacations on a stock farm, at Oconomowoc, Wisconsin, owned by Fred Pabst—you know, the beer man—looking after his prize cattle. When the First World War came along, I was about twelve, and my contribution to the cause was to paint the fencing at the zoo. That was the first year. The second year, they gave four keepers their vacations at the same time, and I took their places. When they came back, I got two weeks off myself."

Bean's attraction to helping construct and run the new Chicago zoo was obvious, and he expressed it with a touch of his usual dry wit. "Introduction of the barless type of construction marked a new epoch in the beauty and value of zoological gardens. No one will return from our Park pitying the 'poor caged animals.' Practically all... specimens will have outdoor range, though protected, of course, from the public. The latter is very important. It is comparatively easy to confine the animals to their places, but we must build strongly to keep the public away from the animals. Someone always wants to put his hand in the bear cage to see if Bruin will really bite, or throw in food to see if he will eat it."

The public would prove Bean right in the years to come.

The Society was fortunate not only in securing the esteemed Ed Bean to head the new institution, but also in hiring Robert Bean, Ed's son, to serve as assistant director. Robert Bean had been serving as director of the San Diego Zoo despite the fact that he was only 25 years old. Practically reared in and around zoos, Robert had always been interested in animals and supplemented his young years of observation and practical experience with animals with two years of zoology study at the University of Wisconsin.

This proposed modern zoo in Brookfield gave the Bean duo a unique opportunity to work together on creating and maintaining what all involved believed to be "the world's greatest zoo." The senior Bean was given an annual salary of $6,000, the younger Bean $3,000.

Above and right: The lion dens (photo, above) and the bear dens (right) are memorable thanks to their distinctive shape and the rock work by Swiss sculptor John Hurlimann.

Top: As early as six years before the zoo opened, Perching Bird House was being built using money made available by the successful 1926 zoo tax vote.

Above: Small Mammal House, begun in 1928, was not finished until early 1935, months after the zoo opened.

Under Construction

The first check from the Cook County Auditor for zoo tax money was received in June 1927 for the amount of $170,000. Field, Clark, and the Beans went to work spending it.

The Board had other tasks during this time, mainly in respect to tax-collection efforts. Just when the first money from the 1926 taxes was coming in, the trustees began exerting pressure on the Illinois House of Representatives to extend the period for the tax collection until December 1930, thus ensuring a complete five-year construction period. Two years had been lost after the 1923 defeat of the referendum. House Bill 398 passed easily, and the Board breathed a bit easier.

Construction continued rapidly in 1928, with Field letting contracts for Small Mammal House, Bird House, the Commissary, and bear dens. Work continued apace on the landscaping, road work, and grading of the rest of the site. The first purchase and planting of Norway maples for the mall area occurred late in the year, although of the 246 maples planted at a cost of nearly $6,600, only 26 survived due to poor drainage.

The pace of work was assisted by a few helpful loans: trustee George Dixon delivered a team of horses and a harness to assist in plowing, and Anton Cermak loaned Bean a saddle horse with which to patrol the park. A milestone was reached on May 7, 1928, when the administrative offices of the Society were moved from 8 East Huron Street in downtown Chicago to the new administrative building at the zoo.

Optimism and energy were running high on the zoo Board in 1928, so high that the trustees briefly considered opening Reptile House to the public that summer. This proved too complicated, but it attests to the enthusiasm of the Society's members.

Along with the Norway maples that still line the malls today, now in stately form, the rock work of the bear and lion dens would become trademarks of the Chicago Zoological Park. John Hurlimann, a Swiss sculptor, was the lone expert on this type of rock work. The trustees set about importing Herr Hurlimann for the task at hand, not easy with the visa and import restrictions of the time. A sheaf of letters exchanged between John McCutcheon and the U.S. Department of Labor attests to the difficulties the Society encountered while attempting to bring Hurlimann here. His visa didn't come through until 1930, and he began work on the bear and lion dens in August of that year.

The Depression Hits

In the meantime, the stock market crash and subsequent Great Depression brought work to a screeching halt. Stanley Field's report for the year 1930 is as follows: "Due to non-collection of taxes resulting in no money being paid to the Society during the year 1929, or during the first half of the year 1930, no constructive work was undertaken during that time. The funds which the Society had on hand were conserved to maintain the necessary force of men adequate to protect the work that had been done on the grounds and the buildings which had been erected, so that due to the buildings not being occupied there would be no unnecessary depreciation."

Field concluded his report to the governing members by stating, "In general, I would say that on account of the non-collection of taxes, the building and construction program of the Society is at least two to two and one-half years behind schedule and you can see that it is going to be absolutely impossible to have the buildings and grounds completed or in presentable shape for 1933, unless there is a substantial increase in the money at the disposal of the Society."

Because of the unanticipated drop in taxes, the Board went back to the House of Representatives, again asking for a two-year extension on the tax levy, to 1932. Again, the House was supportive, and House Bill 758 passed.

Funds weren't available again until the latter part of 1930, at which point the Society went ahead with Hurlimann's rock work on the bear and lion dens, as well as construction of Lion House. Revenue collected from the Forest Preserve District amounted to $450,000 during 1930, and that sum, minus $54,000 set aside until the Board was more confident that additional money would be coming in, was quickly spent on rock work, outstanding contracts, and the minimal Society labor force.

From the very start, the Society was conservative with its cash flow. The Board determined early on that it would only undertake work for which it already had funds in the bank. This was prudent and may have saved the institution when the Depression hit.

It is important to note, too, the distinction made between Forest Preserve District money and Society money. Forest Preserve District money was the revenue obtained through taxes and went directly into construction and maintenance of buildings. Society money was collected through memberships—governing memberships at a price of $100 upon initiation and $25 each year thereafter—and later through admissions, merchandise, food, donations, and other types of earned revenue. Society money was spent on the animal collection, staff, and special programs.

With some embarrassment, the Board went to Illinois officials once more in 1931, asking for yet another extension on the tax levy, this time through 1933 and 1934. Pointing to nearly $1 million in uncollected zoo tax money, Board members appealed to their friends in political seats. Attesting perhaps to how well-positioned the zoo's trustees were, House Bill 1036 passed on June 28, 1931.

The bleak building situation began to ease a bit in late 1931, when tax money started coming in again. Although nowhere near the amount originally promised, every little bit inched the Society's building program forward. In October 1931, Field let contracts on Insect House, Parakeet House, and Pachyderm House.

Pachyderm House, constructed in 1932 at a cost of $250,000, was an engineering marvel. "The large building [at] 110 x 259 feet, largest on the grounds, in no way gains the deplorable importance that such a large structure would attract if it were constructed along conventional lines," said Director Bean. "It is entirely covered with rock work and appears as a large hill or mesa. The simplicity and ingenuity of the construction of the interior of the building is particularly striking.... The building is entirely constructed of metal [sic]; cast monolithic walls, ceiling, arches and floors are employed. There is none of the usual architectural details used for concealing essential structural members. It is the first permanent building of this style to be constructed in America. More was ventured in an experimental way in this building than in any other."

Construction geared up again in earnest in 1933 as the Depression waned and tax money gradually increased, with the trustees hoping to benefit from the Century of Progress Exposition in Chicago that year. Furthermore, one of the conditions in Edith Rockefeller McCormick's gift had been that the zoo open by July 31, 1934, at the very latest. Work began on Aquatic Bird House, North Gate buildings, Australia House, Small Antelope House, Primate House, and the Formal Pool. By the end of 1933, the Society had spent an impressive $2,731,585 on construction over a seven-year period.

Above: Pachyderm House's structure, including huge concrete arches, was part of its appeal, especially as seen through the early vision of Edwin Clark (inset).

Left: Pachyderm House, with its exterior resembling something found in another part of the world, was considered unrivaled in its design when it was erected in 1932.

Right: The animal images on the art deco gates at the north entrance were embossed in aluminum.

Below: Lion House was built when tax money became available in 1930.

Trowbridge Photo

COST OF CONSTRUCTION OF VARIOUS ZOO BUILDINGS

Aquatic Bird House	$ 112,000
North Gate Buildings	$ 30,000
Australia House	$ 51,000
Small Antelope House	$ 53,000
Primate House	$ 225,000
Pachyderm House	$ 250,000

Courtesy the Chicago Historical Society, Trowbridge

Above: Ed Bean enjoys playtime with some of the zoo's first inhabitants: five gelada baboons donated by the Field Museum.

Assembling an Animal Collection

It was an exciting time in the zoo's development. At long last, the Animal Committee could begin assembling an animal collection. In the early days of construction, the Board made a careful decision to delay acquisition of animals until buildings were ready to house the collection and opening day was in sight. With the exception of accepting a few gifts of animals here and there—and many, many more offers were politely declined—the Board abided by this guideline.

In 1930, the Animal Committee, headed by dairy product manufacturer John Borden, began discussions on how to stock the zoo. Some striking differences from modern zoo practices appear in Ed Bean's report to the Committee, which must have been well-received by the many hunters in the group. "Many rare and unusual animals need be acquired, and can only be taken by special arresting expeditions," he reported. "There are certainly a number of sportsmen in Chicago, many are Society members, to whom the capture of living animals...would be fascinating and splendid sport. Forms of great rarity can only be acquired in this way and work of this nature is one of the better and most interesting objects of the Society and should receive encouragement and assistance at the proper time and with the proper people."

Bean went on to elaborate a bit on basic guidelines for the collection. "It is in no ways necessary or worthwhile to show the commoner forms, such as are shown in most parks. Few duplicates of specimen, those shown in the collection in Lincoln Park, [should] be secured by this Society. It is most desirable that some forms be acquired, which are entirely new in American collections; it is likewise desirable for family groups to be secured in preference to single specimen. Not only is the acquiring and displaying of the collection one of the principal objects of the Society, but it is certain it will be its greatest pleasure."

Often, assembling an animal collection of several hundred creatures is a gradual process of fitting pieces together: an elephant here, a few birds there, a primate or two from there.

GEORGE F. GETZ AND LAKEWOOD FARM

George Getz made his fortune dealing in anthracite coal. His interests were many and his generosity legendary in his hometown of Holland, Michigan. One of his interests was boxing. In 1927, he acted as copromoter of the famous Gene Tunney-Jack Dempsey "Long Count" fight at Soldier Field in Chicago. A few years later, he became the Illinois state boxing commissioner.

Getz was active politically as well, sponsoring many dinner parties at his 200-plus-acre home for fellow members of the Republican party. In 1926, he hosted an open party for his friend Fred Green, the Republican candidate for governor of Michigan. Everyone was welcome, and an estimated 30,000 people attended. Getz footed the bill for the ox roast, 18,000 wienies, two bands, and all other costs associated with the huge gathering. In later years, he served as treasurer for the Republican National Committee.

Getz's Lakewood Farm was a sprawling expanse, originally intended as a working farm, but it gradually grew into a private zoo and botanical garden. Getz liked to collect animals from all parts of the world, and once he had them, he displayed them for his neighbors and any visitors to see. The collection started small and gradually grew, as did his visitorship. Eventually, the farm became a well-known excursion for travelers from neighboring states. Open only from Memorial Day to Labor Day, the farm would get as many as 800,000 visitors during the course of the summer. Up until the farm's final two years, admission was free. It was only in the final years of the collection's existence that Getz began charging a minimal fee to help pay for maintenance and upkeep.

By 1933, Getz's energy and interest in the project waned, and he began considering closing the farm. He offered to sell the animal collection to the Chicago Zoological Society and no doubt made similar offers to other institutions. In fact, he had a past with Lincoln Park Zoo in that many of the Lakewood Farm animals went there during World War I. He had no takers for the whole collection, however, and eventually decided to donate the entire assemblage to the new zoo in Brookfield rather than break it up.

As related in *Getz Farm, Lakewood: The Farm that Was a Zoo,* "The animals were transported by truck in various cages. The pythons, 28 and 30 feet long, were placed into large boxes which could be heated if necessary. 'Nancy' the elephant went in a large specially constructed trailer. Ever since her coming to Lakewood, Nancy had an aversion to trucks. Even when the trucks passed near the zoo she would sound her trumpet call to show her dislike. The challenge the farm manager had was to get Nancy into a trailer. He did this by arranging all kinds of leafy boughs to hide the trailer. When she was safely aboard and securely fastened, a tractor backed up to the trailer and she was soon on her way to Brookfield. This transfer, which had to be approved by the Governors of three states, took place on November 2, 1933. George Getz's farm, Lakewood, as a showplace for the public, was finished."

George Getz died in 1938.

The process began in earnest in 1933 under the direction of new Animal Committee chairman Herbert Bradley, a prominent Chicago attorney. Animals were either donated by an individual or institution, or purchased. No special collecting trips were planned, despite Bean's obvious interest. As the first animals were all gifts, the Animal Committee planned to fill in the collection by purchase. The Board estimated the cost of stocking the zoo to be $170,000, whereas only $50,000 was available. A letter sent to all governing members, along with a copy of the Committee's extensive wish list, explained that gifts were welcome and, in fact, needed.

And so arrived the first animals: six lions from E. L. King in Minnesota; 20 wood pigeons and stock doves from Boardman Conover; two Indefatigable Island tortoises from Commander Eugene McDonald; a Mississippi alligator from F. Williams; two lizards from John A. Watson; a Virginia opossum from trustee John P. Kellogg; and a collection of Galápagos Island animals, including penguins, albatrosses, and tortoises, from Thomas Howell. The efforts of trustee John T. Pirie yielded an impressive group of six Kodiak bears, two arctic foxes from Donald MacMillan, and three lions from Thomas Wheelock.

Fellow institutions came through, too, with various gifts: three grizzly bears from the U.S. Department of the Interior; 12 mallard ducks from the St. Joseph, Missouri, Department of Parks; two yaks from the Bronx Zoo; a night heron and a silver gull from the National Zoo; five gelada baboons from the Field Museum/*Chicago Daily News* expedition to Abyssinia; and various others.

Many arrivals were of the tamer variety: turtles, frogs, alligators, snakes, parrots, and other semidomesticated creatures offered by children who loved them and mothers who didn't. At the time, alligators were particularly popular as household pets. As they outgrew their bathtubs, they often ended up at the zoo. At one point, Reptile House had 60 alligators, of which only one hadn't been a gift.

**Above and below:
Among the many
animals donated by
George Getz in 1933
were an elephant
seal (above) and
an elephant and a
giraffe (below).**

However, the heart of the zoo's collection came from one source: George F. Getz's private animal collection in Holland, Michigan. Getz had offered to sell his collection to the Society, but the price was too steep and the trustees decided to pass on the offer. The collection was substantial: 143 mammals, 123 birds, and four reptiles. Director Bean had inspected the collection and found it generally well-kept and healthy.

After some consideration, Getz decided to donate the entire collection to the Society in the interest of keeping it intact. And so, in one move, the Chicago Zoological Society obtained a sizable collection. The moving process for the Getz collection took place in late 1933. The event generated immense press interest, especially when it became necessary to camouflage a truck as a grove of trees to lure an elephant inside.

The rest of the initial collection came through purchases. An important collection of Australian animals, unparalleled in American zoos at the time, was purchased from the Taronga Zoological Park in Sydney for $11,000. The group included 98 mammals, 746 birds, and 32 reptiles. These acquisitions were really the work of Robert Bean, who, because of his work with the San Diego Zoo and travels down under, maintained good contacts with Australian humanitarian and Taronga Zoo Society president Sir Edward Hallstrom, as well as with the Australian government.

Another, newer staff member was responsible for supplying most of the reptiles and amphibians. Grace Olive Wiley came to the zoo from the Museum of Natural History at the Minneapolis Public Library, bringing 236 reptiles and amphibians with her. The Society paid Wiley $260 for the animals and appointed her the first curator of reptiles. She was no doubt delighted with the arrangement, having written McCutcheon back in January 1927 expressing interest in a position with the new zoo.

In 1933, Wiley met with Director Ed Bean. "I cannot express in words how marvelous your zoo seemed to me, and how much I enjoyed meeting you," she later wrote. "I truly found in you and your son, Robert, my kindred spirits—the love for animals and a great appreciation of the wonders of nature. It would give me the greatest happiness to come there and work with you folks where sympathy and understanding is prevalent."

Apparently, Bean was impressed, and Wiley arrived, with her animals, in December 1933 at an annual salary of $1,920. In those days it was highly unusual for a woman to be a zookeeper, let alone a curator, but Grace Olive Wiley was an unusual woman.

GRACE OLIVE WILEY

Born in 1883, Grace Olive Wiley became curator of the Minneapolis Public Library's Museum of Natural History at the age of 40.

She once said, "The fear of snakes is cultivated. We are not born with it. It comes from people saying 'Don't go into that clump of grass, there might be a snake.' Children love snakes as naturally as they love dogs and cats. Don't be afraid of a reptile's tongue. The only animal that can hurt you with its tongue is the human being."

Perhaps her desire to come to Brookfield stemmed from disagreements she had with the museum's directors. She had a particular fondness for cobras and believed that venomous snakes were no more dangerous than nonvenomous snakes when properly handled.

Wiley's bosses in Minnesota feared that her casual handling of these dangerous creatures could be fatal to her and/or her coworkers. They were unsuccessful, however, in changing her practices.

There is no doubt that Wiley had a special way with snakes. In fact, she was reportedly the first person to successfully breed western diamondback rattlesnakes.

Other animal purchases were made through collectors. Generally, the larger, more expensive, and rarer animals (elephants, rhinos, hippos, tigers, and various primates among them) were obtained in that fashion. A price list of available animals from collector Frank Buck gives some perspective on the cost of various animals at that time. (The zoo did not purchase these animals.)

One pair of giraffes	$10,000
One African elephant	$ 3,500
One mountain gorilla	$ 5,000
Two chimpanzees	$ 1,200
Two boa constrictors	$ 150
Hornbills and cranes	$ 200 *per pair*
One pair of Bengal tigers	$ 2,000
One pair of American grizzly bears	$ 300

Several animals, including African leopards and Bengal tigers, were purchased from surplus and duplicate stocks of other zoos, such as the San Francisco Zoo.

Alongside the animal acquisitions, the Society began to assemble a keeper force. Four of the most knowledgeable came from Getz's zoo: twins Marvin and Morris Ryzenga and brothers Fred and Leroy Woodruff.

Lillian Ryzenga recalled how her husband, Morris, accompanied the animals on their journey from Michigan and became employed by the Chicago Zoological Society upon his arrival. Morris was Nancy the elephant's keeper, and he had a good relationship with the gentle pachyderm. After traveling with Nancy and the other animals, Morris had no place to stay. He'd finish up his work, walk into town for dinner and a couple of beers, and then head back to the zoo, where he'd curl up in the hay next to Nancy and sleep a peaceful night next to his warm, trustworthy friend.

Most of the keeper force, however, was made up of neighborhood men looking for interesting work. While many had experience on farms growing up, none had experience with exotic animals. The Beans, Grace Olive Wiley, and the Getz keepers taught them the ropes. It's fortunate the work was interesting, for the zoo pay scale was low and the keepers worked six days a week, with no holidays off.

Above: The zoo's first keepers looked significantly more formal than usual during this gathering.

Almost Ready

With animals in stock, the zoo took on a different character. Local residents began to complain about loud growling, primarily late at night, when sound travels well.

The lion and tiger moats were 24 feet wide, 4½ feet beyond the best recorded jump ever made by a tiger. "We did not really believe [the lions and tigers] could negotiate the deep and more or less invisible pits which separated them from observers, but still we were a little uncertain," remembered John McCutcheon of the exciting day the big cats moved in. "I drove my car to a strategic position opposite, and the ladies stood on the far running board, peering over the top. Mr. Bean, Robert, Herbert Bradley and John Wentworth stood near the pits, their guns poised. I had brought my elephant gun. When all was set, the doors of the inside cages were opened and we waited in suspense. One by one the beasts ambled out and looked around curiously. Then they yawned, found spots in the warm spring sunshine and went to sleep."

Not all experiments with the outdoor, moated enclosures went as well. The Society received a gift of two adult grizzly bears from the U.S. Department of the Interior and promptly released them into their outdoor exhibit area. It seems, however, that the athleticism of a fit bear had been underestimated, for the following morning the enclosure was short one bear.

Not wanting to risk the lives of the zoo's suburban neighbors, in those days before tranquilizers and blow darts, Ed Bean organized a bear hunt. He had little difficulty finding volunteers among the many sportsmen on the staff, on the Board, and in the neighborhood. After several hours of fruitless searching, the bear suddenly startled a member of the party at close range, and the hunter, in a moment of panic, shot the bear in the mouth. The bear ran off, and only after being shot several more times many hours later did he die.

The Department of the Interior, informed of the mishap, generously supplied another bear. The second arrival, judged to be smaller and less fit than the first, also tried to leap the dry moat, as evidenced by the scratch marks on the wall, but failed. It was too close a call for Director Bean, though. He immediately had the moat widened, thus preventing any further bear escapes.

Left: Artist Ben Hallberg rendered this vision of a yard for Australian animals. An exhibit devoted exclusively to animals from down under was highly unusual at the time.

Fine-tuning of animal enclosures continued, and with animals and a work force arriving and the buildings and grounds being completed, the zoo prepared for its opening. The Executive Committee of the Board met often to discuss operational aspects of the zoo and to ensure that work continued on schedule. Of course, Stanley Field, with the able assistance of the Beans, was on top of that all along.

In May 1934, the Executive Committee determined operating hours and admission fees. As had been discussed from the very earliest days of the Society, it became official that admission would be free three days a week, including the busiest days, Saturdays and Sundays.

In fact, the Society's 1927 yearbook had stated that "there will be free admission to the Chicago Zoological Park three days a week—Saturday, Sunday, and one other day. The Park will also be free on all legal holidays and at all times to children under fifteen years of age when accompanied by adults. An admission fee will result in smaller numbers of visitors on the days charged. This will give employees a better opportunity to clean up the Park, to move animals and to attend to all other work incident to caring for the grounds and collection. These quiet days are also an advantage to groups of students or scientists who come to the Zoo for serious study. Finally, the rest is very beneficial to the health of the animals, particularly certain species of nervous temperament."
Admission was set at 25 cents.

July 1, 1934, was scheduled as the grand public opening, and activity moved into high gear in anticipation. Trustee Rufus Dawes, also president of the Century of Progress Exposition, made certain that advertising for the international Exposition mentioned the zoo to attract tourists. Invitations mailed to 5,000 local civic leaders (right) invited them to a special opening ceremony the day prior to the public one. The zoo had its own police force (an unusual safeguard for zoos in those days) consisting of seven men, and this assemblage underwent two weeks of daily training on crowd control, customer service, and giving directions.

The local Brookfield paper, *The Suburban Magnet*, began running front-page stories about progress at the zoo, and practically the entire front page of the June 28, 1934, *Magnet* was devoted to the zoo. Headlines included "Expect 25,000 Visitors at Zoo Opening," "Animal Paradise 8 Years Old; Now Ready for Public Use," and "Modern Noah's Ark Will Open 2 Gates."

Below: Visitors enjoyed John Hurlimann's dramatic rock work, and so did the lions that played on it.

RECOLLECTIONS

Some evenings, when the wind was out of the north and the air was clear, the lions could be heard roaring quite loudly. One would start, and others would join in, adding their voices to the restless chorus as I lay listening in bed in our would-be urban jungle. In my mind, I could see the big cats skulking through the street right under my window.

Brookfield Zoo opened its gates to the public for the first time on July 1, 1934, and I celebrated my 11th birthday on July 4. It was a wonderful birthday present.

Lucille (Gregory) McCusker
Montgomery, Illinois
Formerly of Brookfield

Above: Although much had yet to be accomplished, a 1934 aerial photo reveals the zoo's familiar arrangement. The water tower and chimney for the powerhouse were removed in 1991.

While zoo officials promoted the park as a "dignified scientific exhibit," most papers were more interested in a list of animals and a map of the park. "Yes, it's a dignified scientific exhibit of nearly 3,000 animals, reptiles, and birds," explained *The Magnet*, "but it affords an opportunity to enjoy something better than a Roman holiday in a park-like area that lacks as far as possible that confining atmosphere that one feels when visiting most zoos."

Fourteen years from the date of the original gift and eight years after the successful tax vote, the Chicago Zoological Park was finally ready to open its gates.

The President and Board of Trustees of The Chicago Zoological Society of Chicago request the honor of your presence at the dedication Ceremonies attending the opening of the new Zoological Park in Brookfield, Illinois at eleven o'clock Saturday morning the Thirtieth of June Nineteen hundred thirty-four

Please reply to the Secretary of the Zoological Society at Brookfield, Illinois

---

The Chicago Zoological Park---On It's Opening Next Sunday

A BIGGER AND BETTER BROOKFIELD

THE SUBURBAN MAGNET

No. 10   BROOKFIELD, ILLINOIS, THURSDAY, JUNE 28, 1934   SUBSCRIPTION—$2.00 PER YEAR

EXPECT 25,000 VISITORS AT ZOO OPENING

Shots
ning of The
o Zoo
Editor

That:

MODERN NOAH'S ARK WILL OPEN 2 GATES

Many Song Birds Are Attracted to

VILLAGE EXPENSES EXCEED INCOME BY

Police to Start Drive on Dog Tax

Animal Paradise 8 Years Old

1934 The Chicago Zoological Park opens.

CHAPTER THREE

Enter the Public

(1934)

Aiming Our Arrow at a Star

"Upon behalf of the Chicago Zoological Society, I welcome you here today to share with us a dedication ceremony to which the Society has been looking forward for a long time. There have been dark hours when our hopes of ever seeing this day were very dim, but those times are happily gone by.

"We sincerely hope this visit of yours may be only the first of many. And we also hope that with each succeeding visit you will see improvement—that you'll see the trees in the mall a little larger, the collection of animals a little bigger, the machinery working a little smoother, and, if we can carry our hopes much further, that your initial interest in this project will develop into genuine pride. While much has been done, both above and below ground, I think it is unnecessary to say that the construction program is by no means complete. At present about three-quarters of the originally adopted plan is completed.

"We had hoped to show you a finished product when the Park was opened to the public. But those hopes were born during the days when, like everybody else, we aimed our arrow at a star. Certain things have affected our aim and we must be content with much less than a bull's eye. Realizing this, it is our judgment that an opening now is better than withholding it longer. Some day, not too far ahead, we trust you will see the full program rounded out. Not finished, of course, because we never expect to say it is finished. As new methods of display are developed, there will be changes and additions as there may be freshness and novelty.

"I think we can count on human nature as our ally. Human nature will not change, at least not in its fundamentals, and we know from experience that securely planted within the human breast is a deep abiding interest in animals. The companionship of the boy and the dog is one of the eternal verities. The love of children for animal stories is something inherited at birth and passed down through countless generations. One great object in gathering wild animals into such a modern zoo as we have here is to display them in comfortable enclosures where the spectator is not depressed by their captivity.

"A new zoo is like everything else that is new. It takes some time to get it running smoothly. A new house is not really charming until it has been lived in and the newness softened by love and occupancy."

Right and below: The day before the public was allowed in for the first time, the Chicago Zoological Park hosted local dignitaries for a special ceremony. Speeches were given by John McCutcheon (right) and Illinois governor Henry Horner (below).

With these words, John McCutcheon finally had the pleasure of being master of ceremonies at the opening of the Chicago Zoological Park on Saturday, June 30, 1934. From a temporary grandstand erected on the mall, he then introduced speakers the Reverend John Timothy Stone of the Presbyterian Theological Seminary for the invocation, Forest Preserve District president Emmett Whealan, Chicago mayor Edward J. Kelly, and Illinois governor Henry Horner.

Politically careful, eloquent, and always witty, McCutcheon introduced Democratic governor Horner as follows: "I hope he will find time today to visit the collection. If he should see more elephants than donkeys, I hasten to assure him there is no political significance. The donkey is not wild, at least not as wild as he was three or four years ago, whereas the elephant is now much wilder than he was the same length of time ago. When the donkey becomes as wild as the elephant, we'll certainly have specimens of him in our collection."

Trustee Rufus Dawes, president of the Century of Progress Exposition, was an honored guest, and he said a few words to the occasion. McCutcheon then used the opportunity to applaud the work of Stanley Field and vice-presidents John T. Pirie, John Wentworth, and John P. Kellogg.

"In case you have observed that the President and three Vice-Presidents of this Society bear the name of John," McCutcheon continued, "I wish to assure you that this does not indicate a studied policy of trying to get men of that name." He introduced Animal Committee chairman Herbert Bradley, as well as Executive Committee member and chairman of the Chicago Plan Commission James Simpson. Architect Edwin Clark and Director Edward Bean were also recognized for their efforts over the preceding years. The acting president of the University of Notre Dame, the Reverend John P. O'Hara, concluded the ceremonies with a benediction.

Edith Rockefeller McCormick, unfortunately, had died two years earlier, never to see her land metamorphose into the zoo she had foreseen. With her belief in reincarnation, however, who knows...

The public opening the next day had much less pomp than the official ceremonies, but it was a grand time nonetheless. An estimated 58,000 visitors attended, exceeding the anticipated attendance by 33,000. *The Suburban Magnet* reported that an additional 25,000 were turned away due to traffic and parking problems. Parking spaces for 6,000 cars were available, so latecomers had to park on side streets and walk a healthy distance.

The West Towns Electric railway, affectionately known by locals as the Toonerville Trolley, which conveniently ran right along the southern edge of the zoo, used every available car and ran "zoo specials" all day. It was a madhouse, with seemingly all of Chicago out to see the world's newest zoo.

"THE GREATEST POSSIBLE HAPPENING"

Thousands of little stories were played out on the grand opening weekend. The Riverside and Brookfield papers related some of these "smaller" stories.

"Born with the zoo opening were the new racketeers—the man who charged the visitors a dime to park their cars on his lot and the young boys who charged a dime to watch the cars during the owners' absence. Many fell for the last 'racket' before they realized that there was about as much chance of a thief stealing their cars in the crowded areas as there is of Dillinger giving himself up to police authorities."

"The proprietor of the Standard Shoe Repair shop was seen at the Lion house trying to feed the lion cubs some scraps of shoe leather he had in his pocket."

"One man standing in front of the tiger dens Sunday afternoon made a remark that was typical of statements made by others. He said: 'come on, let's get away from here. I know how far tigers can jump and believe me if one of them fellows decides to get out he won't have any trouble doing so.'"

"The gibbons did their best during the dedication program Saturday morning to lend applause. They uttered their ear-piercing yell at frequent intervals during the speaking, and later when the visitors poured into the monkey house they were the center of attraction as they occasionally gave their yell."

"Even the lions howled several times in appreciation of the dedication ceremonies, once while President McCutcheon was making remarks about the educational advantages of this new institution."

"Cars from Aurora, Kankakee, Joliet, Rockford and other towns were noticed passing through the village in large numbers. World's Fair visitors from other states who were stopping in Chicago, came out to see the new zoo. Local officials said that every state in the Union was represented here last Sunday."

And finally, "As has been chronicled in the columns of this newspaper for the past several years, the Chicago Zoological Park is fast proving to be the greatest possible happening to this village since it was founded."

Not all animal houses were open: the Small Mammal, Perching Bird, and Parrot houses were still unfinished. The lines for the washrooms were endless, the landscaping was still terribly immature, and there were few refreshment stands in sight. It seems, however, that most visitors left enthralled. The 200-acre park, with its impressive malls, bear and lion dens, and magnificent structures, was unlike anything Chicagoans had ever seen before. Hagenbeck's barless zoo concept provided for a real outdoor adventure, with animals exhibited in naturalistic habitats visitors had seen only in pictures.

Right: On opening day, crowds pushed and prodded to see the polar bears.

Left: The Toonerville Trolley was busy, running extra trains to and from the zoo's South Gate.

Below: People from Chicago had never before seen exhibits that separated animals from people seemingly using empty air. This way of seeing animals made standing in front of the mighty bears especially exciting.

RECOLLECTIONS

In the mid- to late 1930s, I can remember going there as a very small child. In the very beginning, we traveled to the zoo by streetcar, which went on a scenic route over a rickety bridge and through beautifully green foliage. The streetcar was so overcrowded that one had to wonder if the bridge would hold up, or if we could hold our breath long enough to get there in one piece because we were smashed in like sardines. The bridge would creak and squeak and everyone would "oh" and "ah." It was great fun!

When I was a young girl, we would go on free days, when the crowds were overwhelming and people from all over the world would come to see the magnificence of the zoo in Brookfield. Of course, we would also go on 25 cent day and pretend we were the wealthy, and have a lot more places to see easier without an enormous crowd to contend with.

Places to visit like Monkey Island, all the bears, regal lions, rare pandas, ivory-tusked elephants, coiled snakes, elderly turtles, exotic birds, silent giraffes, pouched kangaroos, mountain-climbing goats, and a variety of others were always on our agenda. When the end of the day came, we were able to go to the South Gate and board public transportation. The crowds were so massive you sometimes had to wait for the second or third vehicle.

Dolores J. Gordon
Berwyn, Illinois

Attendance continued at staggering rates the following week, providing little relief for visitors' parking or washroom woes. The Fourth of July brought almost 51,000 visitors, and the following Sunday saw that number rise to over 66,400. The days when the zoo charged 25 cents showed a considerable drop in attendance, ranging from nearly 2,000 to over 4,700 that first week. The keepers, as well as the rest of the staff, probably breathed a sigh of relief on days when the crowds let up.

The trustees, on the other hand, must have been euphoric after so many years of struggling with public opinion, financial woes, and other problems. What a success!

1934

The Chicago Zoological Park opens.

'35

Karl Plath becomes the curator of birds.
Emperor penguins arrive, then die.
Small Mammal House, Perching Bird House, Parrot House,
Antelope House, and the Illinois Exhibit open.
Assistant Director Robert Bean is appointed curator of mammals.
Grace Olive Wiley leaves.

'36

The first guidebook is published.
The children's merry-go-round begins operation.
Monkey Island and the Seal Pool open.
Ziggy the elephant arrives.

CHAPTER FOUR

Settling In

(1934-1936)

Right: Foot-weary visitors could rent buggies reconditioned from the Century of Progress Exposition. A person to push it sometimes came along with the buggy.

Some Fine Touches

Once Brookfield Zoo was up and running, the trustees concerned themselves with finishing incomplete exhibits, planning a few new ones, and improving the visitor experience.

In August 1934, they purchased reconditioned buggies and wheelchairs from the Century of Progress Exposition, providing for more visitor comforts at the zoo. (The buggies and chairs could be rented with or without someone to push the vehicle.) The Board discussed other visitor amenities, such as directional signs for orientation, labels for exhibits, permanent refreshment stands, and comfort stations.

In terms of exhibits, final touches were being put on Small Mammal House, Perching Bird House, and Parrot House, with all three buildings opening in early 1935. Construction was underway on Antelope House, on Monkey Island behind Primate House, on a Seal Pool at the western end of the zoo, and on an Illinois Exhibit to feature native animals.

Left: One amenity available to people—one that would be available for many decades—was the attraction of buying peanuts and serving them to the animals.

Visitors flocked to see the new zoo. Attendance for July 1 through December 31, 1934, was 1,292,720 visitors—of which only 99,491 paid admission. Revenue figures for 1934 are remarkably low, particularly in comparison to attendance figures. Income from admissions for the six months totaled just shy of $25,000. Refreshments were by far the largest source of earned revenue, at $53,000. Other sources of earned income included chair and buggy rentals (approximately $2,000), checking fees for dogs and articles (less than $100), and sales of novelties (about $250). There was certainly room for improvement, but it was a start.

The Animal Committee continued its efforts to stock the zoo. One initially exciting but ultimately disappointing shipment of animals arrived: a group of nine emperor penguins, the only such animals in an American zoo. Famous explorer Admiral Richard E. Byrd, back from an early trip to the South Pole, cabled George Getz in May 1935 that he needed money and would sell the penguins he had just brought north. Getz relayed the message to John McCutcheon, who cabled Byrd that "we are deeply interested" and sent Robert Bean (and $5,000) to bring them back in a refrigerated car. At about three feet high each, the penguins would have been impressive additions.

By July 1, after 19 weeks of travel, all nine had died. It was later determined that they perished from aspergillosis, a fungal disease. After delivering the penguins to the zoo, Robert Bean missed the sad event, having left for one of the zoo's first collecting trips, this one to Cairo and Khartoum. In later years, the Society would conduct important research on aspergillosis.

Above: Ill-fated emperor penguins, here tended by keeper Larry Sherman, Jr., arrived from the South Pole in 1935.

Above left: Robert Bean (left) retrieved the emperor penguins. Soon after reaching the zoo, all nine died from a fungal disease.

STANDARD PRICES, 1935

According to *The value of a dollar*, for the cost of zoo admission on "pay" days, a visitor could buy five bottles of Coca-Cola, five Baby Ruth candy bars, a portion of a pack of gum, or part of a roll of film.

Zoo admission	$ .25
A Baby Ruth candy bar	$ .05
A bicycle (top of the line)	$ 34.75
A bottle of Coca-Cola	$ .05
A dozen diapers	$ 1.19
A roll of film	$ .39
An electric iron	$ 3.89
A man's chambray shirt	$ .84
A push lawn mower	$ 5.35
A sewing machine	$ 29.85
A pack of Wrigley's gum	$ .37

Above: Animals arriving at the zoo came in packages big and small. Here a giraffe waits to unload at the North Gate.

Gifts of animals continued to arrive at the zoo. Sometimes the gifts didn't work out quite as planned. A generous offer by rubber executive George B. Dryden to pay up to $20,000 for a pair of Indian rhinos, of which there were believed to be only about 500 in the world, was accepted with pleasure by the Animal Committee. But obtaining a pair of the animals proved difficult because of their rarity. The zoo would not actually exhibit Indian rhinos until well over a decade later, in 1948.

Other animals arrived in a more traditional and time-honored fashion: birth. It was with pride that Edward Bean announced at the 1935 annual meeting that seven lions, one yak, and numerous kangaroos, wallabies, and monkeys, among others, had been born and were thriving in the zoo's first year. As of January 1935, the collection numbered 394 mammals (of 110 species), 392 birds (149 species), and 586 reptiles (155 species).

Curators Come and Go

A few major staff changes took place in 1935. Grace Olive Wiley, the curator of reptiles, did not last long at Brookfield Zoo. After arriving in late 1933 with her large collection of reptiles, she created quite a stir with her unusual techniques for handling venomous snakes.

Ray Pawley, the current curator of reptiles, tells a story about Wiley and keeper Leroy Woodruff. Wiley had invited Woodruff to Reptile House to meet her favorite snakes, king cobras Kingy and Queenie. Wiley took Woodruff behind the scenes and told him to hold his arms straight out. She then unlocked the cobra enclosure and opened the door. One of the king cobras came out of the cage, crawled over the startled Woodruff's arms to Wiley, who was standing next to the keeper, did a loop across both of them, and reentered its enclosure.

Along with Wiley's peculiar methods came fairly frequent escapes, especially as she occasionally neglected to lock cage doors. Former staff member George Speidel recalled that one time three cobras were missing and left unreported for a week, with keepers and visitors walking through the same area as the missing cobras.

Eventually Wiley's carelessness became too risky for the zoo, and Director Bean decided it was time to let her go. The reptile collection she had brought to the zoo stayed behind, as the Society had wisely purchased those animals from her when she first arrived. Although Wiley did appear to have a special touch with venomous snakes and suffered remarkably few injuries or even close calls, she died in 1948 at age 64 from a cobra bite, an unfortunate victim of her own failed theory.

A new curator arrived shortly after (and independent of) Wiley's departure: a curator of birds by the name of Karl Plath. Like Wiley, Plath had written several letters to the zoo expressing interest in a position. His letters to Society president John McCutcheon began in 1924. An amateur ornithologist, Plath's real talent was painting. "I feel that I know something about [birds]," he commented, "as for the last twenty years I have studied them as subjects for my paintings and as inmates of my aviary where I have several varieties, many rare and unusual."

Apparently, Director Ed Bean agreed that Plath could be useful, and he was hired effective October 1, 1935, at $3,500 per year. At the same time, Robert Bean was given the additional title of curator of mammals, even though he still held the position of assistant director. With mammal and bird curators secured, only the reptile curator's position was vacant, and it would remain so for several years.

Above: Although Karl Plath (right) became the curator of birds in 1935, his hobby was painting birds. In addition to his duties as head of the Bird Department, he would create artwork of the avian variety for some 25 years.

RECOLLECTIONS

I had a job as guard at the zoo and in a while was made captain of the guards. We had a force of 21 and were dandies, with white pith helmets, red jackets, fancy blue trousers, Sam Brown belts, and a silver-plated Smith & Wesson revolver. Wow! It had real .38-caliber bullets. We were sworn in by the Brookfield police chief. I must not forget to mention silver-ornamented, bamboo swagger sticks. What a fancy group it was.

Due to a pickpocket infestation, the office was flooded with complaints. All sorts of wallets were stolen, some with big money. It was shameful for the zoo, and the heat was on. The morning [after the opening weekend], workers picked up three bushels of wallets in the bushes, and it continued into the following Sunday. They had us licked until we called in the Chicago Vice Squad. For a while, they were picked up at the gate and locked up for the day and then turned loose, only for them to sneak in another day. They were difficult to apprehend, but we put them out of business.

George Speidel
Former Security Captain

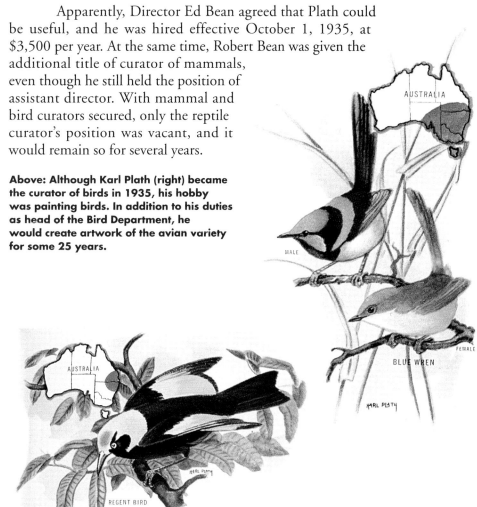

Improving the Visitor Experience

Some manpower assistance came from the government. President Franklin D. Roosevelt's national work assistance programs were tremendously helpful for the zoo, starting shortly before its opening, when dozens of laborers and painters from the Civil Works Administration reported for duty. Over the next few years, many workers from the CWA and the Illinois Emergency Relief constructed roads and walkways, helped construct exhibits, and engineered and built a tunnel running underneath busy 31st Street for pedestrians entering through the North Gate. The Works Progress Administration's Federal Art Project provided artists and sculptors to paint exhibit murals, carve wooden directional signs, design posters for streetcars, create animal figurines for display around the zoo, and construct relief backgrounds for exhibits. These state and national relief programs helped ensure that the zoo opened on time, improved the zoo in the years just following its opening, and provided for beautiful settings both inside and outside the buildings for many years.

THE WORKS PROGRESS ADMINISTRATION

A number of carved, wooden directional signs were created for Brookfield Zoo under the direction of Peterpaul Ott of the Federal Art Project of the Works Progress Administration.

Ott, born in Czechoslovakia in 1895, attended the Royal College of Fine and Applied Arts in Dresden, Germany. After emigrating to America in 1924, he won the International Small Sculpture Competition in 1930 and 1931, the first time the contest was won twice by the same person. He arrived in Chicago and served as WPA supervisor for sculpture and wood carving in the area from 1936 to 1938.

As supervisor for the zoo project, Ott gave final approval to all designs. (He also supervised artists W. A. Gilbertson and E. Viviano, who cast animal statuary in concrete.) After a design had been created by one of seven artists and approved by Ott, the carving took from two to four weeks, depending on the level of detail, by craftsmen employed for the purpose. The signs were carved in fir and finished in lacquer.

During 1935 and 1936, tabletops containing animal images, designed by artist John Winters, were also created for the zoo by WPA artists. Ralph Graham, supervisor of applied arts for Chicago under the WPA, oversaw the creation of the tabletops, which are early examples of the use of inlaid Formica.

Graham had been born in Cheyenne, Wyoming, in 1901 and worked his way through The School of the Art Institute, specializing in oil painting. His work was included in the Century of Progress Exposition in 1933 and was displayed at The Art Institute of Chicago from 1936 to 1939.

As supervisor of 175 WPA artists, Graham was involved in a number of projects, including works for the Chicago Park District, the Shedd Aquarium, the Field Museum, the Art Institute, and Chicago Public Schools, as well as the University of Illinois College of Medicine and Pharmacology, for which he designed beautiful stained-glass windows and murals depicting the history of medicine in Chicago up to 1936. In 1945, following a stint in the U.S. Army, Graham was invited to join the zoo as artist and photographer.

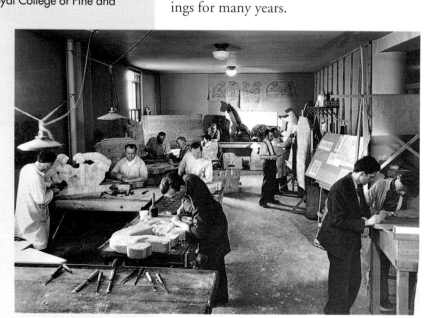

Above and right: In the 1930s, federal Works Progress Administration artists produced many incredible pieces of art, including the tabletops shown above and the posters at right. Some of their pieces are still in use at the zoo.

INFORMATION

ROOKFIELD ZOO

VISIT THE
BROOKFIELD
ZOO

FREE THURSDAY SATURDAY SUNDAY

BROOKFIELD

ZOO

Courtesy Chicago Aerial Industruries 15269

Above: An aerial photo from 1935 shows Monkey Island and Seal Island under construction.

Right: The merry-go-round in the zoo's northwest corner, installed in 1936, was popular as entertainment for kids.

Many improvements visible to guests came about in 1935. Small Mammal House, Parrot House, Perching Bird House, Antelope House, and the Illinois Exhibit were finally complete and opened for the first time, thus demanding a longer visit per guest. Animal identification labels were painted and mounted at the tops of the cages, where they could be seen over several rows of heads on crowded days. Thirty-two directional signs were placed around the zoo, easing visitor-orientation problems.

As of the end of the year, 2,821,492 people had visited the zoo since opening day. Still, only about 7% of those paid for the pleasure, with all others arriving on free days. Revenue figures were up slightly, however, around $135,000 for the year.

Other visitor-friendly amenities continued to spring up. In 1936, the zoo installed a merry-go-round in the children's playground in the northwestern corner. The purchase price and installation cost for the merry-go-round was $2,500, and in the first year alone it brought in nearly that much in revenue. This income was to remain a steady item in the budget for many years.

A guidebook, first introduced on July 4, 1936, also generated revenue for many years. For 25 cents, a visitor purchased a substantial brochure with brightly colored animal images on the cover, a map of the zoo, information about parking and other visitor needs, and page after page of photographs and interesting notes about the animals. The guidebook was published anew each year, with much the same internal content but also updates on new exhibits and a different colorful animal drawing on the cover.

On September 7, 1936, the four millionth visitor entered Brookfield Zoo. Miss Phyllis Gurn of Minnesota was treated like royalty and even left the day the proud owner of a brand new bicycle, courtesy of the zoo.

GUIDE BOOK

Guide Book

GUIDE BOOK

Zoo at Brookfield
Guide Book

BROOKFIELD ILLINOIS

EDWARD KRIMSTON

CHICAGO ZOOLOGICAL PARK
25¢

This page:
The guidebooks published every year offered information important to a zoo visit, updates on animals, and art by Karl Plath, Ralph Graham, and others.

Following page:
A whimsical, engaging map helped visitors find their way.

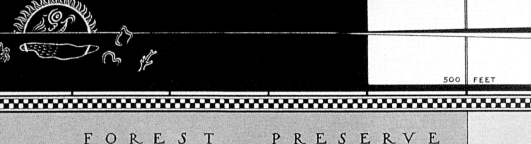

500 | FEET

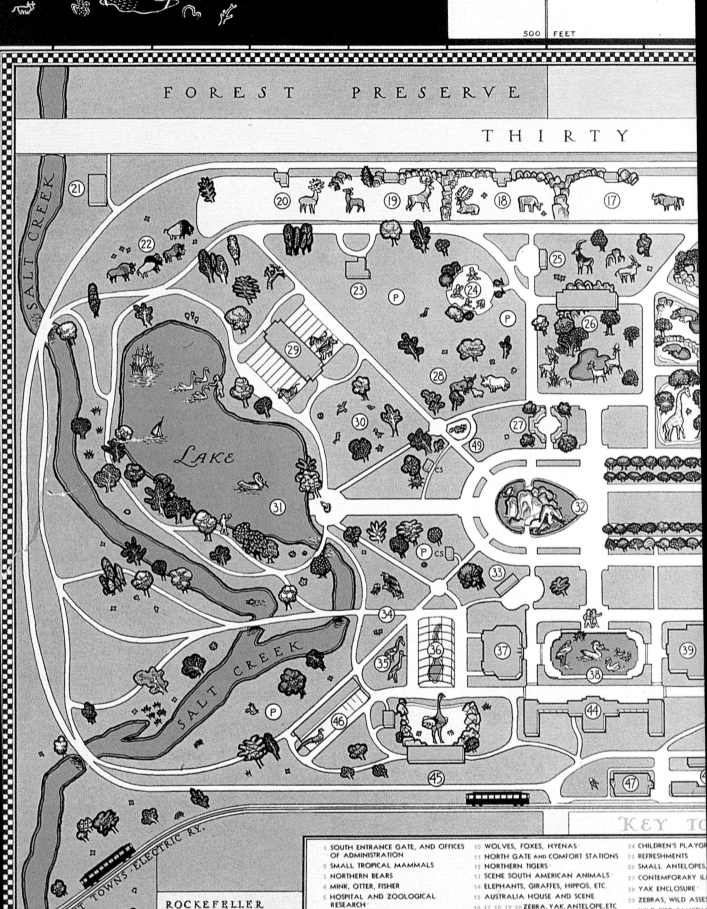

SALT CREEK

SALT CREEK

LAKE

SALT CREEK

WEST TOWNS ELECTRIC RY.

ROCKEFELLER

A.N. REBORI - EDGAR MILLER

KEY TO

1 SOUTH ENTRANCE GATE, AND OFFICES OF ADMINISTRATION	10 WOLVES, FOXES, HYENAS ·
2 SMALL TROPICAL MAMMALS ·	11 NORTH GATE and COMFORT STATIONS ·
3 NORTHERN BEARS ·	12 NORTHERN TIGERS ·
4 MINK, OTTER, FISHER ·	13 SCENE SOUTH AMERICAN ANIMALS ·
5 HOSPITAL AND ZOOLOGICAL RESEARCH ·	14 ELEPHANTS, GIRAFFES, HIPPOS, ETC. ·
6 OPOSSUM, PRAIRIE DOG, ETC. ·	15 AUSTRALIA HOUSE AND SCENE ·
7 NORTH AMERICAN PANORAMA ·	16,17,18,19,20 ZEBRA, YAK, ANTELOPE, ETC.
8 LIONS, TIGERS, LEOPARDS, JAGUARS ·	21 STORAGE BARN ·
9 LARGE ANTELOPES ·	22 BUFFALO AND WILD CATTLE ENCLOS-URES ·
	23 DIRECTOR'S RESIDENCE ·

24 CHILDREN'S PLAYGR
25 REFRESHMENTS ·
26 SMALL ANTELOPES,
27 CONTEMPORARY IL
28 YAK ENCLOSURE ·
29 ZEBRAS, WILD ASSES
30 WILD BIRD SANCTUA
31 AMERICAN WATER
32 SEA LIONS, SEALS,
33 REFRESHMENTS, LUN

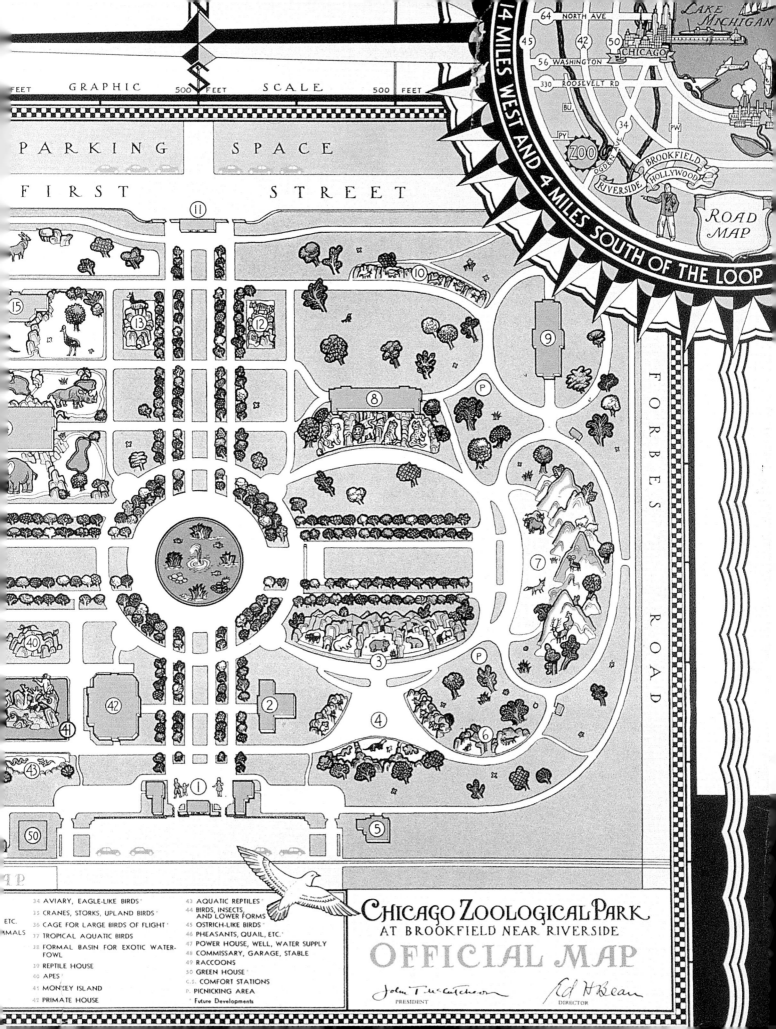

N

GRAPHIC   500 FEET   SCALE   500 FEET

PARKING   SPACE

FIRST   STREET

14 MILES WEST AND 4 MILES SOUTH OF THE LOOP

LAKE MICHIGAN

64 NORTH AVE
45   42A   50
CHICAGO
56 WASHINGTON
330 ROOSEVELT RD
BU
PY   34
ZOO
OGDEN AVE
BROOKFIELD
RIVERSIDE   HOLLYWOOD
ROAD MAP

FORBES ROAD

34 AVIARY, EAGLE-LIKE BIRDS
35 CRANES, STORKS, UPLAND BIRDS
36 CAGE FOR LARGE BIRDS OF FLIGHT
37 TROPICAL AQUATIC BIRDS
38 FORMAL BASIN FOR EXOTIC WATER-FOWL
39 REPTILE HOUSE
40 APES
41 MONKEY ISLAND
42 PRIMATE HOUSE

43 AQUATIC REPTILES
44 BIRDS, INSECTS, AND LOWER FORMS
45 OSTRICH-LIKE BIRDS
46 PHEASANTS, QUAIL, ETC.
47 POWER HOUSE, WELL, WATER SUPPLY
48 COMMISSARY, GARAGE, STABLE
49 RACCOONS
50 GREEN HOUSE
C.S. COMFORT STATIONS
P. PICNICKING AREA
• Future Developments

CHICAGO ZOOLOGICAL PARK
AT BROOKFIELD NEAR RIVERSIDE
OFFICIAL MAP

John T. McCutcheon
PRESIDENT

Ed H Bean
DIRECTOR

CHAPTER FIVE

Panda-monium

(1934-1940)

Animal Antics

The mid- to late 1930s were a great time for Brookfield Zoo. Attendance soared, visitors delighted at the unusual animals and clever exhibits, the work force was generally content, the press favored the zoo, and the trustees continued to dream up new revenue-generating activities. The animals, for their part, kept visitors enthralled and staff members hopping.

In zoos, one animal occasionally acquires "star" status through an event or by virtue of an engaging personality and becomes a crowd favorite. Sally the chimpanzee was one such animal: she "danced" in the 1925 Ziegfeld Follies. While two Russian dancers performed onstage, the audience could see Sally in the wings, dressed in a similar costume and imitating the dance as she was held back by her trainer. Finally, the Russians finished and went off, and on came Sally, going through a burlesque of the whole dance.

Unfortunately, one night Sally apparently became jealous of the young lady she was imitating and bit her in the leg. She was sold to George Getz the following day. Even at Brookfield Zoo, years later, Sally retained some habits that proved amusing. Most notably, she was quite willing to clean her own cage if offered a broom, as long as she received the right reward: a lit cigarette that she would enjoy down to the last puff.

Above: Sally was a favorite of the public, having gotten her start dancing in the Ziegfeld Follies.

Right: Although they did not get along with each other, Miss Suzette and Miss Congo were able to sit amicably for this photo.

Another of the zoo's chimpanzees was less of a ham but was nationally known through her appearances on the silver screen. Meshie, a young female chimp who was brought to the United States in 1929 by American Museum of Natural History curator Harry Raven, came to Brookfield Zoo in 1934 with an unusual background. Raven, a zoologist, had raised Meshie in his home, alongside his children. She became adept at eating with a knife and fork, brushing her hair, and taking baths. She would often ride a tricycle through the exhibit halls at the museum to join Raven in the staff dining room.

Meshie was the subject of two articles in *Natural History* magazine: "Meshie: The Child of a Chimpanzee" and "Further Adventures of Meshie." Her tame disposition brought her much fame, as detailed in one of the articles. "No trouper ever enjoyed success more than Meshie," the magazine asserted. "She became enormously at home on the stage and took all the sittings for movie cameramen, portrait painters, and sculptors in full stride. Paramount bought her film rights, and 'shorts' of her activities have been exhibited on all five continents, to the delectation of the world at large."

Meshie came to Brookfield Zoo when Raven had an opportunity to travel to Burma with famous collector Arthur Vernay. Seeking an appropriate home for Meshie, he chose the zoo, where she lived until her death in 1937.

Other primates colorful in their behaviors were two gorillas: Miss Suzette and Miss Congo. The two females were separated because they didn't get along well. Miss Suzette, however, had a fondness for her keeper, Sam Parrott. Parrott had some unusual gorilla-keeping habits. In his first years as a keeper, he lived in a house on grounds owned by the zoo. Sometimes he would take the two gorillas home with him in the evening and put them in cages he kept there. One evening he went out and apparently forgot to lock the cages. When he returned, the house was a disaster, having been rampaged by two nearly full-size gorillas.

"PRIMATE PARLANCE"

One local poet used her skill to share some of the observations she made while in Primate House. A series by Margaret Yost Zethmayr appeared once a week in the *Brookfield News* under the headline "Our Brookfield Zoo In Rhyme."

PRIMATE SOUNDS

*I find in primate parlance
So much that is not chatter
That I would like to stop a bit
To settle up this matter.*

*The spider monkey travels
With a shrill and mouse-like squeal
Which broadens into chicken squawks
That haven't much appeal.*

*The Rhesus, too, converses
Like a hot and thirsty hen,
While the squabbling brown Doguerras
Bark like puppies, now and then.*

*The gray-caped Hamadryas
Is apt to startle you
With his unexpected motions
And a sudden sharp "Wa-hoo!"*

*The ape, as we have told you,
Has a most unearthly howl:
The Lion-tail coos softly
From his soft, gray beard and cowl.*

*The gray cheeked Mangabey can grunt
Better than a pig:
A miniature lion roar
Makes him feel quite big.*

*The chimps, to show they like you,
Purse their lips and say "oo-oo";
The Orang Utans try to talk
And form a word or two.*

*As I stand vainly begging
Mandrilla Sphinx to talk,
A little Drill next door to him
Gives forth a schreechy squawk,*

*That sounds like any parrot,
While the blue-faced, red-nosed Sphinx
Just yawns and shows his awful tusks
Or sits and thinks and thinks.*

Above: Keeper Leroy Woodruff feeds an elephant seal. Watching employees feed the animals kept people almost as enthralled as feeding the animals themselves...almost.

Right: Cookie, a Leadbeater's cockatoo, was thought to have been acquired in 1934, making her the only animal to survive from the zoo's opening until the present.

Judy the elephant provided an unusual challenge for zoo staff. One day she was to be moved to nearby Lincoln Park Zoo but refused to enter the truck intended for her transport. Zoo officials, after trying all day to persuade the obstinate pachyderm, finally decided that she would walk the 18 miles to the zoo. Judy was accompanied by keepers, excited onlookers, and a squad of policemen during her trek down Congress Avenue. She left Brookfield at 7:00 p.m. and arrived at her new home at 3:00 a.m., with one stop at a Maywood gas station, where she guzzled 66 gallons of water.

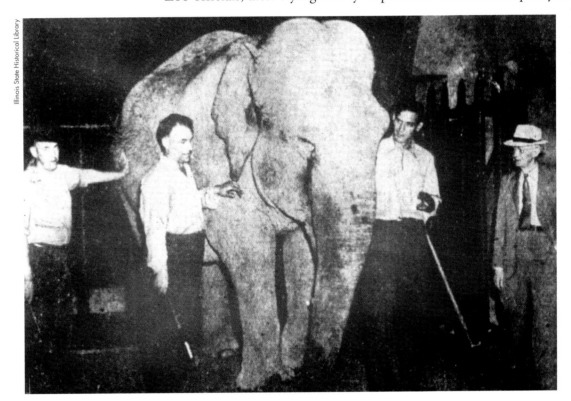

Illinois State Historical Library

Left: Judy proved to be a stubborn pachyderm. She was so opposed to being driven to her new home at Lincoln Park Zoo that officials gave up and she walked to Chicago.

RECOLLECTIONS

We went to the zoo almost every Sunday in the late '30s and early '40s. Every Sunday we would visit the Bird House and one particular cockatoo. I think he waited for us to come see him. My mother would sing "Turkey in the Straw" to him and he would pick up his tin plate and dance around for us. We'd laugh and applaud; my mother would sing again, and he would dance again. We looked forward to visiting him and being entertained and I think the bird looked forward to seeing us.

JoAnne Zick
Naperville, Illinois

A SLIPPERY TOPIC

This excerpt, referencing the Depression, is from a letter Ed Bean wrote to Edmund Heller, director of the Washington Park Zoo in Milwaukee, in February 1935.

"I am quite sorry that you are having banana trouble. I should think it would be possible to absorb the $4,000 cut that your budget had to undergo. Of course we all like to feed bananas and no doubt the monkeys enjoy them, but I believe by substituting carrots, apples, dried fruits and plenty of green vegetables during the summer, the monkeys can survive on a limited supply of bananas. You know, there are any number of families existing without their pie and cake so why not let the monkeys go on a depression diet."

Escapes and Other Mishaps

It is perhaps inevitable in a collection of so many animals that occasionally one gets loose. The first animal to escape from the zoo happened to be a kangaroo. It jumped over a moat, then hopped through the zoo and right out the service gate. The kangaroo hurried over to the Brookfield train depot and hopped down the tracks into Riverside, with zoo officials racing behind.

One employee recalled following the animal in a car. "We were doing sixty and that kangaroo was still ahead of us! We had a hard time catching him because there were no alleys. You'd corner him in somebody's yard and he'd jump over the fence into the next yard, and you had to go all the way around to get over to that side. You won't believe how we finally caught him. There was a fellow sitting on a swing on his back porch, reading a newspaper. The kangaroo sat down right next to him! The fellow didn't know what to do, whether he should jump off the porch or what. But the kangaroo didn't bother him, he just sat there. Finally we got him cornered, and Ed Bean himself tackled him."

Archie Schonemann of *The Suburban Magnet* told his version of the story in the paper's November 3, 1938, edition. "A black-faced giant kangaroo, top heavy with wanderlust, and an insatiable desire to go places and see things, leaped out of his running pen Wednesday morning, and after bounding around in the park for a time, he worked his way out of the grounds and finally was captured on First Avenue.

"At First Avenue, the 'roo was sighted and from this place, the ground crew at the zoological park came upon him with a huge net. Director Bean seized the forepaw of the 'roo, and drawing it down under the arm pit of the other, he raised his elbow up under the jaw of the animal and held him in this position until a net was thrown over the kangaroo's head.

"After the 'roo had been returned to the Australian exhibit, the ground crew returned to their several chores at the park. 'And to think that the director of the zoo, who is twice as old as any of us, had to capture that 'roo single handed,' muttered one of the crew as he walked away."

CHIMP TROUBLE

In "Keeper Aitken is Clawed by Giant Chimpanzee at Zoo," an article in its April 1, 1937, edition, *The Suburban Magnet* gave out some gruesome details about an unfortunate incident.

"Badly clawed by Mike, a 300 pound chimpanzee and his mate, Meshie, Arthur Aitken, keeper in the monkey house at Chicago Zoological Park, is in critical condition at the West Suburban Hospital. Aitken was carrying baskets filled with fruit and vegetables to nearby cages when he passed in front of the chimpanzee cage. Without warning, Mike, the male chimpanzee, thrust his three foot arm through the bars, grasping Aitken's arm. The female, Meshie, rushed forward, and while Aitken attempted to ward off Mike, he with Meshie began jerking the keeper's head and shoulders against the side of the cage. Aitken's left arm was badly lacerated from bites, the muscle below the shoulder and forearm being severed. It was found necessary to amputate one of the fingers of his right hand Tuesday.

"Both of the monkeys were driven to cover by another keeper, Abe Parrott, who on hearing the commotion rushed to the scene with a mop, and wielding it over the heads of the two chimps forced them to retire to the far corner of their cage."

One of the largest animals ever to escape its enclosure was Minnie the elephant. Even more interesting than her escapade is how creatively the January 13, 1938, *Chicago Daily Tribune* described the event on page one. "With a simple home treatment, Minnie the elephant succeeded yesterday in removing from her trunk the wart that has so long baffled the beauty experts at Brookfield Zoo. She unlocked the door of her apartment, smashed some steel gates and fence, and tripped right out of the zoo. And last night, [the keepers] discovered she'd cut the blemish off on the glass of one of the doors she smashed. She just looked smug when they remarked about it, and didn't seem to mind the mercurochrome they put on with a paint brush.

"Minnie, slimmest and most beautiful of the elephants, was gossiping with her bosom friend, Nancy, when something was said about the beauty experts. Minnie smirked and began picking the lock. Although the bolt is hard for the keepers to slide, Minnie pulled it back with her tusk and pushed through the door that the keepers open with a crank. She might have gone out into her front yard, but instead she ambled 200 feet along the keepers path to the commissary. She turned the knob and having the kind of waistline you'd expect of an elephant who never weighs a pound over one ton on the bathroom scales, slipped through. Finding a steel fence between her and the elephant house lobby, she tore the barrier down.

187—Restaurant, The Chicago Zoological Park at Brookfield, Illinois

Above: The Refectory, located at the east end of the zoo, opened in 1939.

Left: Kangaroos provided excitement of various sorts, whether escaping or boxing with a trainer.

A BOXING KANGAROO

Not every kangaroo came from the initial collection. Digger arrived in 1940 via a much different route. On October 31, 1940, *The Suburban Magnet* ran an article called "Your Friends at the Zoo," by Archie Schonemann, about the particularly pugilistic kangaroo.

"Sunday the attendance was 18,567. The crowd was attracted by the fight staged between a kangaroo and a man—the kangaroo being one Digger, and the man, Lindsay Fabre, trainer of the 'roo. The bout consisted of 3 rounds. While most of the combat was fistic with both the 'roo and the man trading punches, the former would balance himself on his tail occasionally thrusting forward his rear legs, with his feet, striking the chest of his opponent who was repeatedly sent sprawling to the far side of the ring.

"More than 1500 persons saw the fight which took place opposite the north entrance to the zoo. Digger was later turned over to the zoo and he has since been added to the 'roo collection in the Australian exhibit. Fabre indicated that Digger had outlived his usefulness as a fighting 'roo; that in addition to using his fore legs to box with and rear legs for heavy duty punches, he had acquired the unhappy faculty of bringing his teeth into play."

"Through the deserted lobby Minnie wandered, as she had seen visitors do, to the main entrance. One door was open. Slender as was her waistline, it wasn't quite slender enough. And so she smashed through the glass and steel of the adjoining door, and departed by them both. Keepers George Lewis and Eli Mark found her sitting on the ice out in front because she'd taken a spill the moment she got out. They said 'There! There!' and helped her up. Gratefully she went back inside with them."

Other problems arose when so many animals needed to be cared for. In the early 1930s, the zoo had some trouble with its bird collection when the United States Public Health Department found psittacosis, a severe infectious disease transmissible from parrots to humans, in one of the king parrots.

Perching Bird House was closed briefly while the Health Department and the zoo decided how to deal with the situation. The service initially asked that all other birds in the cage be destroyed but eventually agreed to allow a special quarantine for the birds in question. Four more parrots succumbed to the disease, but eventually the healthy birds were released back into Perching Bird House and the exhibit reopened.

PANDA-MONIUM

Courtesy Milwaukee Public Museum

Ziggy the Elephant

Among Brookfield Zoo's most famously difficult animals was Ziggy the Indian elephant. Weighing nearly six tons and standing 10 feet, two inches high, he was believed to be the largest land animal in the United States at the time.

Ziggy, short for Ziegfeld, had an unusual background. Florenz Ziegfeld of Ziegfeld Follies was standing at a New York dock one day, watching animals being unloaded for circus head John Ringling, when he spotted a young, 250-pound elephant. On the spot, Ziegfeld decided the elephant would be the ideal birthday present for his six-year-old daughter and quickly arranged to buy the pachyderm. The elephant was somehow maneuvered into a cab and driven to Ziegfeld's estate on Long Island.

Above: Ziggy was one of the zoo's most well-known animals for famous and, later, infamous reasons.

Ziggy, or Herman, as he was then called, did not last long in the Ziegfeld household. He had a tiresome habit of getting wedged in the stairway. His final antic was to smash the pots and eat the plants in the estate's greenhouse during a children's party.

Ziegfeld sold Ziggy back to Ringling Brothers, which eventually passed him on to Singer's Midget Circus. Under the direction of Captain Charles Becker, a 41-inch-tall member of the Singer troupe, Ziggy reportedly learned to play "Yes Sir, That's My Baby" on a harmonica and used a foot-long iron holder to smoke cigarettes. Whenever Captain Becker commanded him to "shake it up!" Ziggy broke into a thunderous, earth-shaking dance.

Once, while on tour in Spain, Ziggy danced a bit too vigorously, and the stage collapsed under his massive weight, much to the panic of the audience. But the elephant saved the day, keeping the crowds from jamming the exits by continuing his dance in the wreckage.

Another of Ziggy's misadventures occurred while Singer's Midget Circus was appearing in Milwaukee during the Prohibition. Lodged overnight in a stable, the inquisitive elephant kicked down a wall and uncovered $60,000 worth of bootleg whiskey that had been stashed behind a false partition. Unfortunately for the circus, the cache belonged to a relative of the local constabulary, and the circus was ordered out of town.

The turning point in Ziggy's career came in February 1936 at the San Diego Exposition. Captain Becker became terribly ill, and a substitute handler assumed charge of the act. Ziggy didn't respond well to a substitute handler and bolted from the grounds. Becker had to leave his sickbed to retrieve the AWOL animal. Some reports maintain that Ziggy attacked and killed a trombone player during his rampage, although there doesn't seem to be much evidence to support the claim.

Although Becker was obviously fond of Ziggy, the circus decided it was time to find the elephant a different home and sold him to Brookfield Zoo for $800. For the price, Robert Bean agreed to have two other elephants delivered to Coney Island later that year. The three elephants were loaded onto a railroad baggage car and, after Ziggy tore down a railway shed and caused a tremendous commotion on the trip, arrived in Brookfield in July. The trio delighted zoogoers with daily performances throughout the remainder of the summer season. In the fall, the two elephants left for New York, and Ziggy settled in at the zoo.

Pandas!

The only animals that bested Ziggy in popularity were the giant pandas, the first of which appeared in February 1937. Su-lin, whose name means "a little bit of something precious," was the first giant panda ever displayed in an American zoo, and he drove attendance up to numbers reminiscent of opening week.

It was only a fortunate accident that Brookfield Zoo acquired Su-lin (or Su Lin, as his name was sometimes spelled). In December 1936, adventuress Ruth Harkness passed through Chicago with the infant panda on her way to the Bronx Zoo. There her negotiations went sour. She asked an astronomical $20,000, over $200,000 in today's dollars. Also, Bronx Zoo officials feared that the panda's bowed legs might indicate rickets. In February, Harkness returned to Brookfield Zoo to temporarily house Su-lin while she figured out what to do next. Su-lin was pampered from day one. In fact, he spent his first night tucked inside a baby's pen with blankets.

"Every possible arrangement had been made beforehand by the Chicago Zoological Society for Su Lin's comfort at the Brookfield Zoo," Harkness later recounted in her book *The Lady and the Panda.* "One end of the Australian House had been cleared for her, and two glass-fronted rooms thrown together. [For a long time, Su-lin was thought to be a "she," but the panda ultimately turned out to be a "he"—hence Harkness' gender references.] There were a new baby's crib and piles of fresh little pink and blue blankets. The crib was too small; Director Bean and his son Robert were astonished that Su Lin had grown so much. There was a new Chinese grass rug on the floor which immediately appealed to Su Lin, since she could get her claws into it and really make progress. But the room temperature was too high; Su Lin's coat was very thick and heavy, and I had always given her as much fresh air as possible no matter how cold the weather. Then when a cageful of wild dingo dogs began to bark, there was no question that the Australian House was the wrong place for a baby Panda.

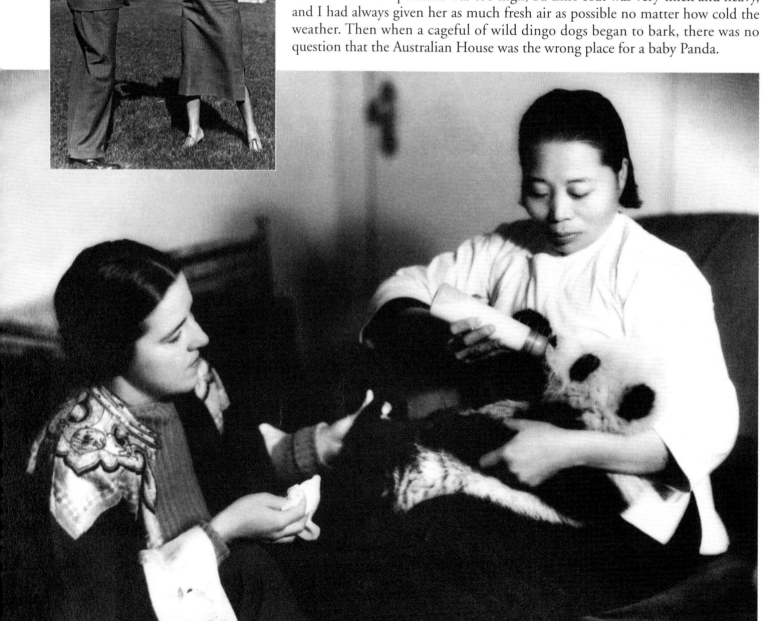

Far left: Su-lin arrived in Brookfield being treated like royalty, as he would be during his entire stay at the zoo.

Below left: In China, adventuress Ruth Harkness (left) gets a lesson on how to feed a baby panda.

Right: A zoo security guard handles Su-lin while the crowd presses in, confident in giant pandas' perceived "gentle" nature.

"The first aid station...was finally decided upon, and Su Lin was given a room to herself with all of the windows wide open. Nothing could have suited me (or Su Lin) better because the next room was the one Miss Mary Bean [Ed Bean's daughter] occupied all day. The Baby's care fell in the hands of Miss Mary and Mr. Robert Bean, and never has one little animal had two more devoted friends. Miss Mary is a registered nurse with special baby training, and Mr. Robert Bean, besides being Curator of Mammals, possesses that natural instinct for understanding animals that is a rather rare thing."

At that point, Su-lin was not on public view. Instead, he was cared for behind the scenes by Mary Bean, who in addition to her first-aid duties often cared for young animals. By April, Su-lin had tripled in size to 25 pounds and was enjoying a daily diet of two raw carrots, half a head of lettuce, three or four stalks of celery, spinach, prune juice and orange juice, vegetable soup and cod liver oil—a far cry from the bamboo ordinarily a staple of panda diets.

A BABY BEI-SHUNG

The December 1983 issue of *Smithsonian* magazine, in an article entitled "First U.S. panda, shanghaied in China, stirred up a ruckus," by Erika Brady, questioned the first association between Su-lin the panda and Ruth Harkness.

"...the story of how Su Lin was obtained is still one of the more perplexing mysteries in the annals of zoological expeditions—a tale as exotic and enigmatic as the giant panda itself. [After Ruth Harkness' husband of 17 months died while on a panda-hunting expedition, she decided to continue his quest herself.] Ruth Harkness evidently was a very lucky person indeed. On one of their first days in panda territory, she and [guide] Quentin Young were prowling the bamboo thickets when Young heard a sound and set out after it. Harkness followed. 'Dimly through the waving wet branches,' she recalled in her book, 'I saw him near a huge rotting tree. I stumbled on blindly brushing the water from my face and eyes. Then I too stopped, frozen in my tracks. From the old dead tree came a baby's whimper.... Quentin came toward me and held out his arms. There in the palms of his two hands was a squirming baby bei-shung.'

"Meanwhile, [collector] Tangier Smith...did his best to discredit Harkness' story. Between the time her party left Chengtu and returned with the panda, he insisted, she could not possibly have set up a base camp and the lesser scout camps as she claimed. What is more, he said, his sources informed him that she had set up a single temporary camp in the vicinity of Tsaopo, and there paid cash for a baby panda being kept for him by one of his hunters. This view is supported by fresh evidence uncovered several years ago by Atlanta attorney Richard J. Reynolds III, who corresponded with several missionaries and animal dealers. They expressed the conviction that Ruth Harkness, whose worldly demeanor did not impress them, purchased the panda—just as Tangier Smith maintained. Unhappily for him, however, the American press showed little interest in his allegations. The late 1930s were discouraging years in the United States, what with the Depression and rumblings of war in Europe; Ruth Harkness and Su Lin provided the kind of charming diversion the nation hungered for."

Above: The public's thirst for all things relating to pandas led to some strange antics—from humans, that is. Here WLS-Radio reporter Martha Gowdy "interviews" Mei-lan.

Above and left: On most days, the crowd around the panda exhibit was many heads deep. The presence of the pandas drove attendance way up. *I'm a Panda* was published to meet the demand for panda paraphernalia. An ashtray featuring a panda served the same purpose. Realizing the significance of "panda mania," Quaker Oats featured Ruth Harkness and Su-lin in one of its ads for oatmeal.

On April 19, Brookfield Zoo bought Su-lin with an $8,750 commitment toward Harkness' next expedition to China. It proved to be a good investment. As the only panda outside of China, Su-lin immediately attracted attention. In fact, the same day the purchase was made, Alexander Wooldcott—columnist, author, and radio commentator—came to the zoo to "interview" the panda. Other newspaper articles and radio stories followed. WLS-Radio even broadcast live from the zoo in June. All this despite the fact that Su-lin was not yet on display.

On August 13, after his new air-conditioned "house" had been completed in the west end of the zoo, Su-lin met the public, albeit only for one hour each day. One Sunday, after Su-lin had been on exhibit about a week, attendance was reported at 53,504 visitors, one of the largest crowds since the zoo had opened.

Su-lin did his part to keep interest high by climbing trees, somersaulting, and staying active. Overnight he became a Chicago attraction. One couple wrote from Australia to say they were coming to America to see the Dionne quintuplets and the giant panda.

"Panda" became a household word. The Society began selling toy pandas (all trademarked, of course). Increased admissions and revenues from panda merchandise eased some financial concerns the trustees had been mulling over.

Child movie star Shirley Temple came to visit the famous animal, accompanied by John McCutcheon, Jr., and left content with an inky footprint of Su-lin, complete with seals of certification. Actor John Barrymore visited as well and had to be escorted by zoo security to prevent him from being mobbed. Other notable visitors included Theodore Roosevelt's son Kermit, Sophie Tucker, Helen Hayes, and Helen Keller, upon whose arm curator of birds Karl Plath deposited a gentle salmon-crested cockatoo so she could feel it.

Right: Su-lin was so popular, he merited a color feature in the *Chicago Sunday Tribune*.

Below: Su-lin (right) and Mei-mei met briefly. Although the crowds would have loved seeing the two popular animals together, the pandas did not get along.

Harkness, after leaving what she thought was a female panda in Brookfield, returned to China to find Su-lin a husband. Disappointed that she was able to find only "another" female, she nonetheless brought Mei-mei, meaning "little sister," to the zoo in February 1938. Unknown to her or zoo staff, Mei-mei was male as well, thus providing the zoo with two male giant pandas, both thought to be female. The introductions did not go well. Su-lin hit Mei-mei on the nose the first time they were together, and they were separated thereafter. Su-lin died of pneumonia a few weeks later.

Mei-mei was joined in November 1938 by Mei-lan, "the little flower," yet another male masquerading as a female. He was presented by *Chicago Daily News* president and publisher Colonel Frank Knox, who had served under Theodore Roosevelt in the Spanish-American War in the famous Rough Riders troop.

Although both Mei-mei and Mei-lan had the same comical appearance and active nature as Su-lin, neither of them ever matched that first panda in gentleness of disposition. Mei-mei was considered mean and Mei-lan even meaner. Upon arriving with Mei-lan, adventurer Rey Scott pointed out his many scratches and declared he didn't care whether or not he ever saw his charge again. Mei-lan bit everyone within reach, including Robert Bean and several keepers.

RECOLLECTIONS

...the giant panda bonanza came into being. It could well be called one of the single greatest coups in zoo history. You had to live through that era in order to understand the immediate popularity and drawing power of that little animal known as Su Lin. It hit the Chicago area by storm and was quickly paid for. Books were written, front page stories, feature stories, radio, Pathe news, magazine stories, and foreign correspondents came almost daily. On a sunlit February Sunday in the Chicago vicinity the little animal drew 40,000 visitors—unheard of during that time of year. What a sight to behold....

It was impossible to obtain panda souvenirs in large enough quantities to satisfy sales. The panda craze was in full sway and the animal has never lost its appeal. To this day panda items are found in stores the world over. We started it all.

George Speidel
Former Security Captain

Above: Mei-lan shows off the exhibit that was created especially for him.

One keeper, Ralph Small, lost his hand to Mei-lan. "About five weeks after I started working at the zoo, I lost my right hand to the giant panda," he later said. "I was replacing the regular keepers, who were off that day. The panda...looked like he was sick.... Director Bean asked me to feel its nose to see if it was cold and wet. If the nose was cold I was supposed to let the animal out into the panda yard. The panda was lying right against the two-inch link fencing on the gate, so I checked it. It was cold, so I let the panda out. Bean asked me to check it again to be absolutely certain. This time the panda was laying down by the larger outside bars with its head up. The panda threw open its mouth and caught me, right at the wrist with the lower jaw, and the upper one caught the fingers. Other keepers came to help me right away. One guy said he pulled some muscles in his back he was pulling so hard. They finally got me loose."

Mei-mei died in 1942 at the age of five. Mei-lan, however, lived until September 1953 to the age of 15. All three pandas went to the Field Museum upon their deaths, and it was there that it was discovered that the trio had all been males. When museum curator Dwight Davis conducted in-depth anatomical studies on the animals, they contributed one last time to the small but growing body of knowledge about giant pandas, confirming the species' relationship to bears.

PANDAS IN THE SKIES

On May 19, 1938, in honor of the 20th anniversary of the establishment of air mail, a special air-mail flight was dispatched from Brookfield Zoo's north parking lot. Over 3,300 envelopes, specially postmarked for the occasion with the likeness of a panda, were officially mailed while giant panda Mei-mei, hundreds of zoo visitors, and local citizens looked on.

Courtesy Brookfield Historical Society

Above: Nancy embarrassed zoo officials when it was discovered that she was not "with pachyderm," despite the giant bash the zoo threw in celebration of her famous pregnancy.

Zoo Babies

Other events that often attract public and media attention are animal births. In the late 1930s, there were several notable pregnancies and, in some cases, births at Brookfield Zoo.

One of the most publicized pregnancies was that of Nancy the elephant, who had arrived (reluctantly) from Michigan as part of the original Getz collection. (It's worth noting that during her time at the Getz farm, Nancy was photographed by Paramount Pictures and actually trumpeted for one of the earliest "talkie" films.)

Below: *Life* photographers were frequently at the zoo, snapping pictures of the latest arrivals.

Nancy had been introduced to the famed Ziggy, and it was soon announced that a baby elephant was imminent. On August 12, 1940, a baby shower of huge proportions was held in and around Pachyderm House, with a reported 40,000 guests in attendance. Nancy was in her finest: a baby-blue and white bed jacket specially designed for her by a tent manufacturer. A baker contributed an enormous cake bedecked with replicas of storks and a baby elephant. Zoo visitors brought baskets of fruits and nuts, and plush toys arrived in quantity. The National Dairy Council even sent a 400-gallon nursing bottle.

The shower was a smash, but as the date of delivery approached and then passed, red-faced zoo officials announced that Nancy's "pregnancy" was nothing more than an inordinate weight gain. Apparently, her earlier acting experience had paid off in cake and presents.

Unlike Nancy, several of the zoo's animals actually did give birth. These new additions received considerable press coverage in those early days of zoo mania, both as the blessed events approached and after delivery. In the early '40s, *Life* magazine covered Brookfield Zoo's notable births, several times devoting spreads to photos of mother and offspring.

Occasionally, the zoo sponsored public contests in search of the best name for a newly born animal. Pamela the giraffe's son Claude was named in this fashion. Over 24,000 children entered suggestions. The second-grader who won received a $50 savings bond.

Bebe the hippo's offspring was dubbed Puddle by contest, with the name winning over such suggestions as Hippotobias, Chihipo, Wimpy, and Man Mountain Dean. Puddle became the central figure in a children's book published in 1936, *Puddle: The Real Story of a Baby Hippo*, and was later sent to the San Diego Zoo in exchange for popular Reggie the elephant seal.

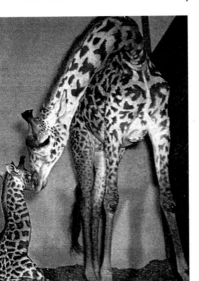

RECOLLECTIONS

About 45 years ago, I named two rhinoceroses at Brookfield Zoo. The Chicago American *held a contest to name two rhinoceroses. I was the first-prize winner of a TV set. I named them Tipsatun and Tipsatuntu.*

Mildred Schuetz
LaGrange, Illinois

Left: Puddle the baby hippo, with mom Bebe, became a star as the subject of a children's book.

Unusual Exhibits

Many major zoos have one or two exhibits that are somewhat unusual, perhaps because they house particularly rare animals or exhibit animals in a distinctly different manner than other zoos. Brookfield Zoo had more than its share of these exhibits.

The zoo's collection of hoofed animals was particularly large for many years. In 1937, the zoo acquired a species never before captured alive: giant elands. These large antelope can reach a height of six feet at the shoulders and a weight of 1,500 pounds. They were on the verge of extinction for many years, and it was only after four years of negotiation with the British Embassy in Washington, D.C. and officials in the Sudan that the zoo secured permission to export the giant elands.

Other hoofed animals that brought Brookfield Zoo acclaim were its many sitatungas. At one time, the zoo displayed over 70 of these small, beautiful animals, which bred especially well. Over the years, the zoo would boast of over 500 sitatunga births. This may be due in part to the claim that while Robert Bean traded many male sitatungas to other zoos, he never parted with a single breeding female. In *The Zoo*, author Peter Crowcroft states that "almost every sitatunga in the U.S. originated from a group at Brookfield."

In its time, the Illinois Exhibit was unusual for zoos in that it tried to draw visitors' attention to animals native to the area. The open-air building featured Illinois mammals such as coyotes, red foxes, squirrels, skunks, minks, ferrets, bobcats, and woodchucks. Usually squirrels aren't thought of as zoo animals, but the exhibit was quite popular.

The Illinois Exhibit also featured murals of buffaloes, elk, bears, and cougars with information about where the last specimen of each was exterminated in Illinois. Also included were records of Native-American tribes that at one time inhabited Illinois.

THE CHILDREN'S PLAYGROUND

In a September 1937 letter to the *Philadelphia Inquirer*, Ed Bean responded to a request for information about a children's zoo within Brookfield Zoo.

"We have a very unique children's playground in the heavily wooded section in the west part of the Park. It is enclosed and has several wood carvings of domestic animals on the archway. Within the enclosure we have sand boxes, teeter totters, lawn swings; around the outer fence we have cages of doves, a nanny goat with three kids, two lambs. The fence is low so that the children may step over and coddle them. At the rear we have monkey town. It is arranged like the face of a sky scraper. On the doors below there is a fire department, police station, barber shop, undertaker, hardware store, and several other business stores amusingly named on the windows. On the upper floors there are ledges below each set of windows, and they are labeled with the various occupations that are found in a large office building. There is a small fire escape at one corner of the building along which the monkeys can climb up, walk along the ledges, go to the hairdresser, justice of peace, lawyer's office, etc. The children and many grownups get quite a kick out of the monkeys visiting the various offices in the building."

Near the Illinois Exhibit was a raccoon enclosure, with a water-filled moat and a center island. Again, it was not a typical zoo exhibit, but the active raccoons proved entertaining.

Finally, mention must be made of the magnificent bear and lion dens. On free weekend days, crowds eight heads deep could often be found in front of these exhibits. No doubt this was due in part to the unique rock work and unusual display techniques first encouraged by the Hagenbecks and later realized by sculptor John Hurlimann.

In the 1930s, the grottos were exceedingly well-populated, with as many as seven lions or eight bears in one enclosure. While staff addressed all sorts of problems with regard to animal management and competition for food and social stature among the group, it was a delight for visitors. Seven lions in one exhibit inevitably makes for much activity and interaction between the animals, elements of a popular exhibit.

Thanks to an active animal collection, innovative exhibitry, and an interested public, the late 1930s were glory years for Brookfield Zoo. They didn't last long, though. Zoogoing and zookeeping took a marked dive in the 1940s, when the nation went to war.

Above: A host of black bears eyes the crowd, probably hoping for marshmallows.

Top: A young girl inspects an elk on a mural in the Illinois Exhibit. The mural detailed the species' history in Illinois.

Left: Over 500 sitatungas have been born at the zoo over the years.

Far left: Robert Bean knew the value of good public relations. Here he chats with WLS-Radio reporter Martha Gowdy as she helps feed some giant elands.

Right: Edward and Robert Bean discuss weighty zoo matters in front of Kodiak Island, which was completed in 1938.

Courtesy Ellen Bean

CHAPTER SIX

The War Years

(1940-1945)

Making Ends Meet

Having survived public opposition in the 1920s and the Depression of the 1930s, Brookfield Zoo faced new challenges when World War II broke out. Attendance dropped by 500,000 in 1939, attributed to poor weather and the possibility that people were staying home to hear news on the radio. With revenues dropping off and the future uncertain, a halt was called on new construction and efforts were made to increase attendance in new ways. Free music and guide services were offered during the summer of 1940, and a publicity firm was hired briefly to increase awareness of the zoo.

"WE THREE"

"THE BEGGARS"

"WE LIKE PEANUTS"

Left: Even in its early days, Reptile House displayed its animals in standard enclosures with "cage furniture" such as branches, rocks, and live plants.

The situation only got worse throughout 1940 and 1941, with fewer visitors and little hope for immediate improvement. The Federal Income Tax Law of 1941 required that an admission tax of 3 cents be collected on all paid admissions and on all persons admitted free on 25 cent days, thereby increasing the admission rates without benefit to the zoo. A bad wind and hail storm later that year and the loss of keepers to the war effort further depressed morale.

Also that year, Ziggy, the Indian elephant famous for stirring things up, did it once again, in a big way. Elephant keeper George "Slim" Lewis was about to bring him in for the day when the giant pachyderm suddenly turned on his keeper.

Lewis later described the attack in *I Loved Rogues: The Life of an Elephant Tramp*. "He whirled on me in a flash. His lashing trunk struck me full force and the blow threw me nearly fifty feet. I landed on my stomach. Before I could scramble to my feet, he was on top of me. His trunk seized me by a leg and he pulled me, face down, beneath his head. I tried to turn over on my back, hoping that if I could face him, he might respond to a command. As I twisted to my side, his tusks grazed my chest and my back and thudded a foot into the ground.

"He jerked up his head and the tusks poised above me. His trunk was curled over, outside the right tusk and around underneath to hold my legs. His tusks were close-set, and there wasn't much room between them, but I managed to twist into that space as they plunged into the ground a second time. Ziggy stabbed again and again. I kept wriggling, and by some miracle, he missed piercing my body. If my nickname hadn't been Slim by rights, I wouldn't be telling the story.

"Once he came so close he pinned my right arm to the ground, and I thought it was coming off. Incongruously for a man still under a bull elephant intent on killing him, I thought, 'How am I going to make a living with one arm gone?'

Above: Visitors are dwarfed by the spaciousness of the free-flight display in Aquatic Bird House and by the building itself.

"Then he got my right leg in his mouth and tried to chew it off. As he worked my foot back toward his great, grinding molars, he had to relax his mouth for another pull, and I jerked the leg free. I didn't see how I could possibly continue to escape the thrusts, pinned down as I was, and half my mind was screaming, 'Go on, get it over with.' The rest was saying, 'Keep trying.'

"I closed my eyes as the tusks descended again, but when I opened them, I was still there and the ivory shafts were buried in the hard ground. Ziggy had thrown his weight into them so hard it took him a moment to pull free. In that tiny interval, I finally managed to turn over so I faced him. As he raised his head, I grabbed one of his ears and he pulled me to my feet. Plastered to the side of his head, I gouged for his eye with my free hand. At the same time, I shouted at him.

Ziggy must have thought he had done the job. He was so startled that I could still fight back, he straightened up and stood still.

"I turned away from Ziggy and went to the moat, walking so he wouldn't get the idea I was in retreat and be encouraged to charge me again. I jumped into the moat and climbed out the other side. At the fence, I turned to look back at Ziggy. He strolled over to where the hook and my hat had fallen when he first struck me. He picked up the hat, twirled it in his trunk for a second and threw it into the moat. Then he did the same thing with the hook. It was a nice bit of grandstanding."

After the attack, Lewis visited Director Bean in his office to beg that Ziggy not be destroyed. Coming from a circus background, Lewis was used to unruly animals being killed, and he pled for Ziggy's survival with tears running down his cheeks. Director Bean decided that Ziggy would be pardoned but, as a safety precaution, that the elephant would be kept only in an indoor enclosure from then on. Later that same day, the indomitable Lewis went back into the yard with Ziggy and, with the help of another elephant, brought him inside. Decades later, Ziggy's circumstances would change the way these animals are managed in captivity.

Ziggy's attack was one of the events that set a somber tone for the zoo. At the 1942 annual meeting, Stanley Field reported, "I think one can only look forward to the year 1942 and the years that are to follow with considerable trepidation. The trustees and Executive Committee will have to exercise much care to maintain what is there now and to keep the park open."

During the same meeting, Director Bean reported that due to men enlisting in the armed forces or seeking war-related employment, "more employees were lost by resignation during the last year than in all previous years since the park opened."

One happy event does stand out: the October 1941 birth of the first black rhinoceros born in captivity. John McCutcheon recalled how he heard the news. "Once in the small hours of night our telephone rang," he said. "This is never a pleasant sound. Brookfield was calling. 'There's a baby rhino!' came Robert Bean's excited voice. 'It's hardly twenty minutes old. There's never been one born in captivity before. I want to tell the committee!'" McCutcheon decided to wait until morning to share the good news with the Executive Committee.

Above: In 1941, Ziggy the Indian elephant violently turned on his keeper, "Slim" Lewis. A passerby managed to snap this photo of the attack.

Above and left: In 1941, Mary the black rhino (above) gave birth to Georgie-Joe (left), the first of the species born in captivity. It was a momentous event considering black rhinos are endangered. A sign (inset) announced the grand birth.

MIGHTY PHARAOH

Former animal collector Walter C. Schulz recalled the capture of the male black rhino, Pharaoh, "...which I followed for 17 days on the foot of the Olessimingo mountain, 90 miles west of Arusha towards lake Manyara. A scratch caused by a lion had injured its anus which a young newly arrived Veterinary declined to operate on, advising to destroy the animal and catch another one. Poor Vet, he had no idea that the capture of a rhino in those days was not an easy task, and was only to be achieved by months-long hunting in the veld, bearing all hardships on a never-give-in basis and constant fight for survival for men and animal alike. I doped the young rhino bull, disinfected the area, repositioned the intestine and stitched up the rectum. The result: this rhino became the father of the first rhino calf born in a zoo."

The successful birth of the black rhino to parents Pharaoh and Mary helped mark the Chicago Zoological Park as a first-class zoo, not just in respect to exhibitry, but also in breeding efforts.

Rhinos notwithstanding, Field's prediction unfortunately came true. In 1943, attendance dropped to 669,769 from 2,089,223 in 1938. Earned revenues fell accordingly, hitting $166,000 in 1943, having reached $290,000 in 1938. The thinking at the zoo was of sheer maintenance and existence rather than growth and improvement. Excess animals were sold, decreasing the amount of food and keepers needed and bringing in a much-needed source of cash. In 1943, the Society raised $23,315 selling animals, and no new animals were purchased. The practice of selling animals, common in zoos at the time, was soon discontinued except to properly accredited and responsible organizations.

At Director Bean's suggestion, Small Mammal House was closed in 1943 due to difficulty in securing and retaining keepers. Reportedly, the closing saved the zoo about $6,000 a year in food and maintenance. Many experienced keepers left to join the military or to find higher-paying jobs in the war industry. There were missile factories and other war-effort jobs in neighboring communities, and they paid considerably more than the zoo. Bean and the trustees tried to keep up by continuously raising pay scales, but they couldn't afford to keep pace.

"On July 1, 1941, the approximate date on which the first man left the Park to enter the armed services, the Society employed 32 men for the care of the animals," Bean reported. "In the three years since that date, 51 men have been engaged—some staying a year and others only a few hours. Today there are 26 men on the keepers payroll—only seven of whom were with the Society prior to July 1, 1941. Most of the new men didn't know a hawk from a handsaw when they came, and I regret I must add that many didn't when they left."

HIPPOS FOR SALE

In January 1943, the *Chicago Daily Times* featured an article called "Wanna Buy a Hippopotamus?" about the practice of selling animals during World War II.

"Unless you have an outsize bathtub, you probably won't be interested, but if you want to pick up a pair of hippopotami at bargain rates, your opportunity is knocking out at the gates of the Brookfield Zoo. Only $4,500 will take away Bebe and Toto, the hefty hippos aged 4 and 3 respectively, whom Robert Bean, assistant director of the zoo yesterday posted for sale along with 5 black bears, 30 baboons, one wildebeest, one hartebeest, one eland antelope and two giraffes.

"Though gasoline rationing has made rather an ugly dent in zoo attendance, Bean said the animals are being sold primarily because they're duplicates.

"A Chicago banker wanted a bear—to eat. And a local firm selling game wanted a bunch of bears—also to be sold to eat. Bean made short work of them, 'Our animals are NOT being sold to be destroyed.'

"The 30 baboons, whom no one has shown any marked interest in acquiring, will sell for $25 apiece, if the buyer takes the lot. Individual baboons run higher. The eland antelope and the hartebeest will go, if they go at all, for $600 apiece, and the wildebeest for about that sum."

Tire restrictions and gas rationing didn't help attendance problems, even eliminating the ever-present school groups from the zoo. The children's polio epidemic that hit Chicago in 1943 further discouraged parents and schools from bringing their little ones to a public place. The popular merry-go-round was temporarily shut down in 1943 to cut down on contact from child to child. A private citizen, a Mr. Harrison, even wrote a letter to the government suggesting that the zoo dismantle its cages and donate the scrap metal to the war effort—a suggestion that didn't get much consideration from the trustees. Taxes, even when collected, were not always passed immediately to the zoo, creating further cash-flow problems.

The zoo managed surprisingly well with all of these difficulties. Since the '30s, the zoo had farmed several acres in the northeast corner to provide fresh, cheap food for the animals. In 1943, 110 tons of green fodder, 13 tons of soybean hay, 12 tons of corn fodder, and 10,000 pounds of pumpkins were harvested on 23 acres of land. This self-sufficiency certainly helped the zoo weather the days of poor supplies.

"Naturally," Stanley Field reported in 1944, "there have been difficulties in obtaining the proper kind of food, such as for instance, the inability to get bananas for the monkeys and the substitution of sweet potatoes. There have naturally been many such changes—but no difficulties whatsoever have been experienced, nor is the health of the collection in any way impaired."

Circumstances eased a bit in 1944 when attendance increased by about 200,000. The trustees, ever hopeful, created a new exhibit wish list that included a gorilla house; a new barless panda grotto; renovations for Small Mammal House, which desperately needed better ventilation and more public space; new paddocks for some of the hoofed animals; and underground wiring for the telegraph and telephone wires. Also desirable but less pressing were a North American panorama, a small hospital, a library and meeting place, and buildings for hunting trophies and animal art. The trustees knew all they could do was dream—new construction wasn't possible at the time—but at least they would be prepared if the situation improved.

When possible throughout the war years, the Board of Trustees set aside extra money in a contingency fund, not knowing how long the war would last or what the future would bring for the zoo. By 1945, the fund had grown to nearly $500,000, a testimony to the Board's frugality and careful planning.

Left: The zoo lost many of its workers, including much of its grounds crew, to World War II.

Below: Commissary manager Frank Snyder (right) oversaw distribution of animal meals, including zoo-grown hay, corn, and pumpkins.

Ed Steiner

"TIRELESS" ZOOKEEPING

In 1942, the Associated Press filed the following report, "Gorillas Join Tire Complainers," about how even the animals were affected by rationing during World War II.

"Chicago, July 15—The scrap-rubber drive hit the gorilla house at Brookfield Zoo. The three ancient tires which Suzette, Congo and Sultan toyed with for their diversion were removed from their cage while they slept. Came the dawn and Suzette, Congo and Sultan obviously were piqued. The keeper deemed it unwise to romp with them until they rise above the pinch of personal sacrifice."

A Tragic Loss

Just as the war situation was looking a little more hopeful and attendance and revenues were beginning a slow but steady upward climb, the zoo was rocked by tragedy. On September 5, 1945, Director Ed Bean was returning from a vacation spent with his sister when his car skidded on loose gravel. The car turned over three times before coming to a stop against a fence. Bean, helped from the car and taken to the hospital, said he felt "a little dazed." Later, however, doctors discovered he had suffered a concussion. The 69-year-old zoo director died shortly thereafter.

With the shock waves still reverberating, the Board of Trustees considered the question of a successor. Everyone knew that Ed Bean, who had been director for 18 years, would be a hard act to follow. The zoo had prospered during his watch. He had fostered good relations with his active Board and created a family feeling among staff, his connections in the zoo world had allowed for many unique animal transactions, and under his watchful eye, the Chicago Zoological Park had gradually come to be. Bean had helped build the zoo into a leading zoological institution.

As assistant director since 1927, Robert Bean was the natural choice to follow his father as director. In 1945, the trustees appointed him acting director, a position he held for two years until he was officially made director. The reluctance to immediately appoint the junior Bean as full-fledged director signified some reservations the Board had about his capabilities. Although exceedingly knowledgeable about animals and zoos, obviously intelligent, well-respected in the field, and a quick study, Robert had one flaw the trustees worried about: he had a drinking problem.

And so a new chapter began for the zoo. World War II ended, Ed Bean was gone, and the zoo moved on.

1945 Ed Bean dies in a car crash.
Ralph Graham is hired as artist and photographer.
Robert Bean is appointed acting director.

'46 Curator of reptiles Robert Snedigar joins the staff.
Insect House opens.

'47 Robert Bean is officially made director.
Ralph Graham is appointed assistant to the director.
A spectacled bear injures a three-year-old boy.
The first photography contest is held.

'48 Ralph Graham captures two Indian rhinos for the zoo.
A child falls into the Monkey Island moat.

'49 John McCutcheon resigns, then dies shortly after.
Clay Judson becomes the Society's new president.
The first *Bandar-log* is published.
Karl Plath escorts a large shipment of animals, mostly birds, from Australia.

CHAPTER SEVEN

Robert Bean's Reign Begins

(1945-1949)

Legends of Robert Bean

Robert Bean

In her book *Animal Gardens*, Emily Hahn quotes several zoo men who commented something to the effect that Robert Bean "was about the best in the business." Throughout his tenure at Brookfield Zoo, never was there doubt that Bean was one of the most admired zoo directors in the world.

A keeper once stated that Bean was "tops" among zoo directors, adding that Bean could get an employee a job at another zoo. At that time, many zoos required civil-service exams of their new employees, but according to the keeper, if Bean recommended the applicant, the test requirements were lifted. The story attests to the zoo director's reputation.

Bean was immensely knowledgeable about animals and well-connected, having literally grown up in and around zoos. Although he never completed his zoology degree at the University of Wisconsin, the years he spent there augmented his practical experience. Also, his international contacts were responsible for Brookfield Zoo's acquisition of the first collection of Australian animals in 1934, and his previous role as director of the San Diego Zoo allowed for healthy relations and animal trades with that organization. His connections and reputation had only grown since 1934 through his collecting trips and travels to other zoos.

Having been present throughout all of Brookfield Zoo's construction, Bean knew every inch of the zoo. "He knew where every nail was that was put in that place," a keeper commented. "He knew where everything was."

Robert Bean's character and talents have made him somewhat legendary. Some people believe he had total recall, that he could remember every phrase he ever heard and every image he ever saw. It must have seemed that way to his employees because he never forgot even part of a conversation. Some maintain that his excellent memory came in handy during his many travels. They say he would note the nicest, newest exhibits in each zoo he visited and come back with all of the mental details necessary to replicate and improve the exhibit for Brookfield Zoo.

RECOLLECTIONS

[Robert Bean's] knowledge of animals, and particularly individual animals, was greater than anyone I have seen before or since. He knew the background of herds of animals we had at the zoo, moreover, I think he knew the backgrounds of their mothers and fathers. [And] he had the respect of his colleagues, absolutely. Moreover, he had a command of the English language that was truly outstanding. When he spoke it was mesmerizing and poetic. He used words extremely well and could communicate beautifully.

Ron Blakely
Later Zoo Director

Most everyone who recalls Bean agrees that he was essentially a good-hearted, generous man. Stories abound about leaves granted on the spot due to family illness, about personal loans he made to employees (many never to be repaid), and about how he would regularly refuse his salary increase, insisting instead that it be split among the employees. Certainly he loved the Chicago Zoological Park, having witnessed its birth and subsequent development.

Also certain is Bean's fondness for alcohol, which diminished his effectiveness and life span as director. Employees would approach Director Bean only after determining his sobriety with the switchboard operator. "It was no use going in if he was in a bad mood," recalled one keeper. Employees kept their distance on those days. He was known to fire employees on his bad days, only to rehire them the next day. The disease was not one he could hide, and the whole institution knew of his problem. It interfered with his ability to make decisions and to lead. The Board struggled with how to manage its highly talented, world-class director with a drinking problem.

New Staff Members

Staff changes helped solve part of the problem by distributing responsibilities. For one, a new curator of reptiles, Robert Snedigar, was hired. Snedigar was a talented man who not only took on the management of a large portion of the animal collection but also began building educational programs for the zoo. He joined the staff in January 1946 after working at the American Museum of Natural History and the Hayden Planetarium in New York.

Without a curator since the departure of Grace Olive Wiley in 1935, the reptile collection needed some attention. Snedigar went to work immediately, attending to both Reptile House and to a new insect exhibit next to Perching Bird House.

Insect House was the first of its kind in the country and attracted local and national attention. Some of its high-tech displays were equipped with a microprojector that magnified amoebas, hydras, water fleas, and other insects.

Snedigar applied himself to other projects, one a series of daily lectures held within Insect House. His knowledge of zoology and animal behavior was wide-ranging, and he had a talent for expressing himself in common terminology. His lectures were popular with children as well as adults. In addition, he found time to write several popular books about animals and was often interviewed by newspaper, radio, and television reporters.

Right: Robert Snedigar strikes a familiar pose as he lectures to a group of visitors. People enjoyed the knowledgeable reptile curator's daily talks about insects and other subjects.

Ralph Graham

Another addition to the staff was Ralph Graham, the artist who had supervised several WPA Federal Art Project programs. Bean hired Graham in 1945 as artist and photographer. By 1945, assistance from the Federal Art Project had ended, and Graham had his hands full in his new position as he wrote the text and painted the artwork on every sign in the zoo, created visitor maps, produced artwork for guidebooks, and photographed births and special events.

Graham must have impressed Bean, for he was appointed assistant to the director in 1947. He continued to serve as artist but took on additional tasks ranging from animal-collecting trips to acting as director during Bean's absences. Frequently, he served as an intermediary between Bean and the staff.

Just as Snedigar and Graham were arriving, other key staff members left. George Speidel, head of security and husband of Mary Bean, Robert's sister, left to become director of the Racine Zoo in Wisconsin. Subsequently, he was to become director of the Washington Park Zoo, filling the same position his father-in-law had held prior to coming to Brookfield Zoo in 1927. Mary had served as zoo nurse and panda babysitter in earlier years.

Apparently, the zoo's trustees were pleased with the new staff members and with Robert Bean's performance in his two years as acting director because in July 1947 he was pronounced director.

HOW TO MEASURE AN ANACONDA

This *Grand Rapids Herald* article of June 26, 1946, describes an unconventional negotiation for the purchase of an anaconda.

"El Diablo was measured yesterday at Brookfield Zoo, but since he kept himself purposely bumpy at the time, despite the efforts of 11 strong keepers to straighten him out, no one is quite certain that the official length of 13 feet 9 inches is correct.

"El Diablo is a 135 pound anaconda from Colombia, in South America, bought in New York a week ago by Robert Bean, zoo director. Louis Ruhe, [the] animal dealer who sold the giant snake asked $450 and said he thought the reptile was between 21 and 22 feet long. The cunning Mr. Bean agreed on the price, but added an offer to pay $20 per foot for each foot over 21 if Ruhe would slash the same amount off for each foot under. Ruhe agreed.

"As a result Ruhe will get only $310, since El Diablo was seven feet under estimate. Bean generously decided not to take anything off for the extra three inch shortage. The snake is the first of his species at Brookfield since a previous anaconda died eight years ago, presumably of a hunger strike. This one, a mere 8 feet long, ate only once of his own volition in more than nine months. El Diablo, if his actions yesterday are any indication, seems nasty tempered enough to eat anything, including a stray keeper or two.

"He glared and opened his mouth in rage when Emil Rokosky, head reptile keeper, dropped a wet sack over his eyes and grabbed him behind the skull. And when 10 other keepers seized him and carried him outdoors like a fire hose, El Diablo formed a series of sulky curves and never straightened out until returned to his glass cage and released, after the keepers wrapped him twice around a tree as a safety precaution."

Right: Because of its length and weight—and perhaps due to its disposition as well—it can be extremely difficult to measure an anaconda, as keepers have discovered.

"I DIDN'T THINK THEY GREW SO BIG"

Insect House drew attention from all over the country, as demonstrated by this May 1947 article in *Nature Magazine* entitled "Pioneering at Chicago's Zoo," by Charles W. Keysor.

"Paradoxically, animals without backbones form the backbone of the Chicago Zoological Park's new Special Exhibits and Demonstrations House. This public collection of invertebrates and local reptiles reveals an unappreciated strata of the animal kingdom to zoo-goers who used to think of the parks only in terms of kangaroos, monkeys and elephants.

"Approximately fifty species of invertebrates are shown to visitors, who marvel at a furry tarantula, a pale scorpion, and a Louisiana centipede, star performers of the invertebrate display. Leeches, diving beetles, and water fleas crawl or paddle about in their sand-bottomed aquariums. Antenna-waving roaches that stalk over the wire walls and ceilings of their cage draw interesting reactions from many visitors. Standing by this exhibit, you might hear: 'Ooh!' or 'I didn't think they grew so big,' or '...and we never did get rid of them.'

"Many citizens of the invertebrate world are too small to be shown without magnification. That is why five-tube microscopes were installed in the Special Exhibits House. Under the 'scopes, many people learned that common butterfly wings are covered with scales. Legs, heads, and other segments of insect anatomy have also been shown...

"Two colonies of honeybees, living in a tall case at the north end of the building, make one of the most popular exhibits. In the summer, the bees have two transparent tunnel exits to the outdoors. The insects, which return heavily laden, almost invariably take the bottom entrance to the comb. To emphasize this activity, Curator Snedigar painted in and out arrows on the lower and upper tubes. Throughout the summer, visitors marveled that the bees were intelligent enough to follow directions!

"Snedigar and [Robert] Bean set a precedent in zoological exhibition that has called public attention to the fascinating invertebrate world. They have been pioneering at the Chicago Zoological Park."

Above: The popular Insect House featured many creatures, including a variety of spiders, like this tarantula (upper left) and wolf spider (above), that people don't normally think of as living in a zoo.

"BEDBUGS AND LICE, FOR GOSH SAKE"

A 1946 newspaper article entitled "Postal Opinion of Bedbug Hunt: 'For Gosh Sake'" explained how Brookfield Zoo came upon a portion of its invertebrate collection.

"Postmaster Michael Colgrass of the Brookfield post office is a patient man, but yesterday he registered a mild complaint. 'We have handled lizards, worms, black-widow spiders, and skunks for the zoo,' he said, 'but now we get bedbugs and lice, for gosh sake. That's really the climax. We get rid of 'em as fast as possible.'

"Meanwhile, at Brookfield Zoo, where shipments of bedbugs and lice from all over the country and Mexico, Nova Scotia, and Cuba have been pouring in in response to a plea by Director Robert Bean for six pairs of bedbugs and six pairs of lice for the invertebrate collection, Robert Snedigar, curator of reptiles and invertebrates, added his plaint to those of Colgrass and Bean.

"'I have about 250 bedbugs now,' he said wearily, 'and I've been threatening to give them away as door-prizes at the 2 and 4 p.m. lectures on invertebrates daily. I'm certainly going to get rid of most of them somehow.' Snedigar said the zoo will STILL pay $6 for the FIRST six pairs of body lice received, but that they do NOT need any more bedbugs or head-lice.

"Snedigar said most of the people sending them in, wrap the packages with superb care; in fact, one woman put so much scotch tape around an aspirin box containing bedbugs that they were dead on arrival."

Rhino! Rhino!

Bean's first major accomplishment as director came the following year with the chance to obtain two Indian rhinoceroses. Back in 1934, George B. Dryden, a rubber manufacturing executive, had offered to pay up to $20,000 for a pair of the animals but not a single cent for a lone representative of the species. At the time, it was thought that there were only about 500 Indian rhinos in the world, and no zoo except the one in Calcutta had a pair.

Animal collector Frank Buck had offered a single rhino in 1935, but it was just one animal and, furthermore, it was missing an ear. In 1936, hopes were again raised when a pair was held in captivity in India, but famine struck the region and the rhinos were released to forage for themselves. In 1948, John McCutcheon induced explorer Arthur Vernay to use his contacts to help secure rhinos from the maharajah in Nepal. Shortly thereafter, Vernay reported that Mr. Roundtree, the conservator of forests of Assam in northeastern India, had granted the Society a permit to export two Indian rhinos. It was just a matter of catching them.

Showing great faith in his artist and assistant, Bean sent Ralph Graham to Assam's Kaziranga Game Sanctuary. Totally inexperienced but enterprising by nature, Graham left in February 1948. His adventure is chronicled in his book *Rhino! Rhino!*, a collection of engaging letters he sent to Bean during the expedition. In the end, the trip took five months, 200 workers, and Graham's undivided attention.

In essence, the capture began with a six-foot pit. After a few days' wait, a male rhino fell in. Through a series of ramps, cages, and ropes, the rhino (named Kashi Ram after Graham's knowledgeable and indispensable guide) was pulled by an elephant to a stockade. A female rhino was caught in the same manner a few days later, and she was found to be pregnant—a bonus. The rhino pair was then taken via riverboat to Calcutta and loaded onto an ocean steamer bound for Savannah, Georgia, from where they were transported by train and truck to Brookfield.

It took 46 days from the female rhino's capture for Graham and his charges to reach Brookfield. Stress, weather changes, and the ocean crossing made for a hard trip for the rhinos, and Graham tried to comfort the animals as best he could. Sadly, the female, named Kamala Rani ("lady lotus"), lost her calf during the voyage. In his letters, Graham maintained that he had asked the men guarding the rhinos to alert him the moment delivery seemed imminent, which they did not do. Expressing anger and profound disappointment, he wondered whether their failure cost the baby rhino its life.

Right: Keeper Cliff Jones tends to his charge, one of the Indian rhinos Ralph Graham captured and brought back from Assam.

Dear Robert —

Excerpts from Graham's letters capture his emotions throughout the venture.

"This has been the most memorable day of my life," he wrote. "As you already know from my cable, we've got our first rhino and he is a beauty. Right now he is a very tired fellow from fighting all day and he is having a well-earned rest and sleep in the stockade. We started to work at seven o'clock this morning and at nine tonight the rhino stepped into the stockade. All materials and equipment were of the crudest sort but at least they served their purpose. It doesn't matter whether we induced the rhino into our parlor by means of offering him a movie contract or by pulling him there in an old-beat-up iron cage; the main thing is—WE HAVE ONE RHINO!" *(February 29, 1948)*

"There is nothing of great importance to report at this time except that the female rhino is a humdinger and she seems to be thriving. She is about the same size as Kashi but a bit heavier in the midriff. The Forest Veterinarian and I (for no good reason) suspect that she is pregnant." *(March 21)*

"It begins to look as though I've caught Assam with its monsoon showing. The weather has been anything but dry for the past week. In fact, it is raining civet cats and mongooses right now. I would enjoy hearing the rain hit the thatched roof and run off to the ground if I didn't worry so much about what the rain will do to the road to Dhansirimukh." *(March 28)*

"I didn't want to be unprepared if Kamala was pregnant and delivered her calf on the trip, so I cut sections of bamboo for bottles. I mootched [sic] a piece of rubber from the boat crew and made it into a crude nipple. Then I practiced milking Kamala for about an hour each day. She was most co-operative—the hussy. There was not enough room in the cage to accommodate a calf so I intended to raise the end gate and have each member of the crew shove a timber across the end, leaving just enough space at the theatre of operations to take the calf and still not allow any possibility of her escape. We practiced this once or twice each day and perfected our technique until we could do it with the precision of a Notre Dame 'B' team." *(May 9)*

"The little calf, a female, had not been taken out of the cage for some time after it was born. I was utterly sick and almost to the point of uncontrollable fury at Bapu and Bunduah, who had not stood watch during the night but had slept and had not noticed anything unusual until the calf was being born. I blame myself for the loss of the calf but in retrospect I don't see how I could have done any differently." *(May 23)*

"This trip has really been the most wonderful experience of my life and I've enjoyed every bit of it except losing the calf. I am more than grateful to you and to the Society for making the trip possible and more important—for having confidence in me to achieve the mission successfully. Brookfield—here we come and will I be glad to see you!" *(May 23)*

Ralph G.

Even without the baby rhino, Graham had succeeded. The zoo finally had its pair of Indian rhinos. Kashi and Kamala settled into their new life in Pachyderm House. Within the next few years, several efforts were made to mate the two immigrants for the purpose of starting an Indian rhino dynasty at the zoo.

The less than successful affair was described in the zoo's 20th anniversary book. "Kashi was permitted to enter Kamala's outdoor enclosure where the pleasant and natural surroundings, it was hoped, might establish the proper atmosphere. Everything seemed to be progressing smoothly until Kashi stepped into her watering place. This evidently constituted a direct personal challenge to Kamala for she immediately rose to the defense of her possessions and order was only restored after they had both been locked up in their stalls. Though the future of their friendly relations began to look somewhat dim by this time, the zoo gave them another try in the summer of 1950. As before, Kashi seemed prepared to be ingratiating and hopes began to revive for a moment, but they were short-lived for he made the fatal mistake of again setting foot in her water. This time tempers ran so high and Kashi laid chase to Kamala with such determination that before it was over she had crashed her way through a fence of twelve by four inch bridge timbers and jumped into the five foot moat surrounding the yard. It was the reluctant decision of all concerned that this particular brand of romance was much too violent for further experimentation, and since that summer of 1950 the two have led peaceful and separate lives."

Kashi and Kamala attracted considerable notice around the country, even being featured in a United States Steel advertisement. The company built and erected the heavy fencing surrounding the rhino enclosures and used the opportunity to boast of the strength of steel.

Other hallmarks of Robert Bean's early years as director were various visitor-friendly programs. To handle the countless questions asked by visitors—ones not easily answered on signs or in the guidebook—the zoo provided an "answer man," Alexander Lindsay. For seven years of summer weekends, Lindsay offered his time, an exceptional memory, an extensive natural-history book collection, and some 5,000 reference cards from a booth set up on one of the malls. Although the most frequently asked question was for directions, Lindsay also responded to ones about such topics as how far a whale can travel before it gets tired, how big a kangaroo is at birth, if animals commit suicide, and if giraffes can swim. (Apparently, the latter question was the only one that ever stumped Lindsay.)

Other programs proved popular, too. Graham designed a charming zoo map that sold quickly at a cost of 10 cents. Also, amateur photographers enjoyed the photography contest, which began in 1947. The contest grew in size each year, and eventually hundreds of entries were received from around the world.

Above: An advertisement by United States Steel featured Kashi Ram inside the enclosure built by the company to prove the strength of its product.

Right: Alexander Lindsay nearly always had the answer as he tackled a mix of mundane and bizarre questions from his booth.

Above: The moat around Monkey Island was at one time filled with water, the only real danger to the boy who fell in in 1948.

In the late 1940s, Bean witnessed events that justified his father's concerns about protecting animals from visitors. In 1948, an off-duty policeman rescued an eight-year-old boy who fell into the moat surrounding Monkey Island. The boy climbed over the guardrail and tumbled into 10-foot-deep water, where he was in more danger of drowning than of being attacked by the animals. The policeman jumped in and pulled the boy out.

This diverted disaster followed an even more dramatic rescue the previous year, when a three-year-old boy climbed over a fence to feed a spectacled bear. The boy gave the bear popcorn and then tried to pat the animal through the cage bars. The bear reached through and grabbed the youngster with one front paw, tearing at the child's arm and leg with the other paw. This time the hero was an off-duty city fireman who hurdled the barrier to rescue the boy. He punched the bear on the nose repeatedly, causing the animal to let go. The three-year-old needed 10 stitches to close up his wounds. Just as Ed Bean had predicted two decades earlier, it was clearly a case of someone wanting "to put his hand in the bear cage to see if Bruin will really bite, or throw in food to see if he will eat it."

McCutcheon Resigns

As the decade came to an end, Board president John McCutcheon announced that he would step down. The news was no surprise to his fellow trustees, for his health had been failing for some time. Yet they were sad to see the end of an era spanning more than a quarter of a century. The mantle passed from McCutcheon to his vice-president and brother-in-law, Clay Judson.

McCutcheon died in June 1949. Judson offered a touching resolution honoring his predecessor's tremendous contributions. "John T. McCutcheon died on Friday, June 10, 1949. From the first days of the Chicago Zoological Society until he became Honorary President last January, he had as President, in his genial and gentle way, presided over its affairs. His keen interest in the zoo at Brookfield, his imagination, his friendships in all parts of the world, and the particular esteem in which he was held in this community, were all vital factors in building the firm foundation on which the affairs of the Society now rest. To the members of the Executive Committee his loss is a personal one."

THE CHICAGO ZOOLOGICAL SOCIETY

CHICAGO   ILLINOIS

Office of the President
Tribune Tower
Superior 0100

Dear Stanley:

The date of the annual meeting of the Chicago Zoological Society is approaching, when a president must be nominated for the coming year.

For twenty-six years I have had the honor, the duty and the pleasure of holding this office, of being the nominal head of an undertaking carried through by men much abler than I, of leaning heavily upon the abilities and energies of all of you. This more than quarter of a century has covered the entire life of the Zoo, its development from a dream to the handsome reality it has become.

But for some time now old Anno Domini has interfered with my activities and prevented my being as useful to the Zoo as I could wish.

The realization, this summer, of a further dream-- the two magnificent Indian rhinos--seems to offer a suitable opportunity for me to retire in a certain amount of vicarious glory, and I hereby suggest that you nominate a spryer man.

With my thanks for your unfailing co-operation, with assurance of my continuing interest, and my best good wishes, I am

Sincerely

In tribute to the man who had nurtured the organization for so long, the trustees discussed renaming the park after McCutcheon, but the McCutcheon family declined the honor.

New president Clay Judson had been involved in the Society since 1934, serving as vice-president for several years and acting as informal legal counsel when necessary. A partner in the Chicago law firm of Wilson & McIlvaine, Judson was heavily involved in civic projects, also serving as president of the Chicago Council on Foreign Relations and the International House at the University of Chicago. Other involvements included membership on the Chicago Bar Association board of managers, as well as trustee roles with the United Charities of Chicago, the Menninger Foundation, and the Francis W. Parker School. He was a busy, industrious, and intelligent man, having graduated cum laude from Harvard University and the University of Chicago Law School. Judson was married to sculptress Sylvia Shaw, the daughter of prominent architect Howard Van Doren Shaw, one of the Society's original governing members, and the sister of John McCutcheon's wife, Evelyn Shaw.

With the passing of the Chicago Zoological Society's gentle leader, and a new president and director firmly in place, the zoo began to strike out in unexplored directions.

CLAY JUDSON

Alice Judson Ryerson recalled her father in *Clay Judson 1892-1960 as seen by Richard Bentley, Alice Judson Ryerson, Ellen Thorne Smith.*

"The first thing I think of when I think of my father is birds. The other day we found a piece of paper in his desk listing important things he remembered. He must have jotted these things down to entertain himself when he was very ill a couple of years ago. Almost one third of the list consists of names of birds and where they were seen. Some were birds he had seen as a boy on canoe trips in the north woods and those particular warblers and kinglets were still vivid in his mind fifty years later, and outranked memories of Harvard and Law School in importance.

"When I was a child...sometimes he would wake me very early on a spring morning, we'd eat a piece of bread and butter and go out into the park while the rest of the city was still asleep. I've forgotten which birds we saw but I can see my father now, holding a pair of field glasses out to me with one hand and pointing intently with the other at a bush or tree where something stirred in the leaves."

THE SHAWS

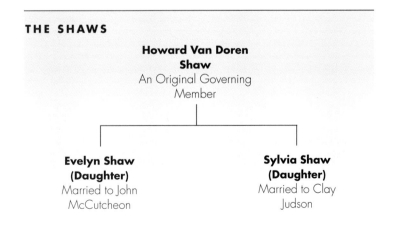

Howard Van Doren Shaw
An Original Governing Member

Evelyn Shaw (Daughter)
Married to John McCutcheon

Sylvia Shaw (Daughter)
Married to Clay Judson

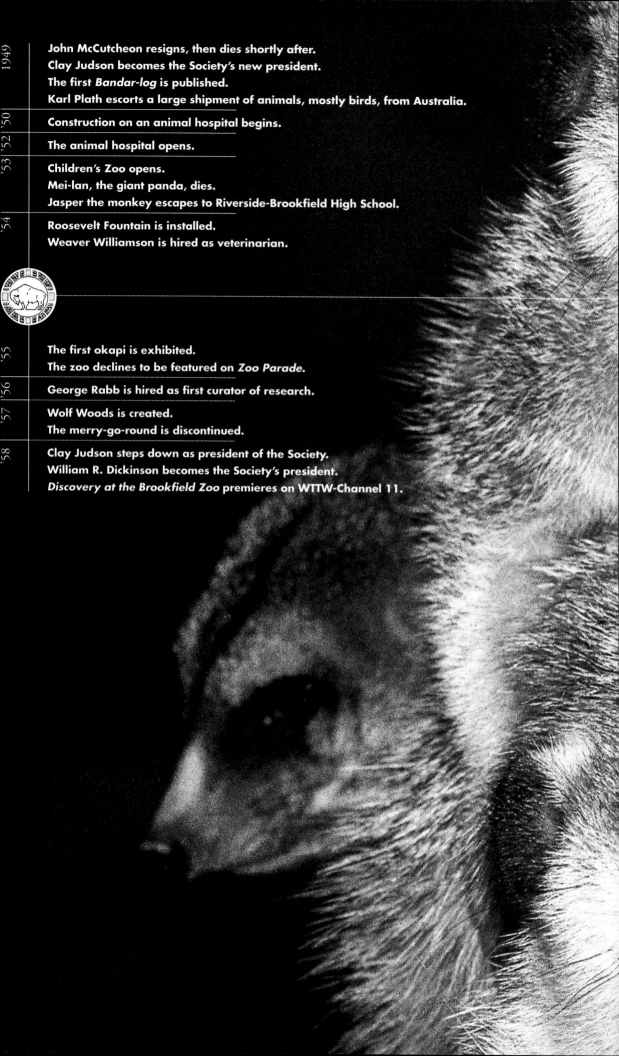

1949
John McCutcheon resigns, then dies shortly after.
Clay Judson becomes the Society's new president.
The first *Bandar-log* is published.
Karl Plath escorts a large shipment of animals, mostly birds, from Australia.

'50
Construction on an animal hospital begins.

'52
The animal hospital opens.

'53
Children's Zoo opens.
Mei-lan, the giant panda, dies.
Jasper the monkey escapes to Riverside-Brookfield High School.

'54
Roosevelt Fountain is installed.
Weaver Williamson is hired as veterinarian.

'55
The first okapi is exhibited.
The zoo declines to be featured on *Zoo Parade*.

'56
George Rabb is hired as first curator of research.

'57
Wolf Woods is created.
The merry-go-round is discontinued.

'58
Clay Judson steps down as president of the Society.
William R. Dickinson becomes the Society's president.
Discovery at the Brookfield Zoo premieres on WTTW-Channel 11.

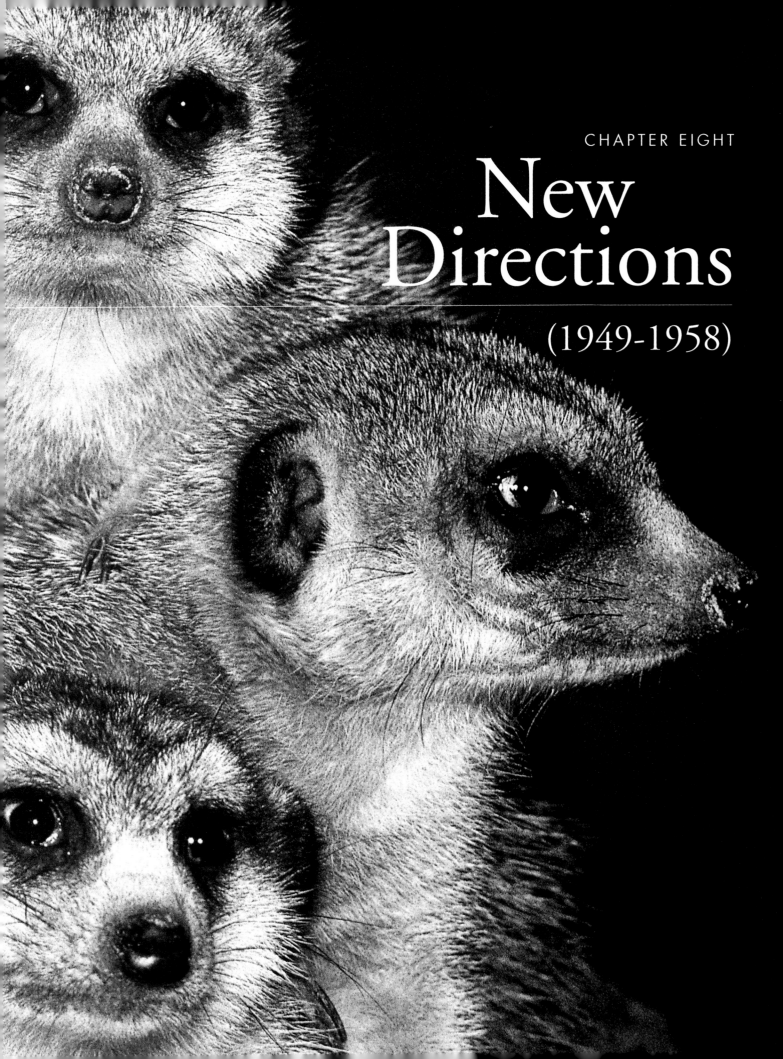

CHAPTER EIGHT

New Directions

(1949-1958)

"It will be the purpose of the Chicago Zoological Society in the years to come to maintain a beautiful, distinguished, and interesting zoological park where old and young may gain health, pleasure, knowledge and understanding, and where, in connection with our great collection of birds and beasts humanely maintained, we may accumulate scientific data of value to all."

Clay Judson
1954 Guidebook

An Animal Hospital

Clay Judson's administration would prove to be one marked by construction of several significant facilities, major advances in the areas of education and research, and notable changes in the animal collection.

From the beginning of the Chicago Zoological Society, when Edith Rockefeller McCormick had stated that she wanted to create an institution that would provide an opportunity for scientific research on animals that might contribute to knowledge about the human soul, the Society had declared that research was a cornerstone of the organization. In fact, it was even a part of the original mission, as Charles Hutchinson had said in 1921: "... the collection, holding, and expenditure of funds for zoological research and publication...." But it wasn't until Judson's time that research really began.

Before the zoo opened in 1934, a Scientific Committee had been created with the primary goal of establishing an animal hospital. Headed by trustee John P. Kellogg, the Committee included two of the country's leading zoologists: Dr. Wilfred Osgood of the Field Museum and Dr. Frank R. Lillie of the University of Chicago. For its first 15 years, however, the zoo had relied on outside veterinarians and regular physicians to care for its massive animal collection, not an uncommon situation for zoos at the time. In fact, the New York and Philadelphia zoos maintained the only zoo animal hospitals in the country until the one at Brookfield Zoo was built.

President Judson gave top priority to an animal hospital and named a Scientific Advisory Committee, consisting of trustee Tappan Gregory, Dr. Alfred Emerson of the University of Chicago, Dr. Smith Freeman of the Northwestern University Medical School, and Dr. Karl P. Schmidt of the Field Museum.

In 1949, the Scientific Advisory Committee formally recommended to the full Board of Trustees the building of an animal hospital, complete with an office and laboratory for the study of animal diseases and needs. For review, the trustees revived plans drawn up by architect Edwin Clark in 1937, then sent an architect from Clark's office to visit animal hospitals around the country to gather ideas. Meanwhile, the Scientific Advisory Committee conducted a careful search for a veterinarian. Eventually, Dr. Donald A. Schmidt (no relation to Karl P. Schmidt) was hired at an annual salary of $4,500.

Plans for the hospital were officially announced in January 1950, and the $269,000 building was completed two years to the month later. (Someone once figured out that the building's cost equaled the profit on 8,633,334 bags of peanuts.)

At the opening of the hospital, Freeman commented on its purpose. It is interesting that at the time even individuals strongly advocating scientific undertakings at the zoo believed in humans' "supremacy over his environment," rather than their role in nature. "It is hoped that special studies will be made by various interested groups of scientists upon certain segments of the zoo's population," Freeman said. "Facilities of the hospital will be placed at the disposal of suitably qualified groups whose interests are compatible with the primary functions of the zoo. In this way, useful information may accumulate which will not only improve zoo practices in general, but will also contribute something to the overall reservoir of knowledge at the disposal of man in his never-ending struggle for adjustment to and supremacy over his environment."

After taking part in planning and constructing the new hospital, Donald Schmidt left for a university post several years later. He was replaced in 1954 by Dr. Weaver Williamson, who would stay with the zoo for many years. Also hired in 1954 was researcher Dr. Evelyn Tilden from the Northwestern University Medical School, who conducted groundbreaking research on aspergillosis, coincidentally the same fungal disease that had killed Admiral Byrd's emperor penguins in 1935.

Weaver Williamson

Right: Dr. Evelyn Tilden (right) and lab worker Ruth Getty conduct research on aspergillosis, a fungal disease.

Children Get a Zoo

Just as construction began on the animal hospital, the trustees received an offer from Charles Ward Seabury, a local philanthropist who headed the insurance firm of Marsh & McLennan, for $35,000 to help build a miniature zoo where children could have actual contact with the animals. Having visited the London Zoo's children's section a few years earlier, Seabury decided that he wanted a large area where children could be taught how to handle animals. He felt that an important part of a children's zoo should be a barn with farm animals so that city children could watch cows being milked and learn about ducks, geese, chickens, and pigs, as well as wild animals.

Edwin Clark went to work once again. Many incarnations of a children's zoo were discussed, including an Old West stagecoach ride with ponies and longhorn steer. The children's zoo was completed in August 1953 at a cost of $95,000. Christopher Holabird, son of a prominent Chicago architect, was hired as superintendent of what was officially dubbed Children's Zoo.

Opening day at Children's Zoo brought several thousand youngsters accompanied by adults. *Life* magazine's photo spread on the opening reported that "some animals fought back. A monkey grabbed a woman's lipstick. A baboon hit a boy. A llama who had had his fill of popcorn discovered a way to say so, and a loud-mouthed mother stalked away, yelling, 'That dirty brazen creature poked me in the rear!' But most of the animals had soon had it. Caesar, the 7-weeks-old lion cub, was pawed so much he had to retire to his cage. While gladdened by the 6,815 first-day turnout, zoo officials decided to put in a few refinements such as a fence to protect the baboons from the youngsters. They also talked of taking some of the animals, who had had as much attention as they could stand, away 'for a little rest.'"

Children's Zoo housed a diverse collection of animals, including a baby Kodiak bear, a lion cub, a young kangaroo, and Melinda the baby elephant, as well as the various cows, ducks, rabbits, llamas, and goats that are part of today's Children's Zoo. It was a combination of animal nursery and domestic animal-petting farm—fascinating for the visitors, no doubt, but difficult to manage.

Above: An attendant gives a baby rhino and a lion cub their baths— an activity unique to Children's Zoo.

Above right: For many adults, the most striking childhood memory they have about Children's Zoo is the chance to walk across the stepping stones.

Above left: Baby elephants were popular in the early days of Children's Zoo, which didn't change its focus to only domestic and native animals until many years later.

A further complication with this type of nursery exhibit is that as the original inhabitants mature, new youngsters need to take their places. In most cases, Mother Nature supplied the infants, but with more exotic species—elephants, for example—new animals needed to be purchased every few years. In fact, Seabury continued to supply baby elephants for several years.

Another difficulty was having these less common animals start out in Children's Zoo. For instance, baby elephant Melinda, upon her release in Pachyderm House, fell in a moat and broke her back legs because she was unacquainted with such obstacles. Although there was great hope of a complete recovery after she was treated for the injuries, she died in 1956.

Sobered by Children's Zoo's unexpectedly costly construction and maintenance, the trustees pleaded their case to state officials for an increase in the property-tax levy for the zoo. The legislators not only approved an increase in the levy from .0038 cents per dollar to .0048 cents, they also allowed the zoo to charge for special facilities. The trustees decided to charge 10 cents for admission to Children's Zoo. In its first year, Children's Zoo and its pony rides, for which there was a separate charge, brought in $20,000, not bad for an exhibit that was open only several weeks. (Until 1969, Children's Zoo was open only during summer.) In 1954, the first year of a full summer season for the new section, Children's Zoo's revenue amounted to $84,000.

Above: A 1953 aerial view of the zoo shows off the completed animal hospital just south of Reptile House and Children's Zoo in the southeast corner (lower right).

Roosevelt Fountain

Another major improvement was installed in 1954 through the connections and urging of trustee Alfred Hamill and his associate, Percy Eckhardt. Both were also trustees of the B. F. Ferguson Memorial Fund, a trust under the aegis of The Art Institute of Chicago concerned with statuary in public places.

In the 1920s, a group of Chicago citizens had formed the national Roosevelt Memorial Association of Chicago to raise funds for a memorial to Theodore Roosevelt. Among the Association's officers were Peter Reinberg and Charles Hutchinson, both also central to the creation of Brookfield Zoo. Other Chicago Zoological Society members involved were James Simpson, John Shedd, and Howard Van Doren Shaw.

The Association eventually turned over some $30,000 to the B. F. Ferguson Memorial Fund. The money in the fund increased over the years, and in 1953, the trust approved a $63,000 donation toward a Roosevelt Fountain at Brookfield Zoo. The Chicago Zoological Society added $35,000, and construction began. Edwin Clark, assisted by architects Olsen & Urbain and Russell Read, designed the fountain. Famed sculptress Sylvia Shaw Judson helped with the design and created sculptures to be placed around the fountain, which was to be located where the zoo's two malls meet, creating a focal point for the park.

At no cost, Sylvia Shaw Judson created four bronze animal-head sculptures to honor Roosevelt, each saluting an aspect of his career: statesman, naturalist, hunter, and soldier. Two American animals, a moose and an elk, and two African animals, a kudu and a buffalo, pay tribute to Roosevelt's efforts to save American wilderness and to his African expeditions. The antlers and horns were cast from originals loaned by the Field Museum. The fountain itself was designed to be 215 feet in diameter, with jets that could be altered for different displays. The center jet was built to shoot as high as 60 feet.

Special guests at the May 14 dedication ceremony included Chicago mayor Martin Kennelly, Forest Preserve District president William Erickson, and Hermann Hagedorn, director of the national Theodore Roosevelt Association. Clay Judson christened the fountain with the words, "There will pass by this fountain every year a million and a half to two million people. It is a significant and artistic addition to this community and a worthy tribute to the memory of Theodore Roosevelt, one of America's great men."

SYLVIA SHAW JUDSON

Born in Chicago in 1897, Sylvia Shaw, the daughter of architect Howard Van Doren Shaw and poet Frances Shaw, was trained at The School of the Art Institute of Chicago and at the Grande Chaumiere in Paris. Her sculptures, many of which featured animals or children, can be found in places as varied as the Rose Garden at the White House, the home of former Philippine president Ferdinand Marcos in Manila, the Illinois State Museum, Morton Arboretum, the Ravinia Festival, the State House in Boston, and numerous hospitals and private residences in the Chicago area.

"In spite of the widening horizons of science and the current preoccupation with space, I am still primarily interested in human beings, and in the creature companions of our pilgrimage," she said in *For Gardens and Other Places*. "There is a thread which connects one generation and one country with another, and which draws us close in a common humanity. This is the thread of authentic experience, simple, homely, fresh, and vivid as the parables. Art which follows this thread lasts a long time and can be widely shared without having to lose its local flavor. It is an art which can be at the same time universal and particular."

Other Exhibit Improvements

At the same time, a mink exhibit was made possible through the gift of the animals by Paul Serbar and a $3,000 donation by long-time trustee James Simpson. For $44,000, a large flight cage was built behind Aquatic Bird House, providing larger birds the opportunity to stretch their wings in an outdoor setting. Also, much-needed renovations within Small Mammal House took place at a cost of $215,000, and construction of a grotto was completed for remaining panda Mei-lan, who unfortunately died soon afterwards, in 1953.

Primate House was renovated in 1954, notable because for the first time in any zoo, the glass partition between animals and visitors was charged with a light voltage of electricity, discouraging the animals from touching the glass. Some of the larger apes had been shattering the glass with regularity, and Robert Bean masterminded this new technique in exhibit design. Plexiglas was also utilized for the first time in Primate House.

In the mid-50s, Perching Bird House's central section was altered to house a $125,000 Freedom Gallery, a large area where a diversity of perching birds flew free. For the first time, people could immerse themselves in the tropical forest habitat.

"It does not now seem so important to aspire to maintain a great catalog of animals as it does to exhibit them with feeling and with the expression of providing the whole story of their mode of living and place in nature," commented Robert Bean on this change in zoo direction. Although not every exhibit or renovation during the period reflects this new attitude, it was a pivotal change in thought about how animals should be exhibited and how visitors should experience exhibits.

One amenity was discontinued in the '50s: the merry-go-round in the old children's playground in the northwest section of the zoo. Prior to the opening of Children's Zoo, the playground had housed domestic animals for petting and even some of the young animals born at the zoo. As such, it and its full-size merry-go-round were very popular. With the opening of Children's Zoo, however, its necessity and popularity diminished. When the Society learned that the rate of liability insurance on the merry-go-round was to be increased, exceeding the ride's annual income, it was dismantled.

Above: Roosevelt Fountain, completed in 1954, features bronze animal heads and plinths that celebrate the career of President Theodore Roosevelt as a naturalist, soldier, statesman, and hunter.

Left: Sylvia Shaw Judson works on the design for the sculptures surrounding Roosevelt Fountain as her husband, Society president Clay Judson, looks on.

Right: The Freedom Gallery in Perching Bird House was one of the first exhibits that gave people the chance to walk right into a rain forest—and into the area in which the animals lived.

Educational Possibilities

Several educational programs were instituted during Clay Judson's tenure. In 1949, a very dedicated governing member by the name of Ellen Thorne Smith (later to become the Society's first female trustee) volunteered to write an informative, occasional leaflet called the *Bandar-log*, whose name came from a play on the Hindu words used by Rudyard Kipling to describe chattering monkeys.

The publication's purpose was to keep the zoo's members and friends informed about exhibits and events. Smith had a delightful writing style, and her efforts won the zoo many more friends and admirers.

It is remarkable that Smith had the time to devote to writing the *Bandar-log* because she was also involved with a great number of other worthy Chicago causes. The daughter of Robert Julius Thorne, the former president of Montgomery Ward & Co., and the wife of Hermon Dunlap Smith, a former chief executive officer of the insurance firm Marsh & McLennan, Smith was a prominent Chicago figure. An accomplished ornithologist, she authored several books on birds. She was a director and former president of the Hull House Association, the founder and first president of the women's board of the Field Museum, and the first female trustee of the Field Museum as well.

An excerpt from the first *Bandar-log* illustrates the engaging yet educational tone of the leaflet. "It seems fitting that the first issue of the *Bandar-log* should deal in detail with two representatives of the monkey tribe, Tia and Pieter, 20 month old baby orang-utans. Two more fascinating youngsters would be hard to find anywhere. They live, for the present, in two 'rest' cages, 3 x 4 x 4 feet, set on a table in a sunny room on the second floor of the administration building. Their schedule is very similar to that of most babies, except that their day starts at sunrise and ends at sunset, and they have no mid-day nap. The night keeper gives them their oranges at crack of dawn—one for Tia, who has a young lady's smaller build, and hence a lighter appetite than the much larger Pieter, who gets two oranges. They play quietly in their cages until the day staff, arriving at nine, give them their cod liver oil. This has vitamins added to it, and an orange flavor, and the young apes smack their lips on the horrid stuff. They love it! Next comes a bowl of Pablum with milk...."

Ellen Thorne Smith

Above: The subject of this man's photo obviously knew a great opportunity for publicity in Small Mammal House.

Above left: The front page of the *Bandar-log* featured Ralph Graham's artwork.

Below: Occasionally, a photographer managed to snap a shot of one of the most interesting—and mysterious—animals of all.

"Although most of the Pablum gets inside the monkeys, there is always the inevitable amount left for the outside, as anyone who has watched a two year old feed himself can readily imagine—and the young orangs don't wear bibs. So next comes a bath. Young monkeys cannot be put into water, so Mr. Robert Bean takes Pieter and Mr. Ralph Graham takes Tia, giving each a thorough sponge bath and a good brushing and combing all over. (No ribbons.)

"Affectionate care is just as important to the well-being of young monkeys as it is to babies, so they are petted and talked to a great deal, especially during bath time. While their rooms are being cleaned, Tia and Pieter are turned loose to play. They romp about and nip each other like puppies, grab each other's toys and race around and around the room with them. Pieter is so much bigger than Tia that it seems as though his playful cuffs may hurt too much—but Tia seems to love it and comes back for more. Their favorite small toy is a blue and white piece of cloth, which they take turns running away with, and then sit down and hold it in front of them, peering out for a most ridiculous peek-a-boo game. They have a wonderful four foot high jungle gym apparatus in their room, made of wood and clothesline, and are proficient trapeze artists, longing already for bigger swings to conquer.

"Shortly after ten they are put back in their cages and at twelve comes a light lunch of milk and wholewheat bread with honey, or jam made with honey. They have another hour's play around 3:30, and dinner is served at 4:30, consisting of Gerber's baby foods—perhaps canned liver puree, vegetable puree, a banana, and some more milk. With the dark comes bed-time."

No doubt that after this article appeared readers took a special interest in Tia and Pieter and all of the animals featured in the *Bandar-log*. In fact, the first issue prompted a poetic letter to the editor from a fifth-grade student in nearby Berwyn.

> *Dear Editor:*
>
> *I enjoy your booklet that we have seen,*
> *And I believe the name is keen.*
> *I thought Tia was nice, and I want to meet her,*
> *Also I plan to come and see Pieter.*
>
> *Sincerely,*
> *Roy Johnson*

Each issue contained in-depth information on a specific animal, updates on new exhibits or renovations, illustrations by Ralph Graham and Karl Plath, and information about new animals. As an example of the latter, the following article appeared in a 1949 issue.

"One of the most exciting events around any zoo is the arrival of a shipment of animals. On May 5th, Mr. and Mrs. Bean went to New York to meet a cargo plane full of animals arriving from Bangkok. On Tuesday, May 10, the Pennsylvanian train arriving at 4:40 in the Union Station was met by representatives of the *Tribune*, the *News*, the *Sun-Times*, and the *Bandar-log* (in the order of antiquity). The first three had sheaves of paper on which to take copious notes and each was accompanied by an efficient looking photographer. The *Bandar-log* representative had lost her pencil, and was accompanied by her husband, who had left his Brownie Reflex [camera] at home but supplied her with moral support.

"The first baggage car contained the shipment: 2 black leopards, 2 reticulated pythons, 2 monitor lizards, mangrove snakes, 1 pair of binturongs, Capuchin and squirrel monkeys, Coscoroba and white swans, a white fronted goose, toucan barbets, many waxbills and other birds, and Mr. Bean. All, except Mr. Bean, were in crates or cages, which surprisingly took up only about a fourth of the car.

"The photographers looked dismayed as in the semi-darkness of the car it was impossible to see much through the cracks in the crates. After the reporters had finished their first barrage of questions, all three photographers begged Mr. Bean to take something out of a crate for a picture. Of course they wanted the leopards, but this was impossible. The next demand was for the monkeys. Mr. Bean said the monkeys were 'nippy.' There were not enough people to hold even the small python. Never have I seen three big men look so dejected. Finally Mr. Bean took pity on them and opened a crate, picked up a white-fronted goose and set it on top of one of the crates near the door of the car. The goose promptly curved its long neck around and bit Mr. Bean's hand. The photographers as one man cried 'hold that pose,' bulbs flashed, cameras clicked, and then, and only then did the goose let go of Mr. Bean's thumb.

BROOKFIELD ZOO

Left: Babe the elephant, here greeted by Robert Bean, was the first elephant in the country ever to be transported by plane.

"One photographer, probably trained to leave nothing to chance, wanted another picture. 'Could you get it to bite you again?' he inquired wistfully of Mr. Bean. Just at that moment the monkey in the crate upon which the goose was posed reached through the chicken wire and pulled out a handful of the goose's tail feathers. The goose naturally thought Mr. Bean was the guilty party and promptly turned around and bit him again! Unexpected though it was, all three photographers were equal to the occasion and quick on the camera trigger.

"The goose was finally returned to its crate, where it indignantly ruffled what remained of its tail, and Mr. Bean looked ruefully at his hand, which undoubtedly felt, although it did not look, the worse for wear. But everyone else was happy, including the monkey, who sat grinning at his handful of feathers.

"The crates were loaded onto carts which took them down to the zoo truck waiting patiently in the lower regions of the station. The animals were promptly delivered to their new home, where you can see them any day. The *Bandar-log* editor resolved to attend the arrival of all animal shipments from this day forward, but never expects to laugh so hard again."

Smith continued to produce the *Bandar-log* for 16 years, never accepting payment for her services. At four to six pages per issue, it was a considerable amount of work, but it is clear from her writing that it was a labor of love. In later years, the trail encircling Indian Lake was named for Smith to honor her for her commitment to the publication and to the zoo.

Television Programs

Recognizing the considerable educational power of the new invention called television, the zoo embarked on a new endeavor: a weekly, 13-part television series called *Discovery at the Brookfield Zoo*, which premiered on April 2, 1958, on public television station WTTW-Channel 11. The Ann Arbor Center for Educational Television offered a $36,500 grant to WTTW to produce the show, with the remainder of the bill footed by the zoo.

Producer and narrator Mary Lela Grimes, who had initiated a well-received *Discovery* program in Boston, wrote each script with assistance from zoo staff. Using zoo animals as examples, each half-hour program was built around a basic biological concept such as adaptations to the environment,

Children's Zoo at the Brookfield Zoo

Greetings from BROOKFIELD ILLINOIS

classification and naming, or general ecology. Sections of each program were prefilmed at the zoo, but the program itself was broadcast live from a studio set made to look like a zoo information booth. Live animals were often incorporated into the studio portion, sometimes against zoo scenes rear-projected onto the background.

Three years before, in 1955, the zoo had declined an offer from NBC Television to be featured in the network's hit show *Zoo Parade*, the precursor to *Wild Kingdom*. Marlin Perkins, then director of Lincoln Park Zoo, was the *Zoo Parade* host, and he was looking for a new site due to conflicts between NBC and Lincoln Park Zoo's parent, the Chicago Park District.

Although the show was tremendously popular, Brookfield Zoo staff were vehemently opposed. They felt that a program such as *Zoo Parade*, which stressed handling animals, was in direct conflict with the zoo's philosophy of exhibiting animals with a minimum of human interference and might harm its reputation. There was also concern about the public reaction to closing down some exhibits for the seven hours on a Sunday it took to film the show. After some discussion, the Society decided to bow to the wishes of its staff and turned down the tempting offer.

Above: Mary Lela Grimes was the writer and host of the popular *Discovery at the Brookfield Zoo* series, which ran for 13 weeks in 1958.

Left: At the NBC Television studios, Robert Bean (center) has a cup of coffee with Don McNeill, host of *Don McNeill's TV Club*, and Bob Hope.

A New Era in Research

Once the animal hospital had been functioning for a few years, the Scientific Advisory Committee turned its attention to the zoo's research program. Although much was learned in the hospital about exotic animals in terms of anatomy, physiology, and illness, there was little actual research going on. Evelyn Tilden, with her studies on aspergillosis, and a few other short-term employees were the exception, but there was no cohesive research program. In 1956, the Committee, with the backing of the full Board of Trustees, asked Bean to hire a curator of research to coordinate such a program.

The Committee drew up guidelines for a research program it hoped would stimulate use and interest in the zoo by students and faculty from the area's colleges and universities. The guidelines stated, "The Chicago Zoological Society is encouraging research projects connected with the animal collection of the Zoological Park at Brookfield...providing that it does not interfere with the health of the animals or the exhibition program. Both basic research as well as short and long term utilitarian research will be considered in the fields of zoology, animal behavior, physiology, pathology, parasitology and evolution."

Committee members themselves conducted the search for a curator, and on November 1, 1956, Dr. George B. Rabb reported to work as the curator of research. Rabb was a trained herpetologist, with an undergraduate biology degree from the College of Charleston, South Carolina, and master's and doctoral degrees in zoology from the University of Michigan. He was one of the very first Ph.D.s to work full-time in any American zoo, and his position at Brookfield Zoo was unique in the zoo world.

Rabb's appearance on the scene was overshadowed by the arrival of a rare female okapi on the very same day, and it is ironic because this quiet man would, in the years to come, chart a new course for the Society. Under the watchful eyes of the esteemed members of the Scientific Advisory Committee, he immediately went to work attracting local students and university faculty members to the zoo.

Mostly, the research conducted with the animals' involvement was successful...mostly. "There was a psychology student who got into intelligence testing of young great apes," Rabb said. "His device was a very simple test of shapes and shade distinctions. Shades of grey and symbols like crosses and triangles were attached above a food well so that they covered the well, and with the right choice, the animal got whatever was in the well. Orangutans are very astute in terms of sizing up problems, but they're also short in their tolerance of challenging activities.

"Once there were three food wells, one with the food reward under it. After a few trials, an orang caught on. On the second day, the student came back and set up the test. The orang solved the problem in a distinctly orangutan fashion: it swiped clean the whole set.

EXACTING SCIENCE

A June 1959 *Bandar-log* article on Surinam toads illustrates the kind of research undertaken at the zoo after George Rabb's arrival in 1956.

"Scientific history is in the making in the Reptile House. The Surinam Toad, *Pipa pipa*, is producing young, and the movie camera remains focused in her aquarium in hopes that she can be caught in the act. So far she has outwitted the camera, but not the sharp eyes of the Curator of Research, George Rabb, who saw one of the young toads pop out of the middle of her back. For that is where she carries her eggs, and where they stay imbedded, passing through the various stages of egg and tadpole, occasionally peeking out to see what the world is like. When all four legs are developed the time comes when they decide they want to enjoy life on their own—or perhaps they just become too big to stay in their incubator. You can see the four young already hatched in the next aquarium, but be sure to look at the honey-comb-like back of Mrs. Toad. After her eggs were laid and fertilized they somehow reached her back, which for a week or two previously had been getting soft and spongy. At first she looked as if her back was covered with tapioca. Gradually the eggs sank in deeper and deeper, and the baby toads started to develop. This process has never before been photographed, and Dr. Rabb and Curator Snedigar will publish a scientific description of the blessed event. There are two other pairs of this strange toad on exhibit, so, someday, it will happen again!"

"There was another student interested in tool use. He provided the orangs with a rod, and he held a bunch of grapes. The orangs were supposed to strike the bunch to get a grape. Sure enough, the orangs caught on and knocked a grape out of the bunch. The second time around, an orang swatted the student and the student dropped the bunch of grapes! An absolutely elegant solution."

Assisted by his wife Mary, Rabb began his own studies at the zoo, primarily researching wolves' social behavior and reproduction in frogs. As part of the zoo's research program, he provided students at universities and colleagues at other institutions with animal materials. One guideline of the research program was that it would not infringe on the health of the animal collection, so often an animal was sent to another researcher after it had died.

Animal Dramas

Of course, throughout all of the construction and the inauguration of new programs, there were still animal dramas.

In the early 1950s, Baby the gorilla arrived at the zoo with scabies, trench mouth, roundworms, and hookworms. He was taken into the Bean household on the zoo grounds and nursed back to health by Jean Bean, Robert's wife.

Baby loved to play out on the grass and one day scampered up a tall oak tree, but he panicked at about 30 feet. Jean called to him, but he ran out on a limb that nearly broke, so instead he gave up and sat, paying no attention to pleas, bribes of food and candy, or his foster mother's tears. Jean was beside herself.

At this crucial moment, Jean's mother arrived for a visit. Proving herself an expert grandmother, she quoted the Bible: "Zecchius, come down out of that tree!" Baby may just have been surprised at being called Zecchius, but he came down and never again ventured off the ground. The Beans raised him in their home for five months, after which he joined the other gorillas in Primate House.

A quartet of young bonnet monkeys created a stir in 1953, regularly escaping from their cage on a crime spree at the zoo. One of the monkeys snatched a baby bottle from an infant, another grabbed the sunglasses from a small boy, and all four stole popcorn, ice-cream cones, gum, pens, pencils, and lipstick from unsuspecting visitors. Always after these frequent antics, the monkeys returned to their cage when summoned by their mothers. Gradually, however, their heads grew too big to fit between the bars, and their thieving ways came to an end.

"UNPARDONABLE CURSING"

A United Press report from November 25, 1952, entitled "Parrot in Chicago Zoo Accused of Vile Language," details a rather amusing anecdote from the halls of Parrot House.

"Authorities said Tuesday they received a letter from a woman who bitterly accused a parrot in the Brookfield Zoo of 'unpardonable cursing.' The writer said the bird, 'a gray, wicked-looking creature' cut loose with a stream of 'vile epithets' as she approached its cage.

"She said the 'rasping volley of words that would cause a sailor to blush' embarrassed her. She suggested the parrot be exterminated.

"Brookfield Zoo Director Robert Bean, after promising to investigate 250 parrots to find the culprit, gave them a clean bill of health for free speech, 'I've interviewed them exhaustively, the strongest words any of them said were, 'Oh fudge.'"

In fact, there was a parrot widely known for its extensive vocabulary, most of it foul. Robert Bean was aware of this the whole time and played along with the story for the sake of publicity. Many offers to adopt the bird came in after the story ran, none were accepted, and the bird stayed put.

Left: To learn more about animals, visitors could purchase an "elephant key" to "talking storybook" machines located around the park.

The zoo's bird collection received a boost when a large shipment of animals, primarily birds, arrived from the Taronga Zoo in Sydney. The Australian zoo had wanted two Kodiak bears, two polar bears, and some alligators. Through his connections to Sir Edward Hallstrom, president of the Taronga Zoological Park Trust, Robert Bean brokered an exchange in which 42 mammals (including 19 kangaroos), 14 lizards, and 283 birds were to be sent to Brookfield Zoo in exchange for the bears and alligators.

Hallstrom also threw in a gift of two pairs of extremely rare birds of paradise. (A few years later, he would generously donate 19 additional birds of paradise and various other animals.) Other birds obtained from the Taronga Zoo collection included fairy penguins, black swans, maned geese, Nankeen night herons, a blue swamp hen, ibises, spoonbills, giant kingfishers, and a plumed tree duck.

AN ACADEMIC MONKEY

Jasper, an enterprising monkey residing in Primate House, decided one day to go on a little field trip, as cleverly detailed in an August 1953 article called "Zoo's Monkey Plays Hooky, Tries to 'Enroll' in School" in Philadelphia's *Evening Bulletin*.

"Chicago, August 31—A monkey named Jasper tried to enroll in suburban Riverside-Brookfield High School today but was rejected for being too mischievous. Besides, he didn't have the required grade school credits. Jasper showed up in the office of Miss Ethel Curtis, dean of girls and the school's registrar, as she prepared to enroll students for the school's new term beginning next week.

"'It was pretty obvious that Jasper wanted to register,' Miss Curtis said. 'At least, he grabbed a handful of applications. But he kept tearing them up as fast as he grabbed a handful.'

"Jasper decided to take a tour of the school before enrolling. He stopped first in the office of the dean of men, L.D. Thompson, where he tried out some of the new physical education equipment. He decided the stuff was too tame. And the adhesive tape didn't taste quite right. Then he began an inspection of the classrooms, leaving a trail of littered papers behind him.

"Meanwhile, Miss Curtis called the Brookfield Zoo, about a block and a half north of the school. She told the director, Robert Bean, that one of his monkeys was trying to enroll at school without proper credits. 'That's Jasper,' Bean said. 'He always was ambitious. Wants to get ahead in this world by making monkeys out of human beings.'

"By the time Bean had arrived, Jasper had tried out several personal theories in the chemistry laboratories and was inspecting the high school's basement. Bean found the monkey sampling some fruit from the lunchbox of electrician Paul Michaels, who had slipped a piece of electrical wire onto his collar."

Curator of birds Karl Plath and his wife, Meta, who flew to Australia to collect the assortment, had an interesting return trip via freighter. They discovered that the eight fairy penguins had to be fed one at a time to ensure that each received its proper share. At a grand total of 96 fish (12 per penguin) this chore took a considerable amount of time. Preparing the food, cleaning all of the cages, and sterilizing 256 food and water pans each day was no small task, either. Nor were the Plaths' nights during the trip peaceful, as a pair of nocturnal sugar gliders (small, squirrel-like creatures) spent their waking hours exercising by running from the shower curtain to the window sill to the light fixture in the Plaths' bathroom.

In the mid-1950s, in the interest of attracting visitors and attention, Bean "rented" Serata, a white python, to show in Reptile House. This unusual creature, which was purely white except for its blue eyes, was so rare that it had been featured in *Life* magazine. Found in Pakistan three or four years earlier, it caused quite a stir because nothing like it had been seen before. Locals argued over whether it was a sign of good luck or bad luck and were accordingly pleased or dismayed when an animal buyer purchased the python to bring it to the United States. The buyer asked such a stiff price for the snake that he could find no buyers, and it traveled from site to site through rentals.

Not all animal events were happy or amusing. In Lion House in 1955, five male lions killed a male leopard. A keeper mistakenly led the five into a cage, unaware that a pair of leopards was in the enclosure at the time. The male leopard, Snowball, attacked the group of lions, perhaps trying to protect his mate. Five against one were poor odds, however, and Snowball was soon dead of a broken neck, administered by a swipe of a lion's paw. The female leopard was unhurt, as were the five lions. It was an awful accident. Saddened and rattled, Robert Bean and the rest of the staff considered how to avoid such tragedies in the future.

Okapis

Brookfield Zoo was delighted to receive another rare animal in 1955, one that created an even bigger public stir than the white python: an okapi. For years, former Animal Committee chairman Herbert Bradley and Director Ed Bean had dreamed of obtaining a pair of okapis, the recently discovered cousin of the giraffe that lives in Zaire, what was then the Belgian Congo. In April 1939, the zoo's hopes were raised when the ambassador to Belgium, Hugh Gibson, arranged for the zoo to buy the next pair of okapis to be captured for $8,000. (At the time, a few trustees wanted the public to see pygmies from the Ituri Forest with the animals, as the Hagenbecks and other zoos had occasionally displayed indigenous peoples with their exotic animal displays—a startling reminder of how much zoos and society have changed.)

World War II intervened, and it wasn't until 1955 that a male okapi was put on exhibit at the zoo, but it was not an animal from the Belgian government, but rather one on deposit from Ringling Brothers, Barnum & Bailey Circus. Due to U.S. government restrictions, the okapi couldn't be exhibited with the circus, so instead he was placed on loan at the zoo with the stipulation that his first-born offspring become the property of the circus.

About the same time, Ralph Graham was given the go-ahead to bring back an okapi from the Congo. He did so, but unfortunately it died in Germany 19 days after its arrival in quarantine. The following year, Graham tried again, this time successfully claiming a young female okapi, a present from the Belgian government. After many years of waiting, Brookfield Zoo had a pair of okapis, a rarity in zoos anywhere. Newspaper stories abounded about this strange-looking creature with striped legs, giraffe-like features, and velvety fur.

TAPPAN GREGORY

During Clay Judson's tenure as president, he was fortunate to have Tappan Gregory serve as Animal Committee chairman. A lawyer by trade, Gregory was an accomplished amateur naturalist who pioneered night photography of animals in the wild. With his appreciation of native American animals, he altered the makeup of the zoo's animal collection by introducing Dall's sheep, red wolves, and fishers, which are related to weasels. After a visit to another zoo, where he saw what he termed an inadequate wolf environment, he returned to Brookfield determined to build an exhibit that would do justice to these fascinating animals. Upon his urging, in 1957, naturalistic Wolf Woods was carved out of the forested area surrounding the lake at the western end of the zoo.

However, some of Gregory's additions to the animal collection were animal-management failures. The fishers, for example, that he trapped at his hunting club in Maine died of viral infections while in quarantine at the animal hospital. The joy of accomplishment felt by zoo staff when the okapi group did well was matched in disappointment when they were unable to unlock the mysteries of fisher care. Pronghorn antelope, too, defied attempts to keep them healthy, testimony to the general belief in the zoo world that pronghorn antelope can't be kept east of the Mississippi.

Right: For this photo, Animal Committee chairman and amateur naturalist Tappan Gregory was on both sides of the lens.

Left: Mr. G was the first okapi born in the United States.

Below: Plans called for a terraced restaurant adjacent to the North American panorama, but neither came to be due to a lack of funds.

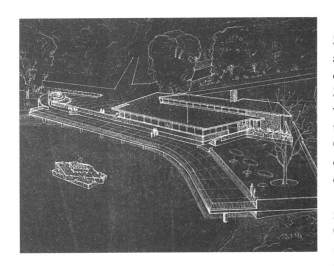

RECOLLECTIONS

[Bill Dickinson] was a friendly guy, a diplomatic type who would get people with differing opinions to come together.... I guess lawyers are good at that. Very friendly, jovial fellow.

John McCutcheon, Jr.
Former Trustee and Zoo Vice-president

The reward for all of this work arrived a few years later. On September 16, 1959, after a sleepless night watch by Robert Bean and Animal Committee chairman Tappan Gregory, Museka the okapi rewarded the zoo with the first okapi ever born in the United States. One headline read, "Okapi is a Poppy," and Brookfield Zoo was thrust into national prominence for its successful breeding of the rare animal. The young male okapi, named Mr. G. after Gregory, was eventually shipped out to Ringling Brothers, as per the original agreement, but the okapi breeding program continues successfully to this day.

Along with the addition of various North American animals, another plan was for a North American panorama west of Salt Creek (the creek that runs through the western section of the zoo) complete with a terraced restaurant and a 150-foot mountain equipped with an elevator for mountaintop viewing. At first, affordable fill to "build" the mountain couldn't be found, but in 1959, the contractors for the nearby Congress Expressway dumped fill from their job site at the zoo. Despite this welcome donation and the desirability of the panorama, there was always a more pressing need for the money required to build the exhibit, and it never came to be.

Judson Resigns

Clay Judson's nine-year stint as president of the Chicago Zoological Society came to an end in 1958, when he stepped down due to poor health. He accomplished a great deal during his tenure: completion of major new facilities, such as the animal hospital, Wolf Woods, Children's Zoo, and Roosevelt Fountain; important advances in education and research; and additions to the animal collection, including the first okapis and many new Australian representatives.

Judson was succeeded as president by his long-time friend and law partner, William R. Dickinson, Jr. A charismatic, jovial, laid-back man who loved animals, children, and the outdoors, Dickinson was a natural choice. A Chicago native, Dickinson received his law degree from Yale University in 1937, joined the firm of Wilson & McIlvaine the following year, and was made partner in 1952. As a close friend of Judson's and as a trustee, Dickinson was intimately acquainted with the zoo's activities and jumped in where Judson left off.

William R. Dickinson, Jr.

1958
Clay Judson steps down as president of the Society.
William R. Dickinson becomes the Society's president.
Discovery at the Brookfield Zoo premieres on WTTW-Channel 11.

'59
The first okapi birth in the U.S. happens at the zoo.
Ground is broken for Seven Seas.

'60
The first dolphins arrive from Florida.
Clay Judson dies.

'61
Seven Seas' dolphin show opens.
Ron Blakely replaces retired bird curator Karl Plath.
Dutch elm disease devastates many trees around the zoo.

'62
Stanley Field steps down as chair of the Buildings Committee.
A miniature railway is installed part-way around the zoo.
Olga the walrus arrives.

'63
Encil Rains is hired as assistant director for management.
Attendance peaks at 2,280,292.
Curator of reptiles Robert Snedigar retires.

'64
Robert Bean is made director emeritus and Ralph Graham assistant director emeritus.
Ron Blakely, George Rabb, Encil Rains, and Weaver Williamson are appointed associate directors. Later Blakely and Rains are made codirectors.
Admission for adults is increased to 50 cents.
The zoo celebrates its 30th birthday.

CHAPTER NINE

Falling Apart

(1958-1964)

Seven Seas

In the early 1960s, Brookfield Zoo achieved another milestone with the opening of Seven Seas Panorama, the nation's first inland dolphinarium. Robert Bean had nourished the idea of a dolphinarium since the building of the original Marineland in St. Augustine, Florida, in 1937. In the late '50s, he finally convinced the Board to go ahead with the project and began working with architects Russell Read and Donald Olsen.

Society president Bill Dickinson had his hands full with the project soon after taking office in 1958. Initially thought to be only a summer exhibit, with the animals displayed in an open-air show, the exhibit turned into a year-round facility—better for the health of the animals. The trustees granted approval for the building in 1959, and Forest Preserve District president Dan Ryan (son of former Forest Preserve District president and solid zoo supporter Daniel Ryan) broke ground in December using the same spade his father had used at Brookfield Zoo's 1922 groundbreaking. Construction was quick, and by the end of 1960, the building was ready to receive its first inhabitants. The dolphins were flown in from the Miami Seaquarium, and by August 1, 1961, they were ready to put on their first show.

Right: Present at the 1959 groundbreaking of Seven Seas were many of the people responsible for opening the exhibit, including (left to right) Charles Sauers, Dan Ryan, Bill Dickinson, Robert Bean, and Evelyn Shaw McCutcheon.

Above: The outdoor pools at Seven Seas were among the most popular places in Chicagoland on bright, sunny days.

Right: Seven Seas was the only place in the Midwest to see dolphins, which are naturally one of the zoo's most popular animals.

Below: Getting wet was part of the fun.

Performing dolphins Vickie, Maggie, Power, and Tommy became overnight sensations. Attendance peaked, even with an additional charge of 50 cents (25 cents for children) to get in. Seven Seas held a thousand spectators at a time, but despite the large capacity, people were turned away from every show, even during weekday "pay" days. Of the first 62 shows, all but three were sellouts.

The dolphins were the stars, but the building attracted considerable attention as well since it was the first of its kind. Highly technical information about tank capacities, water filters, salinization, and corrosion were detailed in the newspapers, alongside engaging photos of the quartet jumping and swimming.

Deterioration

With the huge public success of Seven Seas, Bean had accomplished his dream. However, the price tag read nearly $1 million, and even increased attendance revenues couldn't replace the cost immediately. As a result, much-needed repairs and renovations in the rest of the zoo went unaddressed. Most of the buildings had been constructed 30 years before, and many needed attention in terms of roofing, painting, plumbing, and other basics—far less glamorous than a new exhibit. By the early '60s, the zoo began to look run-down. There wasn't enough money to freshly paint buildings or to fix obviously untended railings and exhibits.

The steam-heating system was the biggest of the problems. Originally using a central, coal-fired powerhouse distributing steam heat to all buildings, the aging system created recurrent problems when it began to collapse. Pipes burst with regularity, and crews frantically dug down to fix the eruptions and restore heat. In 1961 and 1962, the trustees used the few available bits of money to convert the system to a gas-powered one.

To make matters worse, Dutch elm disease hit in 1961, further marring the zoo's beauty. The disease began with one elm just north of Australia House and slowly spread throughout the grounds. Trees were taken down by the dozens. By that time, the zoo had lost its well-maintained appearance.

Internally, things were falling apart. Staff had begun to complain about work conditions back in the early 1950s. At that time, they worked six days a week and holidays for very little pay, so when they were approached by a union, there was some interest in joining in the hopes of strengthening their bargaining position. The trustees, trying to avoid a unionized work force, had responded by granting overtime for holidays and the seventh day of the week worked, increasing wages, granting Blue Cross coverage for regular full-time employees, approving a pension plan, and providing Social Security insurance. These measures had staved off complaints from the employees for a few years.

Wages and conditions, however, were still poor in comparison to neighboring businesses. In 1956, the situation had peaked again, when groundskeeper Ed Steiner circulated a petition among employees demanding raises. He successfully gathered signatures from every nonadministrative staff member. Hoping to avoid another union attack, Judson and Bean responded quickly by offering a five-day work week rather than a six-day week, at a cost to the Society of $65,000 per year. While this adjustment temporarily pleased the staff, bigger problems were around the corner.

Above: Ironically, the zoo's "welcome" sign fell into disrepair, a symbol of the tough times the zoo was undergoing—and one that many visitors probably noticed.

RECOLLECTIONS

[The zoo] was filthy. Grounds [staff] came to work at 8:00 in the morning and worked until 3:00. They didn't even have time to pick up the day's garbage. [The zoo was] selling cotton candy, and the sidewalks were littered with purple cotton candy that had turned black. They were selling peanuts, cotton candy, and sticky marshmallows in Children's Zoo, and the animals would be loaded with goo by the end of the day.

I don't know that Brookfield Zoo was worse than any other zoo in the country. They were all pretty much on the same level. Nickels and dimes were what they dealt in, because there was no real financial support. The buildings were getting old. All the roofs were leaking and the heating plant blew up.

Mary Rabb
Later Zoo Librarian

Left: This once-regal lion had seen better days.

Lower left: No place at the zoo, including Monkey Island, was safe from litter as the grounds crew struggled to keep up with the mess.

Personnel Changes

In the early '60s, it appeared that everything that could go wrong, would. Along with the deteriorating buildings, grumbling staff, and bleak financial situation, retirements and deaths were plentiful.

In a single month, April 1961, death stole away Dan Ryan and trustees Herbert Bradley and Tappan Gregory. Clay Judson had died the previous year, and long-time trustees John Wentworth and Solomon Smith, treasurer of the Society since 1931, died around that time as well. Also, Buildings Committee chairman Stanley Field stepped down from his post in 1962, ending his 36-year reign as head planner and construction overseer. The Board was clearly in a period of transition.

Among the staff, the death of Walter Soderstrom, one of the zoo's original employees, was a great loss. Soderstrom, head of the Grounds Department since before the zoo opened, had been responsible for overseeing all of the original plantings and had since managed maintenance of and upgrades to the horticultural collection. He was a well-respected and central figure at the zoo.

Bird curator Karl Plath, another key player, left the zoo to retire. Having ably served as head of the bird collection and occasionally as artist for 25 years, his retirement was well-earned but sadly received by the staff. He was succeeded in 1961 by Ron Blakely, formerly general curator of Lincoln Park Zoo, who would come to play a major role at the zoo. Reptile curator and ad hoc education program founder Robert Snedigar retired in 1963, leaving another hole in the senior staff.

Amid these departures, a new staff member was hired by the trustees in 1963 to help Bean in his administrative duties. Encil Rains was familiar to the trustees through his work as a management consultant for the zoo. Disturbed by a disgruntled staff, the poor financial situation, and the rapidly declining state of the buildings, the Board had gone to the firm of A. T. Kearney for a management study and to the architectural firm of Olsen & Urbain for a report on the condition of the zoo. The management study suggested several organizational changes, among them a distribution of power that then centered in Bean. Rains, part of the management-study team, was hired as Bean's assistant director for management.

RECOLLECTIONS

When I first started here in 1949, I was making $1.86 an hour. Out there it was $3.00 or something. I certainly could have made more money on the outside. But... I enjoyed it. I also had a couple of part-time jobs to supplement. I'd leave here and go work at the bakery until 1:00 in the morning. Then I'd get up at 6:00 to be here at 8:00 in the morning— six days a week.

Edward Vondra
Former Keeper

RECOLLECTIONS

On one of my Saturdays off, Bob Bean called me. I had drawn up a petition for a raise and I had almost 100% of the signatures in the park: grounds crew, concessions, keepers, all of them.... Bean called me at home and asked if I wouldn't mind coming down to the park, that Mr. Judson wanted to talk to me. He said, "Come down in a good frame of mind!" I said, "I sure will, if everything goes my way!"

We went up to the office, the three of us, and talked things over. Mr. Judson said, "I understand you people want a raise. I'll tell you what we're going to do. We're going to give you a five-day week for what you were making in six." I took it! And they're working a five-day week to this day.

Ed Steiner
Former Groundskeeper

Encil Rains

Ron Blakely

John Lanka Photo

Animal Events

There were some happy moments. One event overshadowed by Seven Seas' grand opening was the birth of a second okapi, this time a female—and the first the zoo was able to keep. Fredricka, named after new Animal Committee chair Fred Pullman, who had replaced Tappan Gregory, bolstered the zoo's confidence in its ability to repeatedly breed this rare species.

The zoo received a generous gift that also helped lift spirits. Mr. and Mrs. Edward Marshall Boehm presented the zoo with the single largest donation of birds ever received from an individual: 60 rare birds of 42 different species, including a woodhoopoe, a cape sugarbird, three species of sunbirds, and two species of solitaires. Mr. Boehm was a sculptor and had kept his own aviary so he could work from live models.

The animals didn't seem bothered by the Society's financial and other woes and continued with their antics. Along with the dolphins, the most popular animals at the time were seven two-year-old orangutans housed in Children's Zoo. Named Stanley, Stella, Spooky, Alice, Katie, Connie, and Sammy, the young primates were a never-ending source of entertainment. They spent their nights in a room near Children's Zoo's kitchen and, much to everyone's amusement, were transported to their daytime quarters in two baby buggies. Stanley inevitably outsmarted his fellow riders, hopping first into one buggy and encouraging the other six to pile in after him. Once the heap was complete, Stanley would wriggle out and jump to the other buggy and ride in style.

Connie had her own tricks. Her favorite pastimes were cruising Children's Zoo's duck pond in her own dinghy (causing the ducks to scatter and the visitors to chuckle) and climbing atop Cookie the young elephant for a high-rise ride. Cookie also had a troop of admirers who were entertained by her diminutive size and sweetness, as well as her tendency to nap with her head in a keeper's lap and her trunk curled around the person's hand or foot.

Right across from Children's Zoo, at Bear Grottos, another comedy was unfolding. Six five-month-old polar bear cubs were discovering the hard way the purpose of the dry moat in front of their enclosure. Unaccustomed to such constructions (unaccustomed to most everything at that age), all six fell into the moat in quick succession. Anticipating this, keepers had padded the bottom of the moat with hay, softening the 12-foot fall. Unhurt but puzzled, the cubs tried their best to climb back up.

Above: Connie the orangutan, a crowd favorite, cruised Children's Zoo's duck pond in her dinghy. She and her fellow orangutans were worth hours of entertainment to Children's Zoo visitors.

Right and above right: In Children's Zoo, playful bear cubs and otters held audiences attentive.

In an article in the *Chicago Tribune*, Louise Hutchinson described the scene. "After a few fruitless attempts to climb back up the sheer 12 foot wall, the little bears had fun. They rolled in the straw till they were four-footed straw men and cavorted in the mud until suddenly they were not polar bears at all. They were black bears. Keepers put a sturdy wood ladder up the side of the moat to the grotto. One little bear mounted three steps—then fell back." With a little practice, some experience, and some growing, the cubs became used to their environment and the endearing antics came to an end.

The bears weren't the only ones hamming it up. A May 1962 article in the *Bandar-log* told the story of an enterprising primate.

"Brookfield's first orang-utan was a remarkable female named Tia, acquired...when the zoo opened. Tia was often fed by visitors, and as you have undoubtedly observed, some of the food thrown by visitors often falls short. Tia loved marshmallows, and one day a little boy threw her a yummy looking one, but it fell outside her cage. Tia tried to reach it with her long arm, and when she could not, she looked hopefully at the little boy. But it was his last marshmallow and no other visitor had any to throw her. Tia studied the situation for a few minutes and then went back to the wooden shelf in her cage and carefully bit off a long splinter, with which she successfully speared the marshmallow. Word traveled quickly, and visitors started throwing food just out of her reach on purpose, and every day Tia bit off a new splinter, using it sometimes as a spear and sometimes as a rake, and every night the splinter was swept away when the cage was cleaned and the sand floor raked.

"Every so often the shelf had to be replaced, a small price to pay for the wonderful show Tia put on for an ever increasing crowd of admirers. One night the splinter was nowhere to be found, which perplexed the keeper as he had seen her using one that day. Tia had buried it deep in the sand, smoothed the floor carefully, and the next morning dug it up, saving herself the trouble of making a new one. After this she always buried the splinter carefully when no one was watching, always in a different part of her cage, and only made a new one when the old one wore out."

RECOLLECTIONS

We used to have three baby chimps who lived in the middle of Children's Zoo. People would always reach out and try to make contact [with the chimpanzees]. As the chimps got bigger, they'd pretend they couldn't reach, and the people would reach in farther and farther. Then the chimps would grab a person's arm, use it as a ladder, and crawl hand over foot up the person, over his or her head, and up the trees in Children's Zoo.

The only way to get them down was to pretend that you were beating up on their favorite keeper, then they'd come down to attack you and protect the keeper. The keeper would scream and yell and pretend to be attacked. That's how we got them out of the tree. This got to be a regular thing. Pretty soon they got wise, and it didn't work as well.

Terrie McLean
Current Keeper

Losing Control

In terms of attendance and revenue, 1963 was a good year. Attendance was a booming 2,280,292, due largely to the popularity of Seven Seas. Earned income was at an all-time high, reaching $1,438,000. Seven Seas was responsible for bringing in $239,000 (only a fraction of its construction costs), whereas Children's Zoo was holding its own by earning $92,000. A new feature, added in 1962, was a miniature railway running part-way around the zoo. It offered both transportation and a scenic journey for foot-weary visitors. In 1963, approximately 400,000 people rode the railway, adding some $80,000 to the revenue column.

LONG-DISTANCE GLARING

Although relations between Brookfield Zoo and Lincoln Park Zoo are friendly today, it wasn't always so. An uncomfortable relationship existed between Robert Bean and Lincoln Park Zoo's former director, Marlin Perkins. John Justin Smith wrote about the two leaders' attitudes in "Our Double-Fisted Hatchet Throwers" in a 1961 edition of the *Chicago Daily News.*

"Among the more interesting creatures to be seen in Chicago's two zoos are the directors. Each denies that his heart contains anything but love for the other. But in some circles it is believed that they might best be billed as the Double-Fisted Hatchet Throwers.

"'Tsk,' said Robert Bean, Brookfield's bushy-browed, sometimes-garrulous, always wonderful boss.

"'I don't think there's any rivalry at all,' said Lincoln Park's silver-maned, clever and nimble R. Marlin Perkins.

"I went into the matter of rivalry with these two gentlemen and came to the conclusion that they're not about to hit each other with hatchets. But there is an undercurrent of keen competition—to Chicago's good fortune. Each is trying to put on the best possible display of animals. The result: We have two world-famed zoos. Let's take a look at the rivalry, though.

"In an effort to support his contention that there is no rivalry, Perkins cited the fact that Bean has often sold him animals. 'We got Judy the elephant from him,' he said. 'Then there was a male wildebeest and a male sitatunga.' Perkins thought for a moment. His silver mustache trembled. The next words slipped out: 'Of course, Robert ALWAYS keeps the female animals.' And why does Bean do this? Well, it's a scientific fact that Perkins can't produce more sitatungas or wildebeests unless he has a breeding pair.

"As for Bean, he has been known to roar like a lion when he reads newspaper reports that Lincoln Park's attendance on a summer Sunday was 60,000, while Brookfield's was 30,000. 'How does Mr. Perkins know how many people were in his zoo?' he asked once. 'He has no turnstiles with which to count the customers. What does he do—total the ears he sees and divide by two?'

"It's a fact that once the newspapers suggested that Perkins' great gorilla Bushman, now deceased, should be mated with one of Bean's lady gorillas. 'Great idea,' said Bean, 'let's go.' Perkins says he doesn't remember the details. But others say that he nearly approved the breeding idea, until he remembered that any baby gorilla would have to remain with Bean's mother gorilla.

"Then there's the matter of a children's zoo. I asked Perkins if he hadn't copied Brookfield's zoo for kids. 'Certainly not,' he said archly. 'We had a small display of baby animals for children two years before Bean did.' But he insisted there was no rivalry...nothing like that. He said he even plans to visit Brookfield soon to see Bean's new show of porpoises.

"Ah, there, Mr. Bean. And peace to you, Mr. Perkins."

The new miniature train was the cause of an uncomfortable but humorous situation at one annual meeting. Before the meeting, the governing members were invited on a tour to see the year's significant births. The new train was designated as the mode of transport for the tour. Unfortunately, whether due to a staff prank or terrible luck, the train ran out of gas just abreast of the garbage pile. And the man with the gas-tank key had gone home! Some governing members walked, others endured the odoriferous situation until help arrived.

Despite the superficial successes, by this time it had become clear to the trustees that something needed to be done about Robert Bean. Notwithstanding his remarkable strengths and his international reputation as "one of the best," things simply weren't as they should be. Bean's drinking, exacerbated by the 1957 death of his wife, Jean, was interfering with his ability to manage his staff and endangering his health.

Bean was losing control of the zoo. In fact, many daily decisions were being made by his long-time secretary, Mae Rose Jana, who had been with the zoo since the late '30s and who had enough experience to know what needed to be done. Young senior staff members like bird curator Ron Blakely, veterinarian Weaver Williamson, and researcher George Rabb were going about their work without much interference or guidance from Bean.

Bean had grown up ensconced in the old-fashioned way of managing zoos: one all-knowing, dictatorial director leading an inexperienced staff—a paternal model of management. The new wave of professionally trained staff members, most of them imposed on Bean by the trustees, reflected a fundamental change in how zoos were run. Other employees sensed the shift from the single leader to a more departmentalized structure. Senior staff members measured their might with much testing, pushing, and pulling. Meanwhile, administrative issues such as building care and financial management were left unattended. Encil Rains was working out his own positioning with respect to Bean, the staff, and the trustees.

End of an Era

In February 1964, the year the zoo celebrated its 30th birthday, the trustees voted to radically change the management of the zoo, hoping to bring a difficult period to an end. At a meeting in President Dickinson's office, Robert Bean and Ralph Graham were removed from their positions. Leadership was temporarily entrusted to four associate directors: Encil Rains for administration, Ron Blakely for the animal collection, Weaver Williamson for health and medical care, and George Rabb for research and education. Ron Blakely recalled years later that the promotions came as a surprise to the four.

Unwilling to fully remove Bean from the institution and hoping to capitalize on his international reputation, the trustees appointed him director emeritus and asked him to tour zoos in Asia, Australia, and India to gather ideas. For his part, Ralph Graham, who struggled with serious health problems, was kept on as assistant director emeritus to advise on specific projects and, from time to time, to make artistic contributions.

With this unusual arrangement, the Bean era came to an end. Begun in 1927 with the arrival of Ed Bean and his son, the dynasty concluded unceremoniously. Over the years—and with more than a few glances back over the shoulder at how things used to be—Brookfield Zoo would struggle to find a new management structure that would bring the zoo into the present. In the meantime, the four new directors needed to address problems that had gone unattended for too long: a zoo that looked shabby at best, neglected maintenance, and an unsatisfied work force.

INTERNAL CORRESPONDENCE

Date: February 28, 1964

TO: ALL EMPLOYEES OF BROOKFIELD ZOO

From: Bill Dickinson

Subject:

For some time the Executive Committee and Mr. Bean have been working on a program whereby Mr. Bean and Mr. Graham could be relieved of their responsibilities in connection with the day to day operations of the Zoo. The objectives of this program have been two-fold:

1. To free up the time of both Mr. Bean and Mr. Graham so that they could advise and assist the Executive Committee on special studies and long-range plans in connection with the growth and future development of the Zoo.

2. To provide opportunity for other key personnel to take over active day to day management of the Zoo while Mr. Bean and Mr. Graham are still available to provide advice and consultation from the broad depth of knowledge of the Zoo which they have acquired over the years.

Accordingly, Mr. Bean and Mr. Graham have been appointed Director Emeritus and Assistant Director Emeritus effective March 2, 1964, and relieved of all responsibilities and authority in connection with operating and administering the affairs of the Zoo.

The responsibility and authority for all Zoo operations will, as of March 2, 1964, be placed in the hands of Mr. Ronald L. Blakely, Mr. Encil E. Rains, Dr. George B. Rabb, and Dr. Weaver M. Williamson.

"THE SEARCH FOR THE DARING"

At Brookfield Zoo's 30th anniversary on July 1, 1964, Seymour Simon, president of the Forest Preserve District, deliberated on his idea of what a zoo should be.

"When I was asked to make this address, I went to the dictionary for the definition of the word 'zoo.' I found that it was 'a place where a collection of wild animals is kept for public showing.' I would like to suggest this as a substitute way for finding the meaning of Brookfield Zoo...just study the responses of the children who stroll these paths every day. They will tell you that Brookfield Zoo is a place of wonder, mystery, excitement, and the greatest of delight for boys and girls. Or look at the faces of the parents of the boys and girls and they'll tell you the same things and even more. They'll tell you that Brookfield Zoo is a fantasy of smell and noise and sights, where there is escape for a grownup into the dreams of childhood. The adults' faces will tell you that Brookfield Zoo provides the closest experience there is to a safari without any actual cost. And the parents' faces will also tell you that this zoo is a place where families can be together and revel in the joy of being together and sharing a common adventure. Where parent and child, hand in hand, can communicate in a deep, clear, and close language of great love.

"What makes Brookfield Zoo such a brilliant achievement is the realization by its leaders that there is always a new challenge to be met, as soon as the present one is conquered. At the end of thirty years of accomplishment, tomorrow, the 2nd of July, is regarded not as a time to relax and rest comfortably in the glow of success, but as a new day, a fresh day, a day of rebirth and rededication, and the continuation of the search for the daring and the adventurous. The zoo has had steady leadership, which has had the courage to back unorthodox approaches and to shrink from the commonplace and the pedestrian. A great amount of peppery showmanship has been present in this zoo, and this explains the vivid, zestful way in which what this zoo has to show has been presented to the public. Finally, the staff at Brookfield has always been indoctrinated with the purpose of a consistent search for the new, the different, the exciting."

Above: Weaver Williamson, George Rabb, Seymour Simon, Bill Dickinson, Encil Rains, and Ron Blakely (from left) celebrate a milestone: the zoo's 30th birthday in 1964.

1964

Robert Bean is made director emeritus and Ralph Graham assistant director emeritus.

Ron Blakely, George Rabb, Encil Rains, and Weaver Williamson are appointed associate directors. Later Blakely and Rains are made codirectors.

Admission for adults is increased to 50 cents.

The zoo celebrates its 30th birthday.

'65

Education gains prominence in zoo goals.

The trustees initiate a fundraising program.

Small Mammal House is renovated.

The Illinois Exhibit and the mink exhibit are razed.

'66

Employees strike for more pay.

Employees sign with the Teamsters Union.

The travel program begins.

John Conrad begins hosting *Zoo World*.

'67

The trustees create a category of nonvoting membership.

Tuesday becomes the only day with free admission.

Three trackless trains are introduced.

Ron Blakely and Encil Rains leave the zoo.

CHAPTER TEN

Struggling Through Transition

(1964-1967)

Multiple Directors

The quartet of associate directors was made up of an unusual assortment. Intended as merely a temporary solution while the Board deliberated on a new director, the foursome was not chosen for its ability to work together. Their personalities were as different as their backgrounds, and it made for an uncomfortable combination.

Encil Rains, a former naval commander with no background in zoos, brought his own ideas about management, organization, and leadership to the group. Ron Blakely, however, was fully a zoo man, having come from Lincoln Park Zoo, where he'd been curator, and also serving briefly as Brookfield Zoo's curator of birds. George Rabb, with his background in research, wasn't technically a zoo man, but he represented and forwarded the academic aspect. Weaver Williamson, as the zoo's veterinarian, was another specially trained individual who added his own sense of priorities.

Right: Ducks congregate on a steamy Waterfowl Lake.

After a few months, it became clear that the zoo's main issues were hammered out between Rains, head of administration, and Blakely, head of the animal collection. Aware of the struggles within the four-person committee, the trustees decided to appoint Rains and Blakely codirectors, with Rabb and Williamson one notch down as associate directors of their areas. The quartet became a duet, but even the committee of two had its problems.

It was no secret that Rains and Blakely had their differences. Functionally, it was an unusual setup. While technically they were codirectors, Rains controlled the finances, requiring Blakely to solicit Rains for every dime spent on the animal collection. Furthermore, the two men's personalities, goals, and philosophies couldn't have been more polar. With their different interests, both struggled to enhance their own programs.

The first sign of tension came in December 1964. When asked to present their budget recommendations to the Executive Committee, Rains and Blakely declared that they were unable to agree on the best action in terms of employees' salaries. For the previous eight years, there had been across-the-board pay increases. Rains, however, thought raises were unnecessary that year and decided the Society could save some money. Blakely, more in touch with the keepers, disagreed, unwilling to open "a Pandora's box of union action." He felt that the employees might have two thoughts: the new administration had done little other than put more rules and regulations into effect, and the paternal approach favored over the years should continue. After listening to both arguments, the trustees agreed with Blakely, and the employees received raises in 1965.

RECOLLECTIONS

I am one of the apparently few people who knew what I wanted to be before I entered kindergarten. I knew I wanted to be a zookeeper. I started work at the age of 15, working summers at the zoo in Lansing, Michigan. Then I went to college and double majored in psychology and zoology and took some education and botany. From there, I went to Lincoln Park Zoo. Marlin Perkins answered my ad, which said, "college graduate, knows how to use broom and shovel, looking for position." I went to Lincoln Park as a zoologist and was later promoted to curator. In 1961, Karl Plath, the curator of birds at Brookfield, announced his retirement, and I had a talk with Robert Bean, who hired me.

Ron Blakely
Former Codirector

Different Agendas

The ideas of numerous zoo directors intersected at the January 1965 annual meeting of governing members. Robert Bean attended as director emeritus, reporting on his trip to an international meeting of zoo directors in Asia. He also outlined plans for an exhibit on hummingbirds. An anonymous member of the Society had offered funding for such an exhibit, provided that Bean assist in its design.

During the meeting, Rains, casting his administrative view on the institution, stated that during the previous year "emphasis was placed on basic departmental organizations and the divisions within these organizations. We feel we are well on the road towards the ultimate goal of a well-organized and administered park where duties and responsibilities are clearly outlined and defined."

Blakely, for his part, urged a new way of thinking about zoos. "Simply exhibiting live animals has been such a good drawing card that for the 7 to 8 thousand years of their existence, zoos have done little more than remain passive recreational facilities," he declared. "The last few years, however, have seen a rather dramatic awakening amongst zoo officials as to their responsibilities, both to the public and to the animals with which they are so concerned. We will, of course, make every effort to utilize the very best techniques in care, cleaning, and safety. While these things are desirable, there is another, more nebulous, sphere which demands our consideration.

"This is the preservation of the very creatures we exhibit. Never...has there been such a rapid decimation of our wild animals. The main cause is simple—more people on a world that is only so big. Where the humans live, the wild animals cannot. Much can be done with education. People that understand animals are sympathetic to their needs and will make efforts to preserve them. Zoos are in an advantageous position to present this education. After all, who can be more convincing than those of us who are already convinced? In addition, we must take positive actions towards propagating these endangered forms. When the day comes that we acquire a breeding farm we will have taken an important stride forward. Until that propitious day arrives, there are positive steps we can take. Already zoos have banded together to compile a blacklist—a list of species so rare in their native haunts that under no circumstances will a zoo encourage their capture by buying them. We now demand to see government permits before buying specimens of a protected species. The day is gone when all we needed to consider was whether the price was right. Now we must consider whether or not we have the moral right."

George Rabb added his opinion, arguing for an expanded education program in order to reach the public in new ways. "Basically these needs revolve about relating the natural world to urban man in meaningful ways," he said.

Aside from these reports, governing members heard about myriad activities and events at the zoo. The variety of happenings must have been somewhat overwhelming. Adult admission had been increased to 50 cents. Over 200 surplus animals had been sold or traded. A dolphin had been born, but it died 17 days later. A new publication, the *Brookfield Babbler*, was afoot. Twelve wild turkeys had been born and subsequently released at the nearby Morton Arboretum. Around the zoo, $160,000 had been spent on repairs and improvements. The house formerly serving as the director's cottage had been converted to education offices. And new staff members included reptile curator Ray Pawley and zoologist Gene Schreiber. It was a time of frantic activity as the zoo struggled to find its way.

Above: New reptile curator Ray Pawley inspects a vampire bat.

Above: The Illinois Exhibit had fallen into serious disrepair by 1965 and had to be torn down.

Right: Trustees Elliott Donnelley (left) and George Beach persuaded fellow trustees to launch an untried endeavor: a fundraising campaign.

Trustee Involvement

The Board of Trustees, aware of the dire condition of the park and of the changes the institution was facing, took on an active role in management. In the past, with Bean at the helm, the Board had generally stayed out of daily activities, with the exception of Bean's last few years. Knowing that the zoo's future depended upon shrewd financial management, the trustees decided to become more involved.

Trustee Corky Hamill recalled how uncontrolled things had become. "Around the time Stanley Field died [in 1964], we had an electrical problem in one of the buildings," he said. "The electric company came in to fix it. They told us that they couldn't replace the wires in the building. Puzzled, we asked why. They informed us that the roof was in such poor condition, the wires simply wouldn't last [due to leakage]. Taking a look up on the roof, we saw that roof tiles were missing and the roof was in horrible shape. Clearly, no one had been up on that roof in years."

How much the average visitor noticed these conditions is hard to say. Certainly parts of the zoo started to look better. Renovations took place in Small Mammal House, and the old Illinois and mink exhibits, both long since closed, were razed due to their poor condition.

A few key trustees stepped up to provide a new level—and type—of support. New president Bill Dickinson expended considerable time and energy holding the park together, Vice-president Fred Pullman became heavily involved in managerial issues, and George Beach volunteered to chair a new Development Committee. Aware that funds for building repairs and renovations were desperately needed, the Board embarked somewhat reluctantly on its first fundraising campaign. Led by an enthusiastic and persuasive Beach, the trustees agreed to try to raise $5.5 million over three years (later lengthened to five years) for restoration projects and new exhibits.

The campaign marked a change in how the trustees perceived their role. Never before had they been asked for money or even been asked to help raise money. In fact, the zoo's Board of Trustees had been the only such board in the Chicago area in which trustees volunteered their time but no money. It was always assumed that the zoo tax collected through the Forest Preserve District would cover the bulk of operating costs and that admissions, merchandise sales, and other earned revenue would make up the difference.

RECOLLECTIONS

At one time, it was necessary for the Executive Committee to take over operation of the zoo. This was when Robert Bean retired. He'd been there for quite a while and was pretty dictatorial in everything he did. I think as he got older, his effectiveness started to deteriorate for one reason or another. But he had a great reputation, and I think he attracted a lot of interest to the zoo, particularly early in the game. I think he was responsible for much of the early part of the success. Then we had an interim period where there were a lot of loose ends that needed gathering.

Frank Farwell
Current Trustee

128

Do monkeys laugh?

Do fish fight?

------- SPECIAL EXHIBITS -------
Live animals in pilot exhibits
showing principles of the natural world.

The trustees felt they should have a new or renovated exhibit to illustrate to prospective funders what the zoo was trying to accomplish. As examples, they chose two very different projects: a renovation of Aquatic Bird House and new refreshment stands in the zoo's west end.

In addition, Insect House was changed into a Special Exhibits building featuring innovative displays on biological principles such as imprinting, dominance, and nocturnal behaviors. The dominance display featured a group of bonnet monkeys, each wearing a collar of a different color. A sign explained the ranking of each monkey within the group and behaviors associated with each rank. Another section demonstrated the concept of territoriality by having two fish, separated by a clear partition, swim toward each other and show "display" behaviors. (In the wild, animals often "display" to attract a mate or repel a competitor for resources.)

NEW AND IMPROVED

The Board of Trustees' wish list for exhibits and renovations, drawn up in 1965, was long. In priority order, it included:

- a new ape house to supplement Primate House and provide more appropriate quarters for the large primates — $ 800,000
- a breeding farm, located away from the zoo, to provide for increased breeding facilities for endangered species — $ 150,000
- a new reptile house as the old one suffered from poor ventilation and inadequate space — $ 750,000
- an addition to the hospital because the building, only 15 years old, was already proving inadequate for the zoo's needs — $ 95,000
- repairs to building roofs, railings, plumbing, and other basic needs — $1,300,000
- improvements to the Freedom Gallery in Perching Bird House — $ 30,000
- a new outdoor predator exhibit — $ 75,000
- remodeling in Lion House — $ 200,000
- a building for jungle animals — $ 125,000
- new restrooms and renovations in the old ones — $ 50,000
- porpoise holding tanks for Seven Seas — $ 250,000
- refreshment buildings and stands — $ 450,000
- a breeding area for large birds — $ 25,000
- an exhibit on predatory birds — $ 50,000
- a plant for disposing of sewage and manure — $ 500,000
- consolidation of the aquatic exhibits — $ 600,000

Other items were informally added to the wish list later, most notably a new Administration and Education Complex to be built at the North Gate entrance.

Above: A little visitor finds something to see at eye level.

Left: The Special Exhibits building, located in the former Insect House, featured a variety of animals to explain basic biological principles, such as monkeys displaying dominance.

Discontent

While the trustees were trying to alleviate financial problems, Rains and Blakely were struggling to keep the work force happy. In 1965, the Teamsters Union made a second attempt at unionizing the zoo. A memo from the directors to the staff explained management's view on the situation:

"Dear Fellow Employee:

"As all of you are aware, the Teamsters are presently attempting to organize our employees. This isn't the first time a union has decided it would like to get its hands in your pockets and it probably won't be the last time. Many of you have asked what our position is regarding this matter and we think you are entitled to a straight-forward answer.

"First, we are a small nonprofit, educational society, and because of this the law does not require us to have a union election or to deal with a union. We view this law as extremely sensible, and have always taken the position that we will not recognize a union.

"More importantly, however, we honestly do not believe we need a union at Brookfield. We always enjoyed a personal relationship and an open door policy that has enabled us to handle our problems as individuals. This system has been both pleasant and effective. We do not intend to allow outsiders to destroy this system and replace it with a labor contract that will require us to treat you as nameless, faceless numbers on one of Jimmie [sic] Hoffa's membership rosters."

Despite the opposition by Blakely and Rains, the employees were determined. In August 1966, they went on a three-day strike for more pay. Uncertain about the zoo's new direction (time clocks had been installed for the first time), untrusting of the new management, and dissatisfied with their meager paychecks and poor benefits, they more or less stuck together. (A few keepers opted not to be included. Some even hopped over remote fences to get in and feed the animals in their care.)

A strike in a zoo is especially touchy because the animals need to be fed and cared for regardless of the political environment. In this case, there were enough curatorial and management staff to pitch in and feed the animals for the three days, although the cleanup was considerable when the strike ended.

In October 1966, a union contract was signed. Animal keepers, groundskeepers, craftsmen, and all but the security, guest services, and administrative staff opted for the union to safeguard their jobs and improve their conditions.

Saddled with the additional personnel expenses created by the union contract, the trustees brainstormed other methods of financial relief. Among them were reducing the number of public free days, increasing admission costs, increasing the tax levy, and instituting a nonvoting membership option. The Board decided to wait until the new Forest Preserve District president was in office in early 1967 before approaching that body with their suggestions.

Major Issues

The mid-1960s were a time of turmoil all over America. Demonstrations about the war in Vietnam and race riots were erupting in towns large and small. For the zoo, times were uncertain and unsettling. Fortunately, both the zoo and the town of Brookfield were spared any real outbreaks. All the same, the zoo, Brookfield, and neighboring Riverside put together "Operation Zebra," a riot-control operation for skirmishes too big for zoo security alone to handle.

Another major issue in the United States in the mid-1960s was equal rights for women. The issue was reflected in Brookfield Zoo's hiring practices. Since the departure of reptile curator Grace Olive Wiley in the 1930s, the zoo hadn't employed any female animal keepers. Women worked in other positions, primarily in food service and office situations, but not in animal care. The exception was in Children's Zoo, where they often were hired seasonally to handle the animals in the petting areas.

As women gradually became more a part of the work force, it began to change the face of zookeeping. Once thought to be a man's job because of the considerable lifting and endless cleaning, the role of zookeeper slowly became less of a janitorial responsibility and more of a nurturing and caring position. This certainly would have happened over time in any case, but the increase in women in the cages hastened its arrival. The "men's club" atmosphere once prevalent in the zoo would soon change, quite reluctantly for some of its employees.

RECOLLECTIONS

There was a fellow who was supposed to go into the Army in the early '60s. He was going to move a baby rattlesnake when he pulled the alarm cord indicating that he'd been bitten by a venomous snake. He was shaking, and he showed me what he said was the bite. I think it was actually a razor cut. There was no mark from a fang at all.

He went to the hospital and even got a vial of antivenin. The fact is, he never should have gotten antivenin until it was determined that he was having some sort of reaction. I think what happened is that he cut himself as an excuse not to go in for his physical for the selective-service call, which was the next morning. However, the antivenin caused such a severe reaction, which sometimes happens, that I think he evaded the draft anyway.

That's the closest that I can say we ever came to any incident here involving a venomous snakebite.

Ray Pawley
Current Curator of Reptiles

ACT OF WAR

The October 1967 issue of *Brookfield Briefs* ran the following item, entitled "Captured Vietnam Snake Arrives at Brookfield Zoo."

"SP/4 Ben Restivo and the patrol he was with moved cautiously through thick elephant grass in the Mekong Delta. It was the end of a patrol and time to clear a camping area. Ben and the patrol began chopping down the grass and then they couldn't believe what they saw—a large curled up Indian Python. For a moment no one moved—the men or the snake. Then the men realized that this Python was in a stupor—it was digesting a large meal it had just eaten. They moved fast and stuffed the snake into a large bag. The next morning they brought the snake back to their base where it remained the camp mascot for nearly a year. During this time it laid a clutch of eggs, but they did not hatch. SP/4 Restivo wrote to Brookfield Zoo from Vietnam and offered to donate the Python to the Zoo. Ray Pawley, General Curator, arranged for the shipment and care of this valuable Python. It is now on display at the Reptile House."

Left: A *Winter Animals* brochure helped people find the most active animals during cold weather.

Advances in Education

Of the many agendas presented at the 1965 annual meeting, education soon came to the forefront. This aspect of the zoo grew intensely in the mid-60s. The trustees agreed philosophically that every exhibit should have an educational purpose. A curator of education was hired, and nearly a thousand signs and labels were produced over a year and a half. As for educational publications, a self-guided tour of winter animals was created, the text for the guidebook was rewritten for the first time in 30 years, and the *Bandar-log*, at that point compiled by George Rabb, was relaunched with a different format that included a dozen pages and a full-color, glossy cover. Education, as one of the four cornerstones of the zoo's original mission, was finally getting the attention it deserved.

The emphasis on education was in part due to Ron Blakely and George Rabb. Their thoughts are made clear in an excerpt from a report they made to the Executive Committee. "We wish to add a note of urgency to the establishment and initiation of the education department. It has become increasingly apparent through the last few years that sooner or later zoos are going to be making spectacular and far-reaching strides in this particular field. Common sense would dictate that this is indeed the only course open to them. The mere exhibition of animals with labels attached, or if you will, the reverse, the exhibition of labels illustrated by animals, is the function that zoos have considered as their excuse for being. More and more, zoo people are realizing the inadequacy of this excuse. We have, not only in every zoo, but in every cage in every zoo, a story to tell, and this story is vital to our public. For the sake of us all, even urban man has to realize that he is, and must function as, a cog in the wheel of nature. Lack of realization of this vital principle is certainly responsible for much of the inadequate legislation and apathetic attitudes concerning our natural resources and environment."

Below: An Indian python made for an unusual camp mascot before being added to the zoo's reptile collection.

Right: Publications were given a new look in the mid-1960s. The *Bandar-log*, minus a hyphen, received renewed attention.

Right: In the mid-1960s, the guidebook was revamped to take into account the zoo's new focus on educating the public.

GUIDE BOOK
BROOKFIELD ZOO

ZOO WORLD

An excerpt from an episode of *Zoo World* demonstrates how education, conservation, and marketing about the zoo were cleverly wrapped up in a conversation between John Conrad and Ron Blakely.

John Conrad: From Brookfield Zoo, located just west of Chicago in Brookfield, Illinois, this is John Conrad with another program called *Zoo World*. We're going to take a look at the grizzly bears today. Ron Blakely, director of zoology, is seated opposite our microphone. Ron, how many grizzlies do we have here at Brookfield Zoo?

Ron Blakely: We have a pair, John, and we also have a pair of the big Alaskan brown bears—the largest of all the land meat-eaters. You may wonder why I mentioned the Alaskan brown bears, but the point of that is that grizzly bears run in size from rather smallish, not much bigger than black bears, to the big Alaskan brown bears. There's no real dividing line.

John Conrad: In looking at the grizzly bear, is there any reason why zoos would want to continue raising grizzlies or keep them from going into extinction?

Ron Blakely: The grizzly is very close to extinction, and when zoos can breed them, they certainly should. We find out that zoos are one of the most potent resources for preserving these endangered species. When we talk about endangered species, we are talking about some thousand different kinds of animals that man is exterminating—more than one species per year.

John Conrad: How does the Himalayan bear compare in size to the grizzly?

Ron Blakely: Himalayan bears are one of the smaller bears. The smallest two bears are the Malayan sun bear and the spectacled bear. The spectacled bear is kind of an interesting little bear, in that with all other bears, at least part of their range is found north of the equator. The spectacled bear is the only bear found consistently just south of the equator. It's a bear that lives in the Andes mountains in South America.

The notion of man being "a cog in the wheel of nature" was a new idea for the zoo. It was a dramatic shift from the 1930s, when the zoo opened with sportsmen at the helm, happy to bring a bit of the wild to the city. Even as recently as the early 1950s, at the opening of the animal hospital, Smith Freeman had talked about "man's supremacy over his environment." By the mid-60s, it was being suggested that humans were part of nature and had a vital responsibility toward the rest of the natural world. Not only did this represent a change in the thinking of zoo leaders, it also posed a daunting educational challenge in conveying to the zoo's visitors the role of humans in nature.

Another type of educational offering was made to the public at large. John Conrad, the zoo's public relations officer, began hosting *Zoo World* in 1966. *Zoo World* was a radio program in which George Beach, staff members such as Encil Rains, Ron Blakely, Ray Pawley, Weaver Williamson, and keepers Bill Huizenga and Herman Buttron were interviewed about topics like animal feedings, animals' habits, and upcoming exhibits. Each 10-minute program was designed to stimulate the public's interest in Brookfield Zoo, and since the interviews were conducted inside the exhibits, background noises by animals and visitors were part of the experience. Conrad was a natural interviewer with a pleasing voice, and the *Zoo World* programs offered both education and excellent marketing.

The zoo was offering different kinds of educational experiences for everyone who visited. For the affluent, the zoo sponsored a four-week safari in September and October 1966, at a cost of $3,000 per person. The group traveled to England, Germany, and Kenya, visiting the Regent's Park Zoo, Whipsnade Park, the Hagenbeck Zoo, and the Kenya Game Reserve along the way.

Another Annual Meeting

Like the one two years before, the 1967 annual meeting proved insightful about the zoo's new direction. Robert Bean was not present, having slipped entirely out of the picture. Along with reports on education, travel, and repairs and improvements totaling $220,000, the governing members heard about the animal collection and a shift in thinking about how to display animals.

As an example of the latter, finches and marmosets had been added to Reptile House's swamp exhibits to make them as naturalistic as possible. Blakely reported that "this type of exhibit is what we are striving for; one that shows the entire biological picture." Combined with the groundbreaking displays in the Special Exhibits building, these represented a move away from sheer recreational viewing and toward a more comprehensive portrayal of the natural world.

The governing members also heard about notable news in the animal collection. Russian ratsnakes had been born—the first such births in the United States. The Bird Department witnessed the first successful zoo hatching of Darwin's rheas. Fifteen sitatunga young had been born, augmenting that population significantly. An okapi calf had been successfully hand-reared. Also, the okapi collection had moved on a generation with the death of Museka, the zoo's first female okapi, and the breeding male, Aribi, being sent to Florida.

During the meeting, the trustees announced to the governing members that a new category of membership would be created in the coming year. Desperate for funds and uncertain about their requests to the Forest Preserve District for increased admissions, fewer free days, and increased tax levies, the trustees decided to go ahead with a nonvoting type of membership. The move would allow for a new channel of revenue without enlarging the governing body unmanageably. The decision would bring benefits for many years.

By the time of the annual meeting, Rains and Blakely had been codirectors for nearly three years. Under the watchful eyes of the trustees—and they were very watchful—the two had made several accomplishments: the growing educational aspect and improvements in the health and maintenance of the animal collection, as well as in the zoo's facilities. But it was still a rocky relationship, far from ideal. The Board continued its efforts to rectify the situation.

If the giddy success of the '30s, '40s, and '50s was Brookfield Zoo's happy childhood (after a long and difficult birth), the '60s would have to be called the awkward teenage years. Over the next few decades, the zoo would transform into adulthood, enduring growing pains endemic to the process. The following two years were to bring some surprises that hastened this growth.

Above: A 1967 snowstorm led to new ways of transporting food to animals. Here, Ron Blakely (left), Ted Borek (center), and Gene Schreiber take advantage of a snowmobile donated by Ted Borek Pontiac.

LELAND LAFRANCE

During the mid-1960s, Brookfield Zoo enjoyed the talents of photographer Leland LaFrance. An amateur who regularly won the International Zoo Photo Contest, he became employed by the zoo, bringing a distinctive artistic quality to the various publications. He had enormous patience, waiting until his animal subjects were behaving in interesting ways and the light was just right for the contrast he wanted.

Clockwise, from top left: Leland LaFrance's subjects included a polar bear, a pair of young Kodiak bears, a young photographer with a llama, an eagle, and a yak.

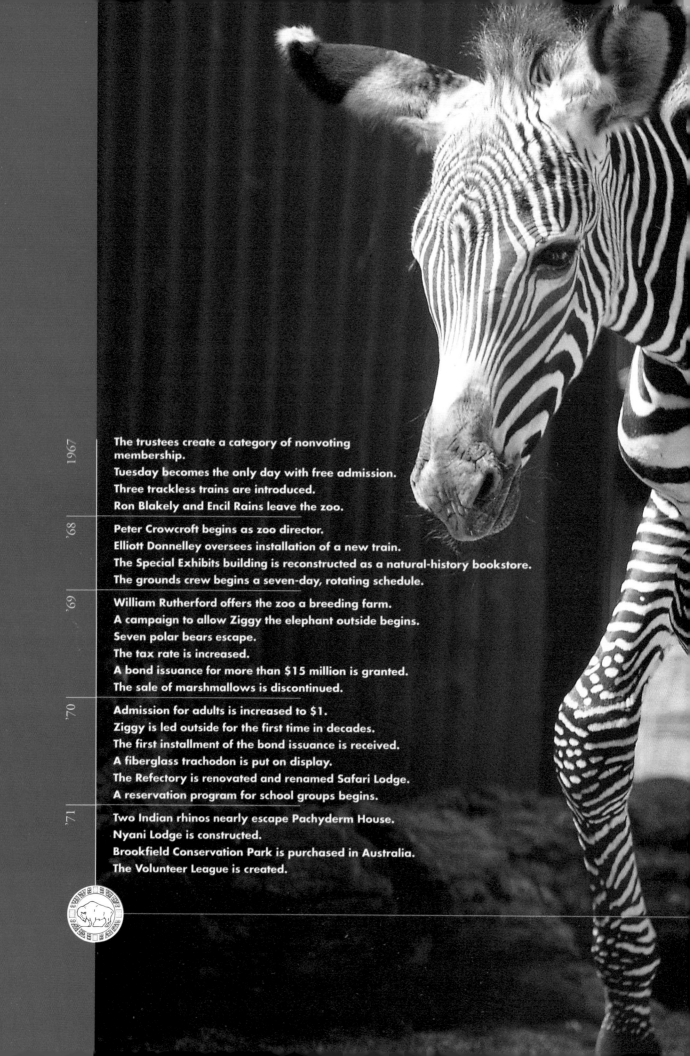

1967

The trustees create a category of nonvoting membership.

Tuesday becomes the only day with free admission.

Three trackless trains are introduced.

Ron Blakely and Encil Rains leave the zoo.

'68

Peter Crowcroft begins as zoo director.

Elliott Donnelley oversees installation of a new train.

The Special Exhibits building is reconstructed as a natural-history bookstore.

The grounds crew begins a seven-day, rotating schedule.

'69

William Rutherford offers the zoo a breeding farm.

A campaign to allow Ziggy the elephant outside begins.

Seven polar bears escape.

The tax rate is increased.

A bond issuance for more than $15 million is granted.

The sale of marshmallows is discontinued.

'70

Admission for adults is increased to $1.

Ziggy is led outside for the first time in decades.

The first installment of the bond issuance is received.

A fiberglass trachodon is put on display.

The Refectory is renovated and renamed Safari Lodge.

A reservation program for school groups begins.

'71

Two Indian rhinos nearly escape Pachyderm House.

Nyani Lodge is constructed.

Brookfield Conservation Park is purchased in Australia.

The Volunteer League is created.

CHAPTER ELEVEN

Fits and Starts

(1967-1971)

Inching Forward

In March 1967, the Forest Preserve District of Cook County approved an admission charge for six days of the week and a charge for parking in the north lot. Brookfield Zoo's Board of Trustees moved quickly to effect these changes, and as of March 21, Tuesdays became the only free days. This was a major change because through 1966 at least 85% of visitors did not pay admission. It meant significantly more revenue but possibly lower attendance. At the same time, the general membership program began. Although the initial response was modest, the program would grow, netting several million dollars in later years.

However, in terms of an overall direction and consistent quality and service, the zoo still had a long way to go. Problems and issues were addressed piecemeal, and most donations for improvements were the work of interested individuals. This remained the trend for several years, until a steadier source of income allowed the zoo's problems, compounded over the previous decades, to be addressed.

The fundraising program, which was meant to alleviate some of these problems, was not progressing as well as the Board had hoped. After two years, the trustees had raised only $870,000 in pledges against the desired $5.5 million. The Board had seen to the completion of renovations to the Formal Pool and the addition of a penguin exhibit, cypress swamp, and riverbank scene in Aquatic Bird House, all showpieces for potential donors. Still, offers weren't forthcoming.

It became apparent that Seven Seas and Primate House were also in dire need of renovation. Work on Primate House couldn't wait because the roof needed to be fixed before too much damage was done to the inside, so the building was quickly and briefly shut down. The wish list kept growing, but the money wasn't there.

Trains

Trackless trains, a 1967 improvement introduced to generate more revenue, proved popular. A miniature railroad running since 1962 had brought in around $50,000 annually. However, the track went only halfway around the park and was used more for sightseeing than for actual transportation. Visitors were essentially on their own in getting around the zoo.

The trustees considered alternatives that might ease both transportation and financial worries. In 1967, Chance Manufacturing Company sold the zoo three "safari trams," which showed off colorful animal patterns, were quieter and more flexible than the old train, and allowed for educational narration during the drive. A zebra train, painted black and white, arrived in June and was an immediate hit. Waiting for seats was the rule until a second train, with a multicolored cheetah design, was put into service. The last of the original fleet, one with a tiger design, went into service in mid-August.

Meanwhile, trustee Elliott Donnelley was contriving to equip the zoo with a proper train. A train buff, Donnelley had connections in the business, a desire to help the zoo, and a generous heart. He oversaw installation of a 2½-mile-long, two-foot-gauge track running around the zoo's perimeter. He then commandeered a diesel-switch engine and three cars, later to be augmented by two steam engines and several more cars, to run the loop. The new train was the real thing. In fact, one of the steam engines was originally built in 1918 and had been in use in Germany's Black Forest.

The train was fully licensed and ran under the name Brookfield, Salt Creek, and Western Railroad. With a schoolboy's glint in his eye, Donnelley, together with Forest Preserve District and zoo officials, christened the train in 1968. Although he shunned publicity concerning his role in the program, it should be noted that he donated every cent.

Left: Train buff Elliott Donnelley (photo, above left) made possible the Brookfield, Salt Creek, and Western Railroad, which complemented the new "safari trams" (photo, left).

Welcome to BROOKFIELD
THIS COUPON BOOK CAN BE USED TO PURCHASE ADMISSION TICKETS TO FOUR ENJOYABLE ATTRACTIONS AT BROOKFIELD ZOO

CHILDREN'S ZOO
SEVEN SEAS PANORAMA
RAILROAD TRAIN
SAFARI TRAINS

PRICE
$1.80
A
$2.35
VALUE

No. 030961

A New Director

For Brookfield Zoo, the late 1960s was a time of fits and starts, transitional leadership, and struggling for funds. In 1968, a new director was added to the mix.

In September 1967, wooed by the opportunity to run the whole show, Ron Blakely left Brookfield Zoo to become director of a new zoo in Wichita, Kansas. It had been a challenging few years for Blakely, and he left a more experienced, wiser, and certainly more jaded administrator. The trustees stepped up their search for a more permanent general director.

Encil Rains didn't stay much longer than Blakely. It had become apparent that controls were lacking in various merchandising and sales areas. Inventories of incoming items didn't always match up with the number of items actually available. A merchandise manager was let go, and it was the final blow for Rains, who was supposed to be supervising that aspect of zoo business. He left as well. George Rabb, who had been serving as associate director for research and education, was asked to serve as acting director until a new one could begin.

The trustees' search had already reached around the world. They extended an offer to Bernhard Grzimek, the director of the Frankfurt Zoo, considered one of the world's foremost zoo experts, but he declined.

They finally found their man in Dr. W. Peter Crowcroft from Australia. When he started in the spring of 1968, he had his work cut out for him. A management report by an outside consulting firm found public service poor and staff morale low. Financial struggles continued, and facilities still needed much attention. It was a difficult situation, with no easy solutions.

Crowcroft, 45 years old, was born in Tasmania. He graduated from Tasmania University and received his doctoral degree from the Bureau of Animal Populations at Oxford University. He had served as curator of mammals at the British Museum of Natural History in London for several years before moving back to Australia to head the South Australia Museum.

Peter Crowcroft

To comprehend Crowcroft's influence on Brookfield Zoo, it is important to understand how his philosophy of zoos departed from those of past directors. The following excerpt from his *Bandar-log* article, "A Zoo Manifesto," summarizes his honest, blunt perspective on the potential and the shortcomings of American zoos. "If you examine [American zoos'] stated functions, you will find the words Conservation, Education, and Research," he wrote. "These are supposed to be just as important in Zoo Philosophy as Recreation.

"Conservation is currently the liveliest of these words, and has been adopted even by minor zoos as a ready path to scientific respectability. In practice, any one zoo can do very little that is significant for Conservation: it is too expensive. There are a few freak co-operative ventures, which may prove effective, and these provide a good reason for overcoming the strangely competitive attitude that is a hangover from the old days. Meanwhile, the real battles of Conservation are being fought by other troops on other fronts.

"Research is still a good word to have on any notepaper. Alas, little of the research that is carried out on zoo premises has any relevance to their collections or their future development. More often than not, it is work that could be done just as well somewhere else.

"Education in a zoo is inescapable and incalculable, and however much people may try to degrade a zoo, they never manage entirely to wipe out its educational function. Somehow the natural beauty and dignity of the animals manage to survive the distractions and elicit a hunger for information.

"There is another word: a battered word which I have never seen or heard associated with an American zoo, but which is emblazoned on that flag I am nailing up. That word is Culture. I aim to help to establish Brookfield Zoo as a great cultural institution...an educational institution in the broadest sense. The great zoo of the future will not be the zoo that breeds the most bongos, or sells the most hot dogs. Its glory will not be measured in terms of the size of its budget, the number of species, the height of its elephant, or the age of its chimpanzee. It will be measured by the extent to which it changes the attitudes of its visitors, and through them, affects the culture of the nation.

"There is a sociological crisis in the United States, and many political and economic solutions are being put forward to solve it. But the only lasting solution is to teach people to understand why they behave as they do, and the appropriate instruments for doing this job are the Natural History Museums and the Zoological Parks."

CHICAGO ZOOLOGICAL SOCIETY

Fifty years after Edith Rockefeller McCormick made her gift of land, Crowcroft's belief that understanding human behavior can best be accomplished through observing other animals—or as he was fond of saying, "the proper study of mankind is animals"—resonated with her wish to build an institution that promotes scientific research contributing to knowledge about the human soul. In keeping with his goal, Crowcroft began planning new exhibits that highlighted the relationship of humans to the rest of the natural world: a major exhibit to feature primates, a display of the major mammal groups, and a "Hall of Man."

His direction and outlook were further articulated in a 1969 policy statement (left) that had the agreement and support of Bill Dickinson. The publication took as its model a similar statement produced by the Forest Preserve District under its longtime superintendent, Charles Sauers, a legendary figure in land management.

A $15 Million Windfall

Crowcroft dreamed big due to the passage of legislation that provided the Society with much-needed funding. After much pushing and prodding from Dickinson's Board members—and helped by a sobering report by consultants MacFadzean & Everly documenting the decrepit condition of the zoo and suggested renovations—the Illinois House and Senate passed Bills 1370, 1371, and 1372 in 1969. The bills, after being signed by Governor Richard Ogilvie, allowed the zoo to remove the 50 cent admission limit on adults, increase the tax rate from .0048 cents to .0058 cents, and most notably benefit from a bond issuance of $15,640,000 for capital improvements. This incredible windfall meant that, after a long financial drought and a relatively unsuccessful fundraising campaign, the zoo could finally begin rebuilding the beautiful park that had fallen into disrepair.

The admission fee was increased from 50 cents to $1 for adults on January 1, 1970, surprisingly affecting attendance only minimally but doubling admissions income for the year. While the increase went toward operating costs, the senior staff and the Board of Trustees began planning how best to spend the $15.6 million allocated for new exhibits and renovations. At the time the Illinois legislature approved the bond issuance, a 6% interest-rate ceiling was imposed. Unfortunately, there was no market for a 6% bond until late 1970, and the zoo didn't actually see the first installment until mid-year. While Crowcroft and the Board wanted the money to begin construction, they were forced into careful planning that may have been overlooked otherwise.

With no zoo experience behind him, Crowcroft cast a fresh eye on the park. He quickly determined his priorities: first, clean up the zoo; second, build new washrooms; and third, focus on the animals. Since the bond-issuance money was held up, Crowcroft had no money with which to institute these changes, so he explored options that cost virtually nothing.

First, he changed the schedule of the grounds crew. He discovered that they worked a five-day shift, with weekends off. While that made sense in many lines of work, it was illogical in a zoo, when the weekends generated the largest crowds and the most litter. In his first session of negotiations with the Teamsters Union, he negotiated a salary increase based on a seven-day, rotating work week. The new schedule, together with new litter containers around the zoo, proved to be a cheap solution for improving the park's appearance. His second priority, additional washrooms, had to wait for the bond-issuance money.

"OLD AND WRINKLED"

It was obvious that the zoo was beginning to deteriorate, as demonstrated by these excerpts from "Brookfield Zoo: Old, wrinkled and poor, but still lovable," a May 10, 1969, *Chicago Daily News Panorama* article by Norman Mark.

"As it approaches its 35th birthday in June, Brookfield Zoo, one of Chicago's prime cultural resources, is beginning to show its age. It is old and wrinkled, and unless it can raise $15,000,000, it is in very serious danger of becoming a second-rate, second-class menagerie.

"Climb, for example, to the top of the Australia House with James B. Riley, the zoo's superintendent of plant engineering and maintenance. The rock work used as toeholds is falling away from the iron rods that form it and the cracked roof leaks. From his vantage point, Riley shows the tar-paper shacks where the ostriches winter; the swamps caused by poor drainage at the end of the hoofed animal and rhea pens, and the asphalt public walkways with their dangerously crumbling edges.

"He says that 22 major buildings need upgrading, that the huge west end of the zoo should be developed, that the hoofed animal barns have no heat and no lighting, that the bars in the Australia House are so rusted they bow outward, that the waterfowl lake 'looks like a crap house,' that the moat [wall] around the baboon island is chipping away, that the kitchens used to prepare food for the birds and animals are clean, but functioning with equipment not acceptable in a slum."

Finding Funding

While Crowcroft and the Board waited for the bond money, they were fortunate to find financial support in unlikely corners.

It looked as if Crowcroft's third priority, an improved animal collection, would be made possible partly through an unexpected benefactor. The zoo had long wanted a breeding farm. In fact, it was at the top of the wish list, second only to an ape house. A small advertisement in a local paper happened to catch the attention of William Rutherford in Peoria, located about 160 miles south of Brookfield. Rutherford, a lawyer who was also the head of the philanthropic Forest Park Foundation, was interested in bettering the quality of life for people. He thought it would be nice to have exotic animals in his part of the state to benefit those around him.

She [the young lioness] would run freely around the yard. If we were having a conversation, she would come around the side of the house and peer around to see you. As long as you looked at her, she would stare, without blinking, and just watch you. But if you turned your back, she would come over very fast, jump up, and with very strong little arms get around your thigh, nip you on the hind end, and run away. Obviously mischievous.

There's a little strip-mine heap of spoil behind the caretaker's house, behind the garage. The young men worked in the garden, and the lion would go up above and look down on them, maybe 10 or 15 feet away, with her paws crossed, and just watch them work in the garden. One day, all of a sudden the lion got up, walked to the back door, picked up the mat, went back to the same place, put the mat down, and laid on top of it.

Eventually the lioness got a little too strong for us. The boys brought her to the house one evening. We had a sweet...German shepherd who was getting kind of old. The cat chased it down the spiral staircase into my den. The dog retreated back up the spiral staircase, with the cat in pursuit. The lioness chased the dog into the kitchen, cornered it, and nipped it in the rear end, taking out a little piece of fur. The dog turned in a fury and made a sound I've never heard a dog make—a scream of fury. It rose up, the hair literally stood up, then it turned and knocked the lioness over. The lioness turned around, ran around the davenport, and climbed up on top. All I could see were two paws and the top of her head peeking over, like one of those cartoons, to see what was going on.

William Rutherford
Former Trustee

Above: One of the first animals to live at McCutcheon Animal Park was a young lioness who raised havoc in William Rutherford's household.

In 1969, Rutherford offered the Society a 400-acre plot of land for its breeding farm. He then went even further, donating $100,000 to get the farm started. The property was inspected, the deed was transferred to the Society, and work began on fencing and other preparations. Jim Fowler of *Wild Kingdom* fame was hired to consult on the design of areas within the farm.

In honor of the Chicago Zoological Society's first president, the trustees quickly decided to name the breeding farm the McCutcheon Animal Park. Several animals were transported to the park, even though it was not yet ready. Two arctic foxes made the trip uneventfully. One young African lioness made a name for herself, living in the caretaker's house, sleeping at the end of his bed, and generally entertaining everyone.

Eventually, as the trustees became more involved in the capital planning process, it became clear that managing a park so distant from Brookfield was not as easy as it seemed, and the McCutcheon Animal Park began to seem less desirable. Staff members were already stretched too thin; revenues for operations couldn't cover even Brookfield Zoo's expenses, let alone additional costs in Peoria; and possible income from the park was negligible.

Progress on the McCutcheon Animal Park slowed, and in November 1972 the Board returned the deed and remaining funds to the Forest Park Foundation. Rutherford was appointed a member of the zoo's Board of Trustees and has remained supportive of Society interests in the years since.

As for the park itself, it has been turned into a zoo of its own, although of a different type. Now known as Wildlife Prairie Park, it focuses on Illinois flora and fauna and displays animals in wonderfully naturalistic settings.

"Free Ziggy"

Although the bond money was slow in coming, other support was becoming increasingly broad-based. A new pool of supporters—school-children—sent money in 1969 and 1970. For safety reasons, Ziggy, the elephant who had attacked keeper Slim Lewis in 1941, had been confined to his indoor stall since the attack. This fact was brought to the attention of several newspaper reporters, who, feeling the situation to be unfair to the giant animal, began a crusade to "free Ziggy." Zoo officials explained that funds were lacking for a Ziggy-safe door that would allow him access to an outdoor yard without mandating human contact with the temperamental elephant. As a result, small contributions, including nickels and dimes, began flowing in.

ZIGGY FUND NEWSLETTER

Brookfield Zoo   Winter 1972-73

BIOGRAPHY OF A BULL!

Early this summer, Dr. Peter Crowcroft, Zoo Director, announced the completion of new quarters for our mammoth elephant, Ziegfeld, or as he is better known, Ziggy. "This work ends a three-year project," he said, "to give Ziggy an enclosure befitting his station as the most famous elephant in the world. A project," he added, "which could not have been accomplished without the uncommon generosity of thousands of concerned individuals, both young and old."

As a result of Ziggy's fame, the Z___ queries regarding Ziggy and ___ endeavors to answer the most ___ as provide an informative bio___ exploits. . . Editor.

Ziggy is the largest___ but he hardly fit that d___ States in 1920. His ri___ "discovered" by Flore___ showman was watchin___ New York doc___

HELP BUILD A NEW HOME FOR ZIGGY!

Above and right: The zoo's Public Relations Department, headed by a creative Phil Cihlar, helped the "free Ziggy" frenzy along, as well as the attendant fundraising effort, by creating Ziggy souvenirs and the *Ziggy Fund Newsletter*.

Schools held collections and sometimes managed to send several hundred dollars. The Boy's Club of Bellwood constructed a five-foot papier-mâché elephant, mounted it on wheels, and pulled it through the village streets, ringing doorbells for contributions. Their labors added $71.01 to the Ziggy Fund. White-elephant sales, car washes, and school fairs were also held in many neighboring communities to aid Ziggy.

One anonymous letter arrived with a crumpled one-dollar bill and a note that said, "I am sending this small amount to help Ziggy. I will have to go to bed without any dinner for the next two nights, but it is worth it." Contributions from all over included $20 from the Philippines and donations from GIs stationed in Vietnam. The *Ziggy Fund Newsletter*, produced by the Public Relations Department, announced that the zoo was selling photos of the elephant and clip-on buttons proclaiming "Help Build a New Home for Ziggy!"

Some Ziggy contributions were larger, including one $700 gift and benefit performances by the Goodman Theater and the Arlington Heights Village Theaters. The biggest boost, however, came from the Chicagoland Buick-Opel Dealers Association, which matched $13,500 raised from individual sources. The large and small contributions added up, and in the end nearly $50,000 was raised for Ziggy's walk in the sun.

Seeking assurance that Ziggy would in fact want to walk in the sun, the zoo scheduled a dry run before any construction began. On September 23, 1970, at 7:30 in the morning, a courageous Slim Lewis, called in from Seattle, led Ziggy through the doorway and into his yard. Television camera crews, newspeople, and a large number of zoo employees were on hand to witness the event.

Ziggy explored the temporarily barricaded passageway with his trunk and tested the specially built ramp with his feet for almost 40 minutes before making the decision to come out. Once outside, he surveyed the area, tested a tree trunk that had grown since he was last outside, then headed for a pile of fruit and hay in the yard. After satisfying his hunger, he roamed the yard and repeatedly rubbed himself against the rough rock work. Then he turned around and walked back inside.

[TRIBUNE Staff Photo: By William Vendetta]

After 30 years of being chained to a wall—except for a few outings — Ziggy is free and in is new stockade at Brookfield Zoo. Some 1,000 persons watched Ziggy walk out.

At Last, Sun Shines for Ziggy

BY SARA JANE GOODYEAR

The big steel doors swung open, there was a great rat-ng of chain and Ziggy lumbered out into the sunlight.

More than 1,000 persons were at Brookfield Zoo for his ming out party yesterday, and despite predictions that the bull elepi.ant might keep them waiting for hours, he was ght on time.

After 30 years of being chained to a wall—except for a w outings in the last year or so—Ziggy seemed delighted be outdoors. He surveyed the cheering, singing crowd d shot a trunkful of dust over his shoulder. Then he ooped up a large mouthful of hay and the children eered again.

her enclosure but after a while, perhaps enticed by Ziggy's interest, she returned.

Dr. Peter Crowcroft, zoo director, said he hopes one day Ziggy may be able to socialize with Babe and also with Millie, another Indian elephant which refused to go out-doors yesterday. That depends, he said, on how Ziggy be-haves across the wall.

Ziggy acquired a reputation of not being much of a gentleman with lady elephants many years ago when he tried to kill one after mating. He was unsuccessful, however. She kicked him flat.

He'll Have Own Pool

Above: The *Chicago Tribune*, one among many publications, took an interest in Ziggy's situation.

Construction began two days later, and the following summer Ziggy's new yard was complete. Invitations were mailed to all donors, and quite a crowd was present when Ziggy ambled out again on August 28, 1971.

Elephant management, in particular handling of notoriously temperamental male elephants, saw changes in the following years. As the incident concerning Ziggy highlights, it is critical to manage the pachyderms without direct contact with the animals. In the years after the incident, Brookfield Zoo, and most major zoos, worked toward the best method for providing the highest-quality care without the risk of injury to humans or animals.

While the camera crews and photog-raphers were awaiting Ziggy outside of Pachyderm House, a potentially dangerous sit-uation was taking place within the building. Keeper Pat Stout went inside Pachyderm House shortly before Ziggy was let out to see how things were going. As he wandered into the keepers' hallway located between the interior exhibits and the "shift" doors to the outside yards, he realized that the doors had been accidentally left open, allowing a pair of Indian rhinos access to the hallway leading outside to the public walkway.

He watched as the rhinos noticed their choices, became overwhelmed, and pan-icked, whirling frantically in tight circles in the hallway. Unsure of what to do, Stout grabbed the only object nearby—a pitchfork—and began waving it to get the rhinos' attention and shoo them into their outer yard. By then, keeper Ron Zdrubecky had arrived, and he ran to close the shift doors that allowed the rhinos access to the hallway. Disaster was averted as the rhinos were inched into their outer yards.

The mass of reporters and photographers on the opposite side of the building—in fact, everyone but Stout, Zdrubecky, and a few other keepers—remained unaware of how close they had come to encountering two Indian rhinos face to face. The pachyderm keepers instituted improved procedures to ensure that the incident was not repeated.

The whole pool, the whole moat, and half the street were flooded, and the bears were swimming across. They had already been out several times. We backed up to the site in a truck and were pumping out the water. We were pumping 350 gallons a minute in each pump, which wasn't even fazing it. That moat holds maybe a million gallons of water.

Joe Chabus and I were up on the back of the truck, trying to watch the bears and watch the equipment to make sure it had gas and stayed running. Once in a while someone would shout, "Look out!" and a bear would make a dart at the truck, then turn around and go back. Well, somebody hollered, "Look out!" and this time the bear didn't turn back. Joe and I flipped backwards over the cab of the truck and ran without looking, because we both knew the bear was behind us. But he wasn't. We ran to the hill in back of Children's Zoo and proceeded to see where the bear was.

The fire department came in after that, and we were moving hoses and getting out of the fire department's way. When we had a chance to sit down, the reality hit both of us: the bear had been right there. Joe was just sitting there shaking, like he had a chill. Kind of earthshaking, when you think about it.

> Pete Price
> Former Head of Utilities

A Polar Bear Adventure

Ziggy's new quarters were matched in public interest by another potentially dangerous episode on July 17, 1969. A five-inch rainfall in the early morning turned the dry moats and roads around the polar bears' enclosure into swimming pools, and seven of the powerful animals escaped. They knew exactly where to go: the snack shop opposite their enclosure, where they had seen visitors purchase marshmallows. They took a swipe at the cash register, then settled into the marshmallow stash for a feast. A night keeper discovered their escape and anxiously called for help.

Crowcroft was out of town, but Associate Director George Rabb and several other employees began using vehicles to herd the animals back into their enclosure. Most of the bears were cooperative, although one wandered into the grizzly enclosure and stayed until he noticed that the grizzly was not exactly friendly. Judging by paw prints, at least one bear wandered as far as the Refectory before ambling back to Bear Road.

Zoo gates were locked to prevent more staff from entering until the bears were again under control. Security and keeper staff took up positions outside the bears' enclosure and shot rifles into the air and into the water-filled moat to discourage another escape. The Brookfield Fire Department was called in to pump the water out of the moats and the road. After several hair-raising hours, the moat was dry and all polar bears were accounted for. No injuries were suffered by bear or employee, although nerves were on edge for hours afterwards. The zoo opened at mid-day. In fact, it was the only time in the zoo's history that it wasn't open all day.

Above and right: A sudden, heavy rainfall flooded the moats fronting the polar bear exhibit, allowing the bears to swim free. With the help of the Brookfield Fire Department (photo, right), the animals were returned to their exhibit.

REPORT 1968
CHICAGO ZOOLOGICAL SOCIETY

Other Improvements

While waiting for the $15 million bond issuance to come through, Crowcroft and the Board oversaw several small improvements that enhanced the visitor experience. A flamingo colony was put on display at Roosevelt Fountain, a prairie dog town was installed in Children's Zoo, security staff were outfitted in friendly green "forest ranger" uniforms, and an annual report was published and mailed—the first since 1933.

A natural-history bookstore, opened in the Special Exhibits building under the guidance of Mary Rabb, was quite successful, selling 8,000 books in its first year and earning approximately $45,000.

Not all of Crowcroft's ideas were implemented. He wanted to rent boats on Waterfowl Lake at the western end of the zoo, arguing that it would provide good fun and good revenue. However, the trustees, claiming the activity didn't fit into the zoo's mission, vetoed the idea.

Another of Crowcroft's efforts never came about due to world politics. The zoo had been trying to secure another giant panda since 1953, when Mei-lan died. Strict trade restrictions with China prohibited the zoo from working with Chinese zoos on an animal trade or purchase. Brookfield Zoo came close in 1972, when Richard Nixon, during his trip to China, was promised two pandas by Chinese Premier Chou En-lai. Senators Charles Percy and Adlai Stevenson, Illinois governor Richard B. Ogilvie, Lieutenant Governor Paul Simon, and gubernatorial candidate Dan Walker all requested that the President consider Brookfield. Chicagoans also waged an impressive campaign by writing letters and making pleading phone calls.

In the end, the pandas went to the National Zoo in Washington, D.C. Crowcroft, however, kept trying. "Now that communications have been opened with the People's Republic of China," he said, "we will renew our efforts to get our own pandas. We have a number of valuable animals that Chinese zoos should want, and I would hope that an exchange might be arranged on this basis." It was one challenge Crowcroft never mastered.

THE NATURE OF BOOKS

In the December 1969 *Brookfield Briefs*, librarian Mary Rabb explained the existence of the zoo's new natural-history bookstore.

"How did the zoo get into the book business? That's a complicated question, but to answer it simply, it is part of the Brookfield crusade—the proper study of man is animals. As in all zoo operations, the aims are to please and inform. It is not the money made in the Book Store that's important. The zoo would probably try to sell books even if the Store was actually losing money. The truth is we are not just selling books, but promoting fuller enjoyment and understanding of the zoo."

DEAR PRESIDENT NIXON

On February 29, 1972, Tony Fuller's article in the *Chicago Daily News*, entitled "Melanie, 7, votes 'Yes' for pandas," focused on the panda issue.

"Melanie Gay Madon is only 7, but the blond second-grader already knows the meaning of political clout. 'Everybody has to tell him he'd be a much better President if he gave them to Brookfield Zoo,' she said Tuesday. Melanie, who lives in Schaumburg, has done her part to let President Nixon know that the two pandas given him by the Chinese should be located in Brookfield.

"The little girl spent all last Saturday composing a letter—the first she ever wrote—to Mr. Nixon detailing the reasons Brookfield would be the ideal spot for the giant pandas. 'I like them (pandas) because they have little ears and almost round faces,' Melanie said in an interview, adding with the sense of a political phrasemaker, 'Pandas are for people.' In writing the letter, Melanie joined hundreds of Chicago area school children who have written the President about the pandas. An intensive drive has been launched to locate the black and white animals at Brookfield, which has a long history of exhibiting pandas.

"Melanie, who has a freckle on the end of her nose and blond hair flowing over her shoulders, expressed confidence in the movement she has joined. 'The pandas are coming...the President is a smart man,' she said."

Right: Polar bears begging for marshmallows was a familiar sight. So many of the sweet confections were thrown each day that the bears bothered to eat only the ones that landed near them.

A less worldly situation—marshmallows—was a hot topic at the Board table in 1969. Trustee Jeffrey Short felt that selling marshmallows and other food to visitors for the purpose of feeding animals was undesirable. He claimed that it interrupted the animals' natural behaviors. Crowcroft agreed. "Instead of the bears carrying on the normal interaction amongst themselves, they were busy standing on their hind legs begging marshmallows from the people," he said.

However, marshmallows were sold at a rate of $2\frac{1}{2}$ tons per summer week, generating significant revenue. Similarly, peanut sales accounted for $40,000 in net proceeds annually. The trustees agreed that feeding in Children's Zoo should continue because the public enjoyed it and it didn't seem to harm the animals. They also said that feeding in the main zoo should be first discouraged, then eventually forbidden, when finances allowed.

The sale of marshmallows was discontinued in 1969, and handouts were printed in 1972 disallowing visitors from bringing in food to feed the animals. (Peanut sales did continue for several years.) The marshmallow ban significantly reduced the sticky litter mess the Grounds Department had been contending with for years, a welcome side effect to the new ruling.

Above: An unusual creature—a duck-billed dinosaur called a "trachodon"—came to the zoo in July 1970. Contributed by the Atlantic-Richfield Company, the 32-foot fiberglass dinosaur was part of the famous Sinclair collection of "terrible lizards" built for the New York World's Fair in 1964. Created by sculptor Louis Paul Jonas, the reproduction was set in the trees northeast of Waterfowl Lake to surprise visitors...and perhaps remind them of the unsettling possibility of mass extinction.

RECOLLECTIONS

I used to feed the polar bears bags upon bags of marshmallows, which the zoo then sold, totally unmindful of what the sugar in the marshmallows might do to the bears' dentistry. I was amazed that everything in the zoo ate marshmallows, and I can well remember trying to get marshmallows from my mother for myself on the theory that marshmallows were good and acceptable for all God's creatures, even me. Mom did not bite, however, and the marshmallows were relegated to the animals. I grew up thinking marshmallows were generically the universal food because everything at the zoo ate them. The polar bears, especially, were exceptional beggars for the marshmallows.

    Judy Baar Topinka
    Current Treasurer, State of Illinois

RECOLLECTIONS

This was the marshmallow capital of the world. More marshmallows were consumed here than anywhere else. Clouds of marshmallows descended on the bears, the giraffes, whatever. I couldn't quite reconcile between concern for these rare animals—Lady Gray's waterbucks and fringe-eared oryx and so on—and people reaching out and offering them these bloody marshmallows. I saw this paradoxical situation—this concern and this professional dimension represented by people like Tappan Gregory—yet here we were, a major purveyor of marshmallows. Very strange.

    George Rabb
    Current Zoo Director

Volunteer Programs

Crowcroft oversaw the formation of the Volunteer League, founded through the efforts of Edith Duckworth and Charlene Carper. The League's most important endeavor was Elephant's Trunk Gift Shop, located in the former Special Exhibits building. More than 60 volunteers managed and staffed the shop, which carried household and gift items with animal themes. Elephant's Trunk Gift Shop was quite popular, grossing $13,000 in its first five months of business. In addition, the League assisted staff with mailings, processing of memberships, and other clerical tasks. Volunteers also worked as educational guides in Children's Zoo, as ticket sellers, and as guides for adult groups from other nonprofit organizations.

Another body of volunteers, the North Shore Association, which served as an ad hoc women's board, helped by conducting benefit events, recruiting new audiences, and raising funds for various projects. Both volunteer groups were excellent ambassadors for the zoo and provided vital revenue.

An Australian Connection

In 1971, despite the disappointment of his failed breeding farm, William Rutherford made possible another program. At the urging of Rutherford and Crowcroft, the Society purchased a 20-square-mile tract of semidesert in South Australia for the purpose of conserving hairy-nosed wombats and studying the effects of grazing and nongrazing by sheep and kangaroos on the habitat. Rutherford's Forest Park Foundation donated the $63,000 required to buy the land, and the preserve, dubbed Brookfield Conservation Park, became the property of the Society.

A local management team, formed to oversee the project, began the process of fencing and restoring the property. The team found that once the sheep, which had been overgrazing for years, were turned out, the native flora came back and even a few species that had not been known to exist there reappeared. For several years, the Society paid the $15,000 to $20,000 annual expenses on the land until it was no longer financially feasible to do so, then donated the reserve to the State of South Australia. Roughly $5,000 was generated annually from wombat-shaped coin banks (opposite) located at the zoo—a considerable amount of dimes and quarters. This "Australian connection" expanded in later years.

And so the Chicago Zoological Society weathered the financially meager late 1960s, picking up new programs here and there as individual donations allowed, hanging tough as it waited for the promised $15 million in bond money. Along with the various new projects, the Board and the staff were still planning how to allocate the money once it was received. When the funds were finally made available, the zoo embarked on a new course.

RECOLLECTIONS

In 1970, I belonged to the Junior Woman's Club of LaGrange, and we decided that our philanthropy for that year would be the zoo. Accordingly, we got in touch with Director Peter Crowcroft and asked if there was anything we could possibly buy for the zoo. He indicated that he had been trying to get meerkats and that it would be possible, within the amount of money we were trying to raise, to import meerkats.

In December 1970, we did a gift and fashion show, all of the proceeds went to the zoo, and they did bring in the meerkats. Dr. Crowcroft and Fred McGuire, who was the development officer at the time, came to the benefit and said to me and Charlene Carper, who was president of the Club, "Gee, I wish I had an organization like this working for me all the time." Charlene and I looked at each other and decided, "Well, we could probably do that."

To that end, we got together a group of women, put an ad in the paper, and in March 1971, 22 ladies met in my home. Dr. Crowcroft and Fred McGuire did a slide presentation for us, and at the end of the evening, 21 of the 22 women signed up to form the Brookfield Zoo Volunteer League. That was the very beginning.

Edith A. Duckworth
Current Trustee

A HOME FOR WOMBATS

The front page of the September 6, 1971, *International Herald Tribune* carried this AP Paris article, entitled "Australia's Persecuted Wombats Get a Little Land of Their Own."

"The Chicago Zoological Society and the Forest Park Foundation of Peoria have gone to the rescue of the hairy-nosed wombat, a furry-nosed denizen of Southern Australia, struggling to live against irate sheep-herders.

"The Society said that with the help of a…grant from the Foundation, it had purchased 20 square miles of former sheepland southwest of Adelaide, where the hairy-nosed wombats can live safely. The sheep ranchers say the wombats tunnel under fences, leaving large holes for sheep to escape through.

"Dr. Peter Crowcroft, director of the Chicago Zoological Society, said the land would eventually be turned over to the South Australian National Parks and Wildlife Commission and then opened to the public."

Above: Prior to the Society's commitment to save the land, Brookfield Conservation Park had been over-grazed by sheep and other animals.

Top: Former Chicago Zoological Society staff member Stephanie Williams and local manager Joe Stelmann helped ensure that Brookfield Conservation Park recovered, slowly and naturally.

1970
Admission for adults is increased to $1.
Ziggy is led outside for the first time in decades.
The first installment of the bond issuance is received.
A fiberglass trachodon is put on display.
The Refectory is renovated and renamed Safari Lodge.
A reservation program for school groups begins.

'71
Two Indian rhinos nearly escape Pachyderm House.
Nyani Lodge is constructed.
Brookfield Conservation Park is purchased in Australia.
The Volunteer League is created.

'72
The Society returns the deed to the breeding farm.
A 40-foot-diameter Society emblem made of flowers is planted near the North Gate.
Visitors are prohibited from bringing in food to feed the animals.
The second installment of the bond-issuance money is made available.

'73
Work begins on Tropic World.
The research program for students is started.

'74
The final installment of the bond-issuance money comes through.
The Board restructures, with the trustees taking on more responsibilities.
Feeding of animals is prohibited except in Children's Zoo.
Admission for adults is raised to $1.50.

'75
At the zoo, the first wombat is born outside of Australia.
Dutch elm disease devastates a number of trees.
Robert Bean dies.
Peter Crowcroft resigns for a job in his native Australia.
William Dickinson steps down as Society chairman.
Elliott Donnelley dies.
Ziggy falls into a moat and later dies of old age.
Corky Hamill becomes Society chairman.
Waterfowl Lake is redesigned and renamed Indian Lake.
The Predator Ecology exhibit is added to Lion House.

CHAPTER TWELVE

Rebuilding

(1970–1975)

The Bond-Issuance Money

The $15 million bond issuance probably saved Brookfield Zoo by rescuing it from its continuing deterioration. Once the first of three $5 million installments came through in May 1970, work started in earnest. Most of the initial money went to functional, rather than display, needs. Underground pipes and electric cables were replaced, buildings were reroofed, greenhouses were constructed, and workshops for craftsmen and groundskeepers were built on the back service road.

In keeping with Director Crowcroft's priorities, public needs were given attention. Parking lots were paved, new bathrooms were built, Nyani Lodge restaurant was constructed, and the Refectory was renovated and reopened as Safari Lodge. Overdue animal needs were addressed as well. Baboon Island and Seven Seas were renovated, and the barns along 31st Street were repaired for the first time in over 40 years. The first $5 million was spent quickly.

Above and left: By the time of the first installment of bond-issuance money, Baboon Island was in desperate need of renovation. George Rabb (above) works on a clay model of the new exhibit.

Right: Nyani Lodge, an eating facility, was constructed next to Baboon Island in 1971.

Above and right: Safari Lodge, once called the Refectory, was refurbished in 1970.

The second installment of $5 million from the bond issuance was made available in 1972. The schedule for Phase II projects included $3 million toward a new ape exhibit; $300,000 for an Asian exhibit; $200,000 for renovations to Lion House's interior; $340,000 for utilities; $200,000 for landscaping at Waterfowl Lake; $150,000 in improvements to Australia House; $150,000 in repairs at Bear Grottos; $140,000 in rock-work repairs around the zoo; and thousands more for roads, water-tank repairs, more roof work, and additional refreshment stands.

It was a flurry of building activity the likes of which the zoo hadn't seen since 1933. Crowcroft's timing was impeccable. Arriving upon the scene just as the bond issuance was granted and other financial restrictions were relaxed allowed him to plan for and oversee repairs and exciting improvements without having suffered through too many of the difficult years. The trustees were heavily involved in the process, with the Executive Committee meeting monthly to keep tabs on planning and progress. The full Board was meeting only three or four times a year, trusting the Executive Committee to make decisions and provide guidance.

Ron Zdrubecky

Above and left: Australia House benefitted from bond-issuance money with a more naturalistic "walkabout" (photo, left) in place of the old kangaroo exhibit.

Operating Budget Crisis

The bond issuance didn't solve all of the Society's problems, however. While capital projects such as new exhibits and repairs were provided for, there was no relief from operating costs. Even with increased admission fees, it was a struggle each year to prevent expenses from exceeding income, and in fact many years it was a losing battle. Cash flow was an ongoing problem, too, as the winter months brought so little revenue that the Society was regularly forced to borrow funds from banks early in the year with the intention of paying them back in early summer.

Originally, the agreement between the Forest Preserve District and the Chicago Zoological Society had been that taxes would pay for most of the zoo's operating costs. Through 1961, more than 70% of operating costs had been covered by taxes. By the early '70s, however, the figure had dropped dramatically, to 39%, while operating costs rose. Gas and water costs alone were up 30%, and it cost money to operate the new programs and exhibits.

It was a challenging time for the staff because they were already stretched thin with additional planning efforts, and the situation was exacerbated by the fact that when staff members left for jobs elsewhere, their positions were left empty as a money-saving effort, increasing the work load on those who remained.

It became necessary to either generate more funds internally or ask the Forest Preserve District for help. Both ideas were tried. The Board raised admission to both Children's Zoo and dolphin shows and increased the general membership fee from $10 to $15. The Society also asked the Forest Preserve District to allow a 25 cent charge for children over six years of age, increase the parking fee, and raise the adult admission charge to $1.50. The increase in the parking fee was approved quickly, but the other issues were held up in committee meetings, leaving the Society in limbo for a time. The situation was so severe that at the February 1974 trustee meeting, President Dickinson stated that the zoo clearly needed Forest Preserve District help "or we would be in serious trouble in 1976."

Even the blessed bond-issuance money was causing headaches. Due to inflation, the original $15,640,000 approved in 1969 had shrunk to an actual value of $11,590,000 by May 1974. Planning had been based on the larger figure, and construction was progressing on many projects. Internal fundraising was needed to make up the difference. The largest portion of the money had been allocated to the ape house, dubbed Tropic World, which was under construction but not going smoothly.

This new facility was being built in the southwest quadrant, where most indoor exhibits were located, to encourage people to make winter visits. Excavation started in September 1973. By early 1974, architectural firm Skidmore, Owings & Merrill was ready to begin construction on the building's shell but needed steel and other materials. The costs had been allocated to the last phase of the bond-issuance money, which had not yet been issued, so construction halted for a while. The project was set back further when one of the lead architects, William Dunlap, died suddenly.

Finally, in late 1974, things began looking better. The Forest Preserve District not only approved the Society's request to increase the gate fee from $1 to $1.50 but also began work on legislation to increase the tax levy for the zoo. The final sale of bonds came through, too, providing the zoo with $5,640,000 for capital projects.

Below left: As construction began on the huge Tropic World, the zoo encountered many obstacles, including lack of money for building materials and the death of a lead architect.

The Board Restructures

Simultaneously, the zoo was trying to determine how best to accomplish planning, fundraising, and construction while still managing daily operations. Peter Crowcroft was the first to desire a new role, requesting as early as 1972 to be removed from zoo operations. In 1974, he more firmly announced to the Board that he wished to do away with the assistant director positions and have instead one deputy director who would essentially run the zoo while he focused on planning and fundraising. After some discussion, the Board agreed and appointed George Rabb deputy director, giving him responsibility for zoo operations.

The Board's structure, too, was under discussion. Crowcroft, more active in Society affairs, wanted to formalize his new role by changing his current role as secretary to that of president of the Board. This move would place him on the Executive Committee and allow him a vote in major decisions. He advocated creating a position of chairman for the volunteer head of the Board. The trustees agreed.

Meanwhile, the Executive Committee, whose members had been meeting monthly for several years, was seeking some relief from its duties. Its members recommended to the full Board that the larger trustee body assume more responsibility and that the Executive Committee be available for special consultation as needed. The idea was accepted, and the Board decided to meet six times a year, with the Executive Committee "on call" for special situations.

The reorganization reflected major changes in the Society, which from the beginning had been run by the few involved trustees on the Executive Committee, with the full Board merely rubber-stamping decisions. The director had overseen zoo operations and had worked closely with the Executive Committee on policy and planning. Giving the Board more responsibility and essentially removing the Executive Committee from the picture encouraged greater participation from all trustees and spread responsibility among them. For the first time, the director was involved in Society issues.

Also, for years, managing the zoo had been the full extent of the Society's activities. The reorganization reflected other involvements: the Australian wombat reserve, planning new exhibits, overseeing construction, and that gnarly matter of fundraising.

RECOLLECTIONS

While the general concept of naturalistic exhibits for primates had been agreed upon, the details of habitat required more information and material than could be found in the literature. Since we had determined that the African section [in Tropic World] must come first, a staff expedition to Uganda was undertaken in 1971 by our former curator of primates, Ben Beck; the late Richard Earle, senior artist; and myself.

In the Kibale Forest, the Maramagambo Forest, the Bwamba Forest on the lower slopes of the Mountains of the Moon, and the Bwindi Forest, where gorillas still roamed, the work began. We measured trees; photographed rocks; sketched scenes; read humidity levels; taped bird songs, insect noises, and primate calls; and observed monkeys using their environment and interacting. We returned from the expedition inspired and literally put that energy into a model that would change many times as we tried to fit visitor and primate into relatively small replicas of forest settings.

George Rabb
Current Zoo Director

Animal Management

Amid the construction and restructuring, the staff was dealing with its usual share of animal-management issues. The wild duck population on Waterfowl Lake, normally about 500, blossomed suddenly into about 2,000, requiring 4,000 pounds of corn and grain at a weekly cost of $400 to $500. The overcrowding, coupled with drainage problems in the artificial lake, caused an inordinate number of duck deaths each year. Botulism was suspected. To cut back the population, the zoo exported hundreds of ducks to the Rockford area several years in a row.

Waterfowl Lake was added to the schedule for renovation work and was subsequently emptied, mucked out, and redesigned, with changes to the islands and the addition of the Ellen Thorne Smith Nature Trail. The lake was rechristened Indian Lake in honor of those believed to have lived in the area long before.

The Bird Department was struggling due to strict U.S. import restrictions on birds and budget-induced staff shortages. The zoo had been without a full-time curator of birds for many years, with curator of reptiles Ray Pawley valiantly trying to wear both hats. The import restrictions had a silver lining, though, in that they forced the zoo to build breeding cages and bolster its ability to encourage breeding among the existing population.

Breeding programs generally were going well... too well, in some cases. The African lions were a prolific bunch, which was great for the public, as it loved little lion cubs, but it posed a problem once the animals grew. Lions were abundant in zoos around the country, and it became difficult to find homes for the overgrown cubs. After much discussion, staff decided to vasectomize Lord Sparks, a particularly productive lion. It was one of the zoo's first forays into controlled breeding.

The already massive sitatunga herd was growing exponentially as well, as was the meerkat population. In 1973, for successfully breeding hingeback tortoises, Brookfield Zoo received the American Association of Zoological Parks and Aquariums' Edward Bean Award, named after the zoo's second director, who was long involved in the AAZPA and strongly advocated breeding programs. That year also brought the first litter of second-generation sand cats born in the country.

In 1975, the zoo proudly announced the birth of a hairy-nosed wombat, the first one born outside of Australia and the only second-generation hairy-nosed wombat born in a zoo. Even more exciting, Aussie left his mother's pouch prematurely and needed to be hand-raised. Peter Crowcroft personally took over the feeding, and Aussie soon flourished. He became a media star, with newspapers and television stations across the country showing photos of his "hairlessness."

Y'S GREAT ESCAPE

In May 1973, an apparently terrified visitor wrote to the *Chicago Tribune* about a shocking encounter at the zoo. The question posed by the writer ran under the headline "Ours Not to Wander, Y..."

"Q.—Several weeks ago I was taking a leisurely walk thru the Brookfield Zoo when I got the scare of my life. I was approaching the baboon island when suddenly one of those ugly creatures let out a shriek, made a dash for the wall of the moat, and in two seconds had leaped onto the sidewalk. I almost panicked, because I thought for sure he would come over and start ripping me to shreds; but fortunately he ran away. Did the zoo people ever catch him? Are they making sure the primate monster doesn't get out again?

"A.L.H., Brookfield

"A.—A Brookfield Zoo spokesman said you must be talking about the great escape of 'Y,' a 47-pound, four-year-old baboon on March 16. He said the 48 baboons on the island were being shepherded into their cage when suddenly Y, apparently in a dither over the intrusion by keepers, broke ranks and split for the wall. He was captured with tranquilizer guns and a net, we were told. Metal protrusions on the wall of the moat, which he used to climb out, have been covered so Y can't get a grip next time he feels the call of the wild, the spokesman assured us."

Above left: To eliminate overcrowding at Waterfowl Lake, hundreds of wild ducks were lured into a trailer and transported to Rockford.

Left: By virtue of his birth, Aussie the hairy-nosed wombat became famous as the first of his kind born outside of Australia.

Above: In 1973, the first litter of second-generation sand cats ever born took place at the zoo.

Above right: The *Brookfield Bison* kept employees and zoo friends informed about the latest zoo news.

Wombats weren't the only ones being hand-raised. An article about a special primate ran in a 1973 issue of a zoo publication called *Brookfield Bison*. "'In a unique experiment,' according to Dr. Ben Beck, Curator of Primates, 'Brookfield Zoo is now hand-raising an infant orangutan with a minimum of human contact. Hand-raised orangs frequently grow up socially and sexually maladjusted if, while young, they are exposed only to humans and never to other orangs. Consequently, the baby will be raised in front of the orang enclosures in an ordinary baby crib at the Primate House during the day. At night, Keeper John O'Connor and his wife, Judy, provide feedings at their home.'

"The appealing female was born on May 14, to Ginger, a Brookfield Zoo orang on breeding loan at the Como Zoo in St. Paul, Minnesota. The baby female, named Hahna after Brookfield's keeper Walter Hahn, had to be taken from her mother for treatment of low grade pneumonia. The baby has recovered completely but could not be returned to the mother as her milk had dried up. The decision was then made to bring the baby to Brookfield and hand-raise her.

"Visitors are able to observe the baby at all times behind glass in the zoo's Primate House. The crib has been placed in front of the enclosures of the other orangs to provide visual and vocal contact. Keepers feed the baby near the bars of the orang cages so she can see the other orangs at close range as well as smell and touch them."

There were failures alongside the successes. The Dall's sheep were breeding, but the younger generations were routinely lost to infection, mystifying the staff for years. The okapi breeding program was going well, with calves born almost every year, but their survival rate was about 50%, with many fatalities caused by injuries induced by the mother. A pregnant female polar bear died after being attacked by a male bear in a mysterious incident.

These events were reminders that, as with any science, there was still much to be learned about the behavior and management of animals in captivity. As stated in the 1973 annual report, "Some species, such as the tiger, are now bred in zoos as a matter of routine, and we are getting better at breeding many others. But others again, cannot be maintained and bred without further study, and time is fast running out. Zoology is still at the horse and buggy stage, and the horse is starving to death. To ignore research is as shortsighted as ignoring roof repairs. It is much worse, for while we might maintain a zoo without buildings, we cannot do it without animals."

Above: The student research program accommodated young scholars' research projects by providing an opportunity for close-up, direct observation of their subjects, in this case a reindeer.

The Student Research Program

A new venture, the student research program, was one attempt to add to knowledge about zoo animals. Through grants from individual trustees, the zoo sponsored student research projects on animal behavior—for example, infant behaviors in grey kangaroos, vocal behaviors of 13-lined ground squirrels, gibbons' bipedal locomotion, and cheetahs' urine marking and associative behaviors—conducted during the college scholars' summer vacations. Local university students also used the animals for their independent studies during the school year. As well, staff research projects continued, covering such topics as primate development and social behavior in baboon troops and wolf packs.

In the October 1971 edition of the *Brookfield Bison*, Ben Beck, curator of research, told of how, while studying tool use in guinea baboons, he had come across an adult female who he suspected was partly blind because she groped for her food on the floor and had trouble orienting threats against other troop members. In response, he took the female to Dr. Samuel Vainisi, an ophthalmologist affiliated with the Illinois Eye and Ear Infirmary.

"Dr. Vainisi peered inside the sedated female's eye with an ophthalmoscope and his enthusiastic interest was quickly evident," Beck wrote. "Dr. Vainisi explained that the baboon appeared to be suffering from binocular macular degeneration. In short, the light-sensitive cells which are involved in seeing fine detail and color had degenerated in both eyes. Her vision was probably quite fuzzy, colorless and confined to the 'corners' of her eyes. Dr. Vainisi wanted confirmation of his diagnosis since the same malady is very common in humans and had never been reported in a non-human primate. A long battery of tests was performed, photographs of the interior of the eyes were taken and a line of physicians examined the baboon (somewhat warily, I may add, as most were used to looking only into human eyes). Dr. Vainisi's diagnosis was confirmed and his feeling about the importance of the case was underscored; our baboon had symptoms very similar to those of many visually handicapped people and it was most helpful to have a similarly afflicted monkey available for research since the cause of the disease is now known. Our celebrated baboon is now

Above: For decades, the zoo has studied wolves' behavior. A group howl is a bonding behavior, part of wolves' greeting ceremony.

housed with a young male on the north wall of the Primate House. She is on a special diet and we are hoping she will breed. Dr. Vainisi and I are preparing a paper on our findings and he hopes to be able to examine the eyes of all the island troop when they are weighed next December.

"This tale demonstrates again that pursuing a superfluous and seemingly trivial observation can have important consequences. Furthermore, it shows that basic research on problems with little direct relevance to the human condition often yields unexpected benefits for our health and happiness."

By the 1970s, Brookfield Zoo was finally participating in the four cornerstones of its mission: education, recreation, conservation, and research. It is interesting to track how the emphasis on these four elements changed during the institution's history. Certainly conservation and research were lacking when the zoo first opened its gates, and even education didn't get much attention until the 1960s. Gradually, as societal awareness of conservation problems grew, as zoology advanced as a science, and as the zoo grew more able to handle all aspects of its mission, the emphasis shifted away from primarily recreation to include the other three dimensions.

"I'M GOING TO WEE ON YOUR KNEE"

A 1975 press release put out by the zoo illustrated the fact that there was always something remarkable going on.

"More than 1,000 youngsters attended Brookfield Zoo's children's Christmas Party on Sunday for visits with Santa in the Children's Zoo barn. Requests to Santa centered on toys and animals with a few notable exceptions such as:

- a 3 year old girl who asked for a baby brother or sister because she was lonely.
- a 7 year old girl who wanted all the animals in the Children's Zoo.
- a 5 year old boy with a notable empty space in his smile asking for two front teeth.
- 4 year old twin brothers who asked Santa to 'make mommy and daddy not fight so much and love each other more.'
- and a 4 year old boy who asked only that Santa please hurry up and see him. When Santa asked why, the earnest youngster said, 'because if you don't I'm going to wee on your knee.'"

Visitor Amenities

While most visitors weren't aware of trends behind the scenes, other changes and improvements were very noticeable. By 1974, the Board finally felt that the zoo was financially stable enough to survive without income from peanut sales, and, with the exception of Children's Zoo, feeding of animals was prohibited. A few visitors who enjoyed that type of interaction with the animals grumbled, but most were supportive of the policy. Other additions around the zoo were ramps installed to make exhibits accessible to people in wheelchairs and children in strollers, as well as international-style signs and maps to help orient visitors of all nationalities.

Employees noticed that few people were reading signs and labels. Many visitors seemed to read the first line and then move on. To engage readers more, writers began using humor and catchy phrases. For example, one sign, still in place today, explains why so many hoofed animals enjoy "Mud - - - Glorious Mud!" Other catchy titles included "Mrs. Gray's Wha-cha-ma-call-it" and "Phew! What Stinks?" Once snared by the headline, many people were intrigued enough to read on. Signs also emphasized a certain aspect of an animal's life or behavior instead of simply its species, taxonomic name, and geographic range.

Occasionally, the writers were a little mischievous, as illustrated by a sign installed adjacent to an exhibit displaying no animal, only a basket of roses.

UNICORN *Monoceros mysticus*
Distribution: Old World with valid subspecies from India, Japan, China, England and Scotland. No fossil record. First report India ca. 1000 b.c.
Habits: Fierce, strong, solitary, shy, starry-eyed. Attracted to maidens. Feeds on roses.
Economics: Drinking cups from horns used to counteract poisoning attempts; market declined with advent of gunpowder.
Conservation: General extinction attributed to education. Continues to exist in protected communities such as James Thurber Reserve, Columbus, Ohio.

A father-son interaction, overheard at the unicorn exhibit, went as follows:
Son: Daddy, there's no such animal as a unicorn.
Impatient father: Don't be stupid. Can't you read the sign?

Perhaps not every sign brought about enlightenment, but the unicorn sign and others like it were evaluated for effectiveness, offering a beginning understanding of visitor behavior.

Another change affecting the visitor experience was the implementation of a reservation program for schools. A favorite destination for field trips on nice spring days, the zoo overflowed with school groups. After one particularly overcrowded day, the zoo began requiring schools to make reservations in advance to control the number of schoolchildren and provide adequate numbers of adult supervisors.

"One day, there were 300 buses at the zoo," recalled Reptile House keeper Terrie McLean, formerly a Children's Zoo keeper. "We had hundreds of day-camp kids with two or three little counselors busy talking about their boyfriends and not controlling the kids, who ran wild. They had little duffel bags for their lunches and possessions, and they took most of the guinea pigs, rabbits, tortoises, mice, anything that would fit in their duffel bags, and cleaned us out. It was like being invaded by locusts. For about three days, these animals would keep showing up. The kids brought them home, and their parents would say, 'You can't keep that.' So we'd find guinea pigs in boxes here and there. It was crazy. Within a month after that, they starting requiring reservations and would not allow that many buses in."

MUD - - - GLORIOUS MUD !

Animals have many biological and psychological needs that must be satisfied within the home range. Feeding, watering, loafing, sleeping and toilet areas are but a few of these needs. Sometimes the MUD WALLOW is a need. Mud not only cools, it crusts on the animal and protects against biting insects. In some cases, mud even camouflages. Besides all this, wallowing in the mud might be fun!

UNICORN
Monoceros mysticus
DISTRIBUTION: Old World with valid subspecies from India, Japan, China, England, and Scotland. No fossil record. First report from India, ca. 1000 B.C.
CONSERVATION: General extinction attributed to education. Continues to exist in protected communities such as James Thurber Reserve, Columbus, Ohio.
ECONOMICS: Drinking cups from horn used to counteract poisoning attempts; market declined with advent of gunpowder.
HABITS: Fierce, strong, solitary, shy, starry-eyed. Attracted to maidens. Feeds on roses.

Right: One of Peter Crowcroft's attempts at beautifying the zoo was a 40-foot-diameter Society emblem, located north of Roosevelt Fountain. Later, the emblem was moved north of the North Gate.

Below left: In the 1970s, signs around the zoo were rewritten in a more engaging style to attract more readers—and impart more knowledge.

"A Botanical Slum"

Upon his arrival at Brookfield Zoo, Crowcroft set about rectifying what he declared "a botanical slum." In addition to the greenhouses erected through the bond issuance, Crowcroft pushed for more formal gardens around the zoo. By 1972, he had overseen the creation of a 40-foot-diameter emblem of the Chicago Zoological Society, located between the North Gate and Roosevelt Fountain, consisting of 200,000 alternanthera and 8,000 marigolds. The formal plantings he encouraged, together with his crusade to clean up the zoo by offering more garbage cans and staggering the schedule of the grounds crew, beautified the park significantly.

Unfortunately, Dutch elm disease hit for a second time in 1975, destroying a great number of the magnificent towering trees. During an approximately 15-year period, the zoo transformed from a forested park to a planned garden.

MAKING GRASS

"Feeding 2,000 relatives calls for budget stretcher," an article by Robert J. Herguth that ran in the *Chicago Daily News* on February 8, 1975, drew attention to Brookfield Zoo's growing interest in horticulture.

"You have 2,000 distant relatives living with you. Your food bill is $4,500 a week and getting bigger. Your favorite grouchy live-in cousin weighs 13,000 pounds and needs 400 pounds of victuals daily or he gets even grouchier. What to do, what to do?

"If you're Peter Crowcroft, and you're director of Brookfield Zoo, you use on-site hydroponic farming to cut food costs for the 2,000 varied animals under your, uh, wing.

"Brookfield's hydroponics machine, 9 by 9 by 25 feet big, is in the zoo's commissary. The commissary manager figures the machine saves the zoo $5,000 a year in food bills. At Brookfield's hydroponics 'farm,' water is used instead of soil as the basic nutrient in which barley grass is grown from seed. Brookfield harvests 800 pounds of barley grass a day from the machine's 56 big plastic trays."

"This is how a zoo should be—a happy marriage of display and breeding area. In fifty years, we may still have some animals left to see, thanks to places like this."

Gerald Durrell
Author and Conservationist
During a 1973 visit to Brookfield Zoo

"Peter Crowcroft's...real legacy was the upgrading of the appearance of the park. In fact, I remember seeing him the day he had a check for $2 million in his pocket—I can't remember the amount exactly—and he said, 'Do I look like a happy man? I have a check for $2 million and I get to plant with it!'"

Edith Duckworth
Current Trustee

Eras End

In 1975, the Society said farewell to a number of people with long involvement in the zoo. Robert Bean died in March. Although he hadn't been involved with Brookfield Zoo for several years, his death resounded loudly among the trustees and staff. He had been an anchor for the institution for many years, and, together with his father, had been central to the zoo's development.

At the same time, Director Crowcroft decided to move on. His native Australia beckoned with a position as director of Sydney's Taronga Park Zoo, the institution from which Robert Bean had started Brookfield Zoo's Australian collection. The dynamic period of exhibit planning and construction was nearing an end as the bond-issuance money was exhausted, and the zoo seemed ready to branch off in new directions. The Illinois General Assembly took a moment to honor the outgoing director with the following unusual resolution:

"Whereas, many species of animals, once plentiful, are being saved from extinction by the men and women who staff zoological institutions and who dedicate their lives to the study and to the care and feeding of the Earth's fauna; and

"Whereas, The Chicago Zoological Society maintains one of the outstanding zoos in the world at Brookfield, and its excellence is largely attributable to Dr. Peter Crowcroft, who has been its director for the past seven years; and

"Whereas, Scientists and administrators of Dr. Crowcroft's excellence and outstanding capability are very rare, and his shoes will be difficult to fill; therefore be it

"Resolved by the House of Representatives of the 79th General Assembly of the State of Illinois,...that we wish for Dr. Crowcroft...many years of health, happiness, and prosperity in Australia."

Society president Bill Dickinson stepped down as well. Having headed the Society for 17 years and suffering from ill health, he yielded the presidency but remained on the Board of Trustees. During his tenure, he had overseen construction of Seven Seas; a period of transitional directors; implementation of numerous educational programs; several economic crises; a difficult fundraising campaign; and the branching of the Society into new directions, all of which supported the zoo's original mission. His administration spanned a busy and crucial time for the institution.

Trustee Elliott Donnelley died the same year. The resolution honoring the train buff highlights the generosity and energy the vibrant man brought to the zoo. "Elliott Donnelley became a member of the Chicago Zoological Society in 1965 and two years later was elected a trustee and a member of the Executive Committee. In that capacity, he took an energetic and constructive part in planning and supporting the enhancement of the Chicago Zoological Park at Brookfield. The most visible evidence of his enthusiasm and generosity is the steam railroad, whose resplendent colors, nostalgic contours and marvelous sounds have brought excitement and pleasure to hundreds of thousands of zoo-goers of all ages. During his years of service as a trustee, Elliott Donnelley contributed over a million dollars to the zoo, more than anyone else..."

The public and the press were most interested in another 1975 departure: the death of mighty Ziggy. In March 1975, Ziggy survived a bizarre accident when he tumbled into the moat inside Pachyderm House. The story was relayed to the public in a press release. "It was the shift door wheel that got Ziggy into trouble, and it was the same wheel, and the promise of the lady waiting behind it, that got Brookfield Zoo's rogue elephant out. On Sunday morning, as keeper Ed Sykes turned the wheel to open the shift door, inquisitive Ziggy reached around with his trunk to give an assist, as he had tried to do many times before. Ziggy reached a little further this time, however, and lost his balance. Keepers rushed to get straw into the moat, while the elephant first straddled the ten foot width. Then, Ziggy's 13,000 pounds slowly fell to the bottom, ten feet below.

"Efforts to right the huge male Asian elephant continued for six hours, finally succeeding when chains girdling the animal were hooked to two 50-ton winches on tow trucks. The trucks pulled.

"LOVE, ZIGGY"

A strikingly atypical letter to concerned visitors about Ziggy pretended to be written by the elephant, an approach that had never before been taken by the zoo. Although educational in certain ways, the letter, dated April 14, 1975, refers to what Ziggy "thinks," "feels," and "hopes," all attributes a scientific institution such as Brookfield Zoo refrains from making.

"I am telling this to my keeper, as I cannot spell as well as he can.

"In front of me, on a big, big bulletin board are all of the drawings and letters you sent to me after my fall. Though I did not hurt myself badly, it did kind of hurt my pride that I lost my balance and fell in my moat. But now I am up out of the moat, and can see all of your pictures and notes to me and they cheer me up. Widget, my girlfriend, lives next door and she can see them, too. She thinks you are all wonderful.

"Many of you drew pictures of bars on my home, but there aren't any. In my room, there is a big tree trunk that keeps me from leaning over the moat. My room is being painted now and I am in a room next door, that does not have a tree trunk. Maybe that is why I fell in the moat. Probably just like you at recess, when you are always trying to skip rope a little faster or jump a little higher or farther, I am always trying to break my past moat-leaning records. Last time I just went a liiittle too far.

"Anyway, as you probably heard, I broke a few inches of ivory off my beautiful tusks, which were my pride and joy. They grow back, you know, but very slowly. I guess I can wait, though. I also scratched my face, but when you come to see me it will all be healed. If you see something dark on the side of my head then it will be my musth gland—something like a runny nose, only just boy elephants have it and it doesn't mean they have a cold.

"The worst part of the fall was that I sprained my trunk. It is still a little sore. So Widget and I have not been able to hold each others' trunks, as we are used to doing. Also, when I was in the moat, I lost my appetite. I made up for that as soon as I had all four feet in my room. All that night and the next day I ate. My keepers gave me some special treats, like bananas, along with my usual bushels of apples, carrots and vegetables, grain, bread and hay. I have a pretty big appetite when I'm not in a moat. I eat 400 pounds of food a day, which is probably more than ten of you weigh all together. I weigh somewhere between six and seven tons, which is between 12,000 and 14,000 pounds. No one is sure how much I weigh because it's hard to find a scale big enough to weigh me. It would be even harder to get me up on it, I can tell you.

"By all this, you can tell that I am quite big, and I have a big heart to match. My heart gets sad sometimes, just like yours, and I turn to my friends to make it happy again and cheer me up. Such a big task takes a lot of friends. That is why I am so happy when I look at your drawings and read your letters.

"It's not always easy, I know, but try to be good. And remember that you have a friend at Brookfield Zoo who is thinking of you and hopes to see you soon.

"Love, Ziggy"

Left: The magnificent rogue Ziggy had an extraordinary life, but age caught up to him in 1975.

Below: Ziggy sports a broken right tusk, the result of his disastrous fall into the moat in front of his indoor stall. Many well-wishers sent cards expressing concern.

The chains cut into the cement top of the moat. To the cheers of dozens of Brookfield Zoo staff, the elephant rolled onto his stomach. Then Ziggy stood on his feet.

"As far as zoo staff was concerned, the worst was over. The rest was only a matter of hard work, they thought. After a quiet night in which Ziggy rested while a keeper kept him company and fervently hoped the animal wouldn't lay down, the work began. Over the next eight hours, shifts of zoo groundsmen and keepers brought in an estimated 1,500 wheelbarrow loads of gravel to construct a ramp in front of the entrenched elephant. By 4:00 p.m., 100,000 pounds of limestone had been placed at a 45 degree angle in front of Ziggy. Keepers then loosened the chain connecting Ziggy's rear leg to a building I-beam, and then tugged another chain wrapped around his huge front leg. Nothing. Food was offered. Apples, carrots, hay, some of the 400 pounds of the daily diet he was used to and hadn't tasted in almost 30 hours. Still, he wouldn't climb the ramp. For over an hour Ziggy stayed in the moat, as zoo [staff] schemed over further incentives. Then keeper Leroy Woodruff, Jr. suggested that the attraction of other elephants might be used to entice Ziggy. The shift door on the side of Ziggy's stall, the one that keeper Sykes was opening when the elephant attempted his near-fatal assist on the wheel, would be the key. The door opens onto the stall of Widget, a 21-year-old female African elephant that Ziggy is known to like. The final psychological strategy adopted was simply to open this shift door and depend on Ziggy to respond, which he did."

Ziggy lumbered up the gravel ramp and turned into his stall. Those overseeing the event breathed a huge sigh of relief. They had reason to worry because over 100 media people were crowding the scene. Had Ziggy turned to them rather than into his stall—and nothing prevented him from doing so—there would have been chaos.

Ziggy did survive the frightening episode, but he didn't live much longer. On October 27, he laid down and never got up. An autopsy revealed a stress fracture on his ribs, most likely from his fall, but the cause of death was old age. The newspapers carried the news of the elephant's death, and public reaction was intense. It is remarkable how well-loved the massive animal was, despite the fact that he had attacked his keeper. Ziggy led a long and colorful life, and it was simply his time to go.

1976 George Rabb is appointed zoo director and Society president.
Claus Hagenbeck visits the zoo.
The tax levy increases from .0058 to .025 cents.

'77 The first docents are trained.
The Parents Program begins.
Ellen Thorne Smith dies.
Two marabou storks escape.

'78 Sylvia Shaw Judson dies.
Mary the black rhino's 45th birthday is celebrated.
A fire starts in Seven Seas.

'79 The Scientific and Educational Advisory Committee becomes the SEACON Committee.
An exhibit worker dies during construction on Tropic World.
Affie the elephant arrives.

'80 Samson the gorilla comes to the zoo.
Two grey-headed kingfishers are the first born in captivity.
An arena is built inside Children's Zoo.

'81 Corky Hamill steps down as Society chairman.
Penny Korhumel becomes the Society chair.

CHAPTER THIRTEEN

New Faces

(1976-1981)

"When I talked to George, I was very impressed with his mind, or perhaps intellect is the word. He was terribly quiet, dark, reserved— and brilliant."

Peter Crowcroft
Former Zoo Director

BROOKFIELD ZOO

Chicago Zoological Park
BROOKFIELD, ILLINOIS 60513
(312) 242-2630 -:- (312) 485-0263

May 29, 1975   **FOR IMMEDIATE RELEASE**

In the move to their new summer quarters, Brookfield Zoo's giant tortoises held their own mini-race today. The race began at 10:30 this morning, when the three largest tortoises—Peter, George and Weaver (named after zoo director Dr. Peter Crowcroft, deputy director Dr. George Rabb and zoo veterinarian Dr. Weaver Williamson, respectively)—made their way out of their grotto.

Based on past tortoise race records, which have Peter winning three contests to George and Weaver's two each, Curator of Reptiles Ray Pawley said he expected Peter to win. This wasn't the case, however, as Fast Peter made too wide a turn coming out of the building and was overtaken by both George, the eventual winner, and Weaver.

Rabb at the Helm

Slow and steady wins the race, as they say. Twenty years after arriving at Brookfield Zoo to head the new research program— and after witnessing several changes at the level of director— George Rabb assumed the top job.

"After considering potential candidates for six months, the trustees are happy to conclude that we had the most competent person right here," said new Board chairman Corwith Hamill in a January 1976 press release. "Dr. Rabb has devoted 20 years to Brookfield Zoo and is intimate with every nook, cranny and occupant. He is also highly regarded in the zoological community."

Rabb raced some stiff competition to the director's position. After Peter Crowcroft left the previous year, the Board conducted a national search for a director. But as Bronx Zoo director William Conway commented to a trustee, "I don't know why you're looking around, you've got the best man in the country right there." Rabb's primary competition came from within Brookfield Zoo.

George Rabb

Dr. Gil Boese, associate director of development and education, was the other chief candidate. The Board argued over which route to take—the conservative, academic animal man versus the less predictable, more gregarious administrative candidate. In the end, the conservative approach won.

Boese stayed with the zoo for several years and was even appointed a vice-president of the Society, an unprecedented honor for a staff member. He eventually left to become director of the Milwaukee Zoo, the same post both Ed Bean and George Speidel had held previously.

Unlike the giant tortoise named after him, veterinarian Weaver Williamson wasn't in the running. Several years prior, he had been bitten in the hand by Sally the chimpanzee, a bizarre occurrence considering Sally's usual friendliness. The bite resulted in infection, and a long series of medications began. Williamson, always a first-class veterinarian with a remarkable talent for quick and accurate diagnoses, never quite recovered from the injury. Over the years, he wore many hats in addition to his veterinary duties, including acting director for zoological operations after Ron Blakely left, associate director, and head of the animal collection.

Above: Two giant tortoises race at their own pace, with the victory prophetically going to George, in 1975's meet.

Corky Hamill

Rabb was also appointed president of the Chicago Zoological Society, assuming the role Crowcroft had fought for. In his new capacity, Rabb worked closely with the new chairman of the Board, Corwith "Corky" Hamill. The two began working closely on a presentation to the state legislature concerning changes in the tax rate, admissions, and other matters. Fortunately, they had the support of Arthur Janura, the general superintendent of the Forest Preserve District, as well as George Dunne, president of the Forest Preserve District.

Corky Hamill

Hamill was a new type of chairman. "The first president was John McCutcheon," he explained. "He was a good president; he had a lot of connections and people trusted him. When he died, his brother-in-law Clay Judson became president, and when Clay retired, his law partner Bill Dickinson became president. It was a very close-knit situation there. That was up until 1975. Those three people had run the Zoological Society since its inception."

For the first time in its history, the zoo had a new chairman and a new director simultaneously, perhaps why the duo was able to truly turn from the past and look to the future, changing the institution's direction and dynamics. "The Board was mostly people like myself, who were children or grandchildren of the original members," said Hamill. "They were getting pretty stale. When I became chairman, I tried to get new blood. They were all nice people, but it was their fathers who were originally interested, and they were just coming along for the ride."

Hamill wanted the people on his Board to have three qualities: prominence in Chicago society; a home somewhere close to the western suburbs, as most previous Board members had resided on the North Shore; and the ability to lend a professional hand in the zoo's development. Being a trustee took on new meaning. Board members were asked to lend their professional expertise, share the responsibility of running the organization, and make use of their personal and professional contacts for fundraising and other purposes. It was a much harder role, but it was also more fulfilling.

Committee Activities

A good example of the Board's new responsibilities was the Scientific and Educational Advisory Committee. Although the zoo had limited staff concentrating on research and education, the Committee took seriously its role of overseeing those aspects of the zoo's mission. In 1975, it set some ambitious goals: develop a program for docents (volunteer educators), expand the adult-education program, develop sensory-input opportunities for handicapped visitors, and, ultimately, construct a building for education with two full-time staff members. Once approved by the full Board, the Committee quickly had a docent program running. The education building took a little longer.

Training for the docent program began in July 1977, and it was an academic boot camp. Trainees were instructed in zoo history, general operations, the physical layout of the zoo, and the biology of reptiles, small mammals, and primates to prepare them for the tours they would give to school groups and the public. Classes were held every Friday for eight weeks (later doubled to 16 weeks) and lasted three hours each. In addition, applicants paid a $25 tuition fee and made a commitment to volunteer one day a week for at least six months.

Right: Docents sometimes lead visitors on tours of the zoo or help children learn about the animals they see.

Below: In 1984, primate keepers Vince and Carol Sodaro received a SEACON grant to participate in rehabilitation efforts for orangutans in Borneo.

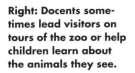

It was education on a whole new scale. Within a few years, over 100 docents had been trained and put into action, and Brookfield Zoo had an education corps.

In 1979, the Scientific and Educational Advisory Committee was reformed into the Scientific, Education, and Conservation Committee, also called the SEACON Committee. Previously, the Board had been unable to back worthwhile conservation projects because of a lack of funding. SEACON was created to provide funding for conservation research in the form of seed money, which a scientist could use to gain enough data to attract money from a larger granting institution, or small-dollar projects, which provided enough financial support to allow a researcher to convene a symposium, finish a project, or pay for a study from start to finish. Funding mostly came from contributors interested in conservation projects and, later, from a 10% allocation from the Society's annual fundraising effort. Bill Dickinson himself financed a lengthy documentary on sea otters only to have all of the film destroyed in a California fire.

SEACON grants were, and still are, typically quite small, but sometimes they reap big rewards. One SEACON seed grant of $1,400 helped a researcher obtain a grant of over $118,000 from a large funding institution. Another group of researchers began with only their own money and SEACON seed money, subsequently attracting more than $100,000 from other sources.

Over the years, projects supported by SEACON have included participation by zoo staff and others in research on mountain gorillas at Rwanda's Karisoke Research Center, part of a long-term study begun by Dian Fossey; rehabilitation of Bornean orangutans; underwriting for the International Snow Leopard Trust, a study of snow leopard ecology in India; training in animal management or behavioral research for Chinese, Kenyan, and other conservationists; and studies on the principle of echolocation in dolphins.

A Bleak Financial Picture

Financially, Hamill and Rabb inherited a discouraging situation. At the 1976 annual meeting, they announced that by the end of April, the Society would have an operating deficit of over $1 million. The zoo had been running a deficit each year for years, and the accumulated total was staggering.

To an untrained eye, it would appear the institution was doing well. The $15 million bond issuance had provided funds for much-needed repairs and dynamic exhibits, the staff was more professional than ever, programs such as the safari trams and the student research program were well-received, and the animal collection seemed healthy. But behind the scenes, things weren't going well.

In fact, the Board even discussed closing the zoo for the winter, but the idea was rejected because the animals still needed to be cared for, making the savings inconsequential.

Having appealed in 1974 to the Forest Preserve District for an increase in the tax levy, the zoo was anxiously awaiting a decision. The District sympathized and agreed in principle, but the rate was set by state law, necessitating legislation in Springfield. Under the guidance of George Dunne, the Forest Preserve District and Board members lobbied their friends and colleagues in the legislature. Although a bill that was approved by the House, the Senate, and Governor Dan Walker authorized an increase in the tax levy from .0058 cents to .025 cents per $100 assessed property valuation, the zoo never realized the full increase due to a change in the valuation system.

"This change is vital to Brookfield Zoo and has been needed for several years," Hamill later said. "It was originally planned that taxes would support the zoo's basic operations, but with inflation of the last 10 years, the zoo's financial situation has changed drastically." He went on to say that taxes once sustained 70% of the budget but had dropped to only 30% in recent years.

The tax increase was good news, but the actual increase didn't benefit the zoo until 1978, after taxes had been collected at the new rate set under the new valuation system. From 1974 to 1978, things were pretty lean.

Left: Early in the Parents Program, one person adopted an ostrich wing for $25...bringing up the question of how much the legs or the neck would have cost.

The staff and trustees explored ways to raise more money. One of the most successful enterprises was the Parents Program, in which individuals or groups donated a sum roughly equivalent to the cost of feeding an animal for a year, becoming "adoptive" parents to that animal. The 1977 brainchild of governing member Penny Korhumel and Darcy Donald, animal adoptions became tremendously popular after the first adoption, a pair of irresistible polar bear cubs, was offered.

The Parents Program soon needed full-time staff to tend to the constantly ringing telephones. Kind-hearted and enthusiastic Mari Paget was hired as the program coordinator, and she had natural sales instincts. One woman desperately wanted to adopt an ostrich but couldn't afford the full price, so Mari let her adopt an ostrich wing for $25. Some parents took strong interest in their adopted animals, often calling Mari for updates when they didn't have time to visit.

Other revenue-generating projects included Polo Day in nearby suburban Oak Brook, during which all proceeds went to the zoo; a brief foray into the business of selling animal art, as cheetah prints by Kenyan artist Simon Combs went on sale at $125 per print; and the creation of zoo holiday cards, of which over 20,000 were sold.

PRINCE CHARLES' BEAR

The Parents Program was so popular, even Prince Charles became involved, as explained in a press release dated December 16, 1977.

"Among the people who have become Brookfield Zoo Parents by paying for an animals' food costs for a year is a new name—His Royal Highness Prince Charles, Prince of Wales. A 22-year-old woman, Nancy Luebben, of Los Alamitos, California, has requested a Christmas Parenthood for the Prince of Wales. His Royal Highness will be sent a packet of Christmas Parent benefits early next week; the envelope awaits a picture of Nancy, which she wishes enclosed with a note to the Prince.

"Ms. Luebben, who met the Prince in Los Angeles this fall, said she thought of the gift after reading about Brookfield's adoption program in the Los Angeles Times. 'I know he loves animals and so do I,' she said. 'What do you give the man who has everything? This seemed the perfect gift.'

"The adoption packet will include...an adoption certificate that will read 'His Royal Highness Prince Charles...The Chicago Zoological Society welcomes you to its family of Brookfield Zoo Parents. This certifies that you have adopted Mary, the polar bear, for one year. Thank you very much for your support.'"

RECOLLECTIONS

One woman who called owned a business called Hippo Hotdogs somewhere on the north side. She wanted to adopt a hippo, which was $3,000. I said, "That's great. Now there's only one little orphan left," because two of the three hippos had been adopted. I didn't think much of it. I was just glad for the large donation. She called back about half an hour later and said, "I can't bear to think of that one being an orphan, so I'll adopt him, too." She sent me a check for $6,000!

Mari Paget
Former Parents Program Coordinator

Final Bond-Issuance Projects

Some of the last money from the bond issuance went toward Predator Ecology, an extension to Lion House that broke new ground in exhibit techniques. The staff cast and hand-formed epoxy to accurately simulate desert, mountain, and forest scenes. The first part to open, the Sahara Desert scene, won the American Association of Zoological Parks and Aquariums' Exhibits Achievement Award. The finest tribute to the exhibit harked back to the zoo's beginning. The words came from Dr. Claus Hagenbeck during his visit in 1976. Standing on the bridge between the two mountain settings, he remarked, "If grandfather could only have seen this!"

The Lion House renovation also included clever mechanisms that encouraged cats' natural behaviors. Sand cats pawing at a hole in the rocks as though to catch mice or other prey tripped a switch, activating an electronic system that deposited food in another crevice. They didn't always receive food, so sometimes several trippings were necessary. Nearby, a pair of pumas stood on a particular tree limb or rock ledge to activate an artificial marmot. To receive a food reward, they had to dash across the enclosure and grasp the marmot before it disappeared. In another display, Siberian tigers had to jump into their pool, climb onto a ledge, then pull on the leg or rib of a model of a disemboweled deer. Meat was deposited intermittently in the deer's body cavity.

The displays were popular with many visitors (although not for the faint of heart) and increased the felines' activity levels and natural behaviors. Unfortunately, the cats proved too powerful for the displays. Eventually, after fixing the mechanisms time and again, the staff dismantled them.

Above: Using models, preparators went to great lengths to make sure the displays inside Predator Ecology simulated natural settings.

Left: A tiger walks past his prey—in this case an artificial deer—designed to stimulate the cat's natural feeding behaviors.

Tropic World

Meanwhile, work was still underway on Tropic World. The trustees dubbed the massive building "Dickinson's folly" due to the many problems and delays in finishing it. Aside from the architect's sudden death, the early obstacles were structural. The roof leaked in four different ways, and whenever the suspected problem was resolved, another leak popped up. Initially, the building was designed with an economical and attractive curved Teflon roof, but the idea was scrapped when the manufacturer wouldn't guarantee such a structure in Chicago's climate. Later, delays were caused by escalating steel prices, so the exhibit was redesigned using other materials. Environmental and economic concerns entered into planning and construction debates as well. Solar panels were not practicable at the time, and placing skylights on the north side of the building was a compromise between illumination needs and heat-load considerations.

Some problems centered around the exhibit's novelty. Nothing like it had ever been built before. First, the building was huge. At 110 feet wide, nearly 500 feet long, and 80 feet tall, it was by far the largest zoo building in the world. Second, no one had ever tried to recreate a rain forest inside a building. Who knew how to maintain temperature and humidity levels in a building that size, and who could really advise on creating waterfalls and rain systems? The problems were a natural part of creating a revolutionary exhibit.

One tragedy associated with the construction of Tropic World happened in 1979. Zulfi Memidovski, an exhibit preparator, fell to his death while working in the building. He had been cleaning an area on the third floor when he apparently lost his balance and fell about 14 feet. His coworkers were on break and didn't discover what happened until they returned. In a coma, Memidovski was taken to the hospital, where he was diagnosed with a concussion and internal bleeding. He later died from the injuries.

THE TRIALS OF TROPIC WORLD

On August 31, 1981, Dori Meinert of the *Chicago Tribune* wrote about the special considerations that arose during construction on Tropic World.

"Glazed ceramic tile was being laid on the hidden holding cages beneath the [Tropic World] exhibit, where animals will return each night to be fed and examined for health problems. The zoo had paid a premium price so that only chip-free tiles would be used. Chipped spots could harbor human bacteria that can cause diseases to which primates are extremely susceptible.

"The job foreman, being economically minded, couldn't be convinced of this danger, however. He let the work continue, adopting the usual standards of the industry, which allow a certain number of chipped tiles. Curator of Primates Ben Beck's arguments for conservation spent, he vowed to come in each night and break all the tiles until the job was done right. Overnight, the foreman was convinced.

"Beck also battled with an architect over the width of a zookeepers' corridor between the cages. His point was made when, in Frankfurt, Germany, they watched zookeepers' eyeglasses and hats torn off by caged monkeys as the men carried a sick monkey down a corridor that proved too narrow. 'It was a lesson I couldn't teach him,' Beck said."

The staff began preparing for the eventual opening of Tropic World. New decisions had to be made: which animals would be compatible in each section, what to do with Primate House residents without new homes in Tropic World, and how to obtain appropriate birds and other animals.

Although collecting trips had become rare by the 1970s, two expeditions were made to capture birds for Tropic World. In 1977, curator of reptiles Ray Pawley joined with representatives from the Milwaukee Zoo and Lincoln Park Zoo to collect birds in Kenya. Several years later, new curator of birds Dennis DeCourcey led a group of members and keepers to Peru to capture Amazonian birds.

Birds, defying zoos' attempts to breed them in captivity, were practically the only creatures still to come from the wild. By the '70s, almost all new mammals were captive-bred and obtained either from other zoos or, occasionally, from animal dealers. Zoos across the country were slowly but steadily moving away from competitive relationships to more cooperative associations.

Some of the Kenyan birds did all they could to leave. On two occasions, shortly after their arrival, marabou storks flew out of their outside enclosure. The birds' wings had been clipped to

Above: "Dickinson's folly," as Tropic World was known, took nine years to construct.

prevent such a mishap, but apparently the procedure wasn't done properly. The first bird flew around the zoo, perching on trees and on top of Tropic World. It eventually picked up a thermal and soared 2,000 feet up. After contacting the media with a description of the bird, the zoo received more than 50 calls about sightings from as far away as Wisconsin and Indiana. Most of

HIPPOS, CROCODILES, AND AN OCCASIONAL BIRD

In an article called "Perspective: To Catch a Wild Bird," which ran in the August/September 1980 issue of *Animal Kingdom* magazine, Ray Pawley recalled an exciting episode during his 1977 trip to Kenya to collect birds for Tropic World.

"One evening Jonathan Leakey asked me to join him in collecting some wading birds for the Milwaukee Zoo. He warned me about the difficulties: 'We'll go out between sunset and moonrise, when darkness will be on our side. We must wade through deep mud to get to the birds, and we must stay clear of hippos, but we'll have battery-powered headlamps to help.'

"[On a mud flat that was part of the delta at the mouth of the Ndau River] Jonathan and I set down our bird crates and strapped on our battery packs and headlamps.... Our objective was to creep as close to a selected bird as possible under cover of darkness. We would have to keep our lights focused at the bird's eyes and avoid placing any part of our bodies or nets between the light beam and the bird's field of vision. A mix of skill and luck could produce a successful netting, but there would be only one chance per bird: A near miss and the bird would be gone....

"Shoes and socks, I quickly learned, were useless and could easily be lost in the muck. Jonathan cautioned that one must proceed carefully to avoid stepping on thorny acacia branches...that might be as much as two or three feet below the surface. One might be ankle-deep in mud but, within two steps, could be knee- or even crotch-deep. Hands and arms were useless to aid in locomotion of this kind; legs and feet took all the work load. The effort was exhausting."

Pawley wrote that after he swung at a yellow-billed stork with his net, then missed the bird, "the stork's takeoff produced a domino effect. The sound of beating wings grew to a roar and lasted for several seconds as hundreds of birds, most beyond the range of my light, took to the air. That was it. I scanned the area with my light...not a bird to be seen.

"Continuing to search for other birds, I heard repeated surface-water splashing a few yards away. Jonathan had told me that a species of catfish frequents the delta shallows and that several catfish can sound like a charging hippo. He had mentioned crocodiles, but said that none in Lake Baringo had ever attacked anyone. I made my way across one of the delta channels, and, as I approached a grassy shore, there arose suddenly a greater commotion of splashing accompanied by loud grunts and coughs. I promptly 'reversed gears' on the premise that catfish do not make loud grunting sounds.

"In heading back to our rendezvous I did manage to net a spur-winged plover. When we rejoined forces Jonathan displayed a blacksmith plover and a ruff. At the boat we sloshed around in lake water to rinse off as much mud as possible, then placed our crated birds amidships and headed back by moonlight (it was close to 11:00 p.m.). As we glided through the water Jon pointed out the deep red eyes of hippos and, farther along, the shiny red eyes of at least six or seven adult Nile crocodiles. It was an exciting experience, but it was good to get back and unload the birds, examine and bed them down for the night...and head for the showers."

the calls described great blue herons, not marabou storks. The bird was finally recaptured in Lake Geneva, Wisconsin, with the help of local residents and police.

The second stork, perhaps inspired by its friend, tried the same trick a few weeks later. Not long thereafter, the storks were shipped to the Los Angeles Zoo.

Above: The zoo's marabou storks took unexpected flight in 1977.

Departures, Arrivals

Rabb was fortunate to inherit Brookfield Zoo's most professional and diverse work force ever. As director, Peter Crowcroft had hired the zoo's first full-time animal behaviorist, a veterinary pathologist, a full-time development director, a new curator of birds, a new superintendent of Children's Zoo, a new curator of research and education, a curator of public relations, a full-time photographer, and a fully staffed Design Department. (To provide adequate room for the Design Department, Crowcroft had had Parrot House converted into studio space.)

Rabb continued the trend, hiring veterinarians Frank Wright and Janis Ott, associate director of development and marketing Ted Beattie (later to become head of the Shedd Aquarium), associate director of administration Jeff Williamson (currently director of Phoenix Zoo), assistant director of planning Paul Joslin, graphic arts manager Hannah Jennings, and administrative assistant Ralph Piland, among others.

Along with the more professional staff came involvement in international zoological and conservation efforts. Both Edward Bean and Robert Bean had had involvement in the International Union of Directors of Zoological Gardens and impressive international connections, but the zoo's participation in large conservation efforts had been minimal, partly because few conservation efforts were underway in the institution's early years. In the 1970s, however, the zoo's scientific staff began representing the Society at meetings around the world.

In 1978 alone, zoo representatives participated in meetings of the American Association of Zoological Parks and Aquariums, the International Union for the Conservation of Nature, the Animal Behavior Society, the American Society of Mammalogists, the First International Symposium on Birds in Captivity, the Illinois Endangered Species Board, the American Association of Zoo Keepers, the International Marine Animal Trainers Association, and the American Society of Ichthyologists and Herpetologists, among others. Several staff members served as officers of these and other organizations.

Clearly, zookeeping was a different undertaking than it had been in the 1930s. The staff list began to resemble more a university roster than a zoo personnel list, with Ph.D.s, DVMs, MAs, and other advanced degrees proliferating.

As the texture of the staff changed, several long-time employees departed. Mae Rose Jana, who joined in 1937 as administrative secretary to Ed Bean and retained that position through several directors, retired in 1975, taking with her a thorough knowledge of zoo operations and a rare historical perspective. Charles Christensen, who served as associate director of administration for eight years and continually struggled with tax-levy increases and tax collections, retired in 1977. Ed Steiner, who headed up the grounds crew, retired in 1979 after 42 years of service. He had been responsible for the petition that won employees a five-day work week in 1956.

Other breaks with the past were more final. Sylvia Shaw Judson, creator of the sculptures at Roosevelt Fountain and two figurines at Children's Zoo, as well as widow of Clay Judson, died in 1978. Her sister, Evelyn Shaw McCutcheon, wife of the Society's first president, had died the previous year.

Ellen Thorne Smith, founder of the *Bandar-log* and its author from 1949 to 1965, died in 1977 as well. A devoted member of the Society since 1958, she had continually applied her time, wisdom, and energy to good care of the animals and attention to the zoo's horticulture. In her later years, she championed a nature trail around Indian Lake, and today the trail is appropriately named after her.

By the end of the 1970s, few trustees or staff who remembered the beginnings of the new zoo in Brookfield remained.

Chairman Hamill was busy fortifying the ranks. His crusade to infuse the board with new blood (ironic since he himself was a descendent of a founding trustee) was working. Many of the new trustees—including Edward McCormick Blair, Jr., Edith Duckworth, Dennis Keller, Penny Korhumel, Norris "Mike" Love, Jerry Manne, and Louis Schauer—would play major roles in the Society.

Below: Artist Sylvia Shaw Judson was renowned for focusing on children in her work. In her two statues standing outside the entrance to Children's Zoo, she captured the magic and wonder to be found inside.

New Animals

Several prominent new faces belonged to other members of the animal kingdom. In preparation for the opening of Tropic World—whenever that might be—Brookfield Zoo secured, through a breeding loan from the Buffalo Zoo, a male gorilla by the name of Samson. Strikingly handsome, he would become a favorite of keepers and visitors. Another notable addition was Affie the elephant, who came from the Indianapolis Zoo. Although nowhere near the size and stature of Ziggy, Affie would also become an oft-recognized animal.

The role of animal "star," once filled by Ziggy, had fallen to a creature who had arrived in 1962 weighing a mere 250 pounds. Tipping the scales at nearly a ton, full-grown Olga the walrus had grown into a crowd favorite, with her very own fan club, by the late 1970s. She knew how to work her audience. She blew kisses with her flipper, whistled at passersby, and occasionally drenched her unsuspecting onlookers for the sake of surprise and entertainment. Olga basked in human attention.

Above and left: Samson was a magnificent silverback gorilla, popular with visitors and female gorillas. He sired several offspring, adding to the small numbers of this endangered species.

OLGA THE WALRUS

"Love is 1800 lbs of Walrus" claimed assistant lead keeper Randy Brill in the headline of an article he wrote for the January 1979 *Brookfield Bison*.

"Since her arrival in 1962, Olga has been Brookfield Zoo's ambassador and one of the most popular animals in the park.

"Olga's media work has always been top notch. More than one television reporter has fretted over upstaging by the crafty walrus. A complete professional, Olga once showed just how fine she could hone her sense of tact. In 1976 inflation had hit everyone hard, including Brookfield Zoo. Using our Most Expensive Eater as backdrop, new Director George Rabb was interviewed on camera regarding Brookfield's financial situation as we asked for more help from the Cook County Forest Preserve District. A weighty interview.

"Suddenly, Olga's head cocked and streams of water were sent in all directions—all except one, that is. Lights, lenses, reporters, and crews were dripping. Olga's boss was dry, however, and her reputation as an ambassador took on yet another facet.

"One of the most important additions to Olga's life was a friend. We knew that isolation from other animals would have long-range negative effects. At that time, the possibility of another walrus was risky as well as too expensive, but Olga was in luck. Over in the Children's Zoo lived a small harbor seal named Amy, who could easily share Olga's home and provide the necessary companionship.

"Olga and Amy together is a sight. Visitors delight in their antics—Olga sitting on the bottom of the pool with her head well above water, cradling Amy in her flippers as a mother would an infant, or Amy acting like a walrus calf, riding around the pool on Olga's back.

"In addition to Amy's companionship, Olga has devised several games and tricks over the years which she uses for some grand entertainment. We've already given you a preview of her forte—drenching the visitor. Here's how it goes. On a typical warm summer's day, visiting crowds will gather around Olga's pool and stand in groups four or five people deep. Always amazed at the sight of such a large animal floating and moving about in the water, they become glued to their spots as if hypnotized and watch the crafty walrus for minutes on end. At this point, Olga has what is indispensable to her favorite ploy—victims.

"While calmly swimming about and watching the crowd, Olga is secretly filling all the available space in her mouth and cheeks with water. When she has taken in as much water as she can, the walrus locates some unwary observers and heads for their side of the pool. Suddenly, with a move made as easily as the blink of an eye, she raises her lips just above the surface and lets go with a blast of water that might have come from a firehose. It drenches with some precision. The people closest to Olga are hopelessly confined by the crowd behind them and take the full force of the assault. Olga rolls in the water with glee and moves back to the center of her home awaiting the next opportunity."

Opposite and above: Olga the walrus was one of the zoo's most famous animals, no doubt because she hammed it up in front of admiring audiences, especially during her birthday party (photo, opposite below). Amy the harbor seal (top photo, above) was Olga's pool pal for many years.

In 1978, another zoo favorite celebrated her 45th birthday by literally attacking her "birthday cake." Caught near Mt. Meru in Tanganyika (now Tanzania), Mary the rhino had arrived in 1935 with her mate, Pharaoh. She captured headlines in 1941 when she gave birth to Georgie-Joe, the first black rhino born in captivity. (Mary and Pharaoh produced Robert R. three years later.) She was almost as old as the zoo.

Mary's birthday was an event. WGN-Radio's Wally Phillips devoted 20 minutes of his morning show to singing songs to Mary, a huge birthday sign was strung up in her enclosure, and about 400 visitors and staff donned party hats and serenaded the grande dame. Mary hammed it up, several times circling and charging her cake, which was made up of apples, bananas, oranges, grass, onions, and yogurt, her favorite foods. Acting more like a two-year-old than her age, she ended up with much of the treat on her face.

Birthdays aside, every day seemed to bring another incident. One involving an ostrich highlights the vigilance keepers must maintain every day. "The rule here is that when you take a padlock off a door, you close the door, hang the padlock on a wire, and click it shut," said reptile curator Ray Pawley. "An ostrich was in Aquatic Bird House's outside flight cage. A keeper set the padlock down for an instant, took two or three steps into the enclosure, and then remembered she had to click the lock shut. When she turned, she saw the lock in mid-air. The ostrich had grabbed it and flipped it up in the air to catch it and swallow it. The keeper made a lunge for the bird and grabbed it around its neck. She felt the padlock slide past her fist into the ostrich's stomach.

"We had to take the bird to the hospital. The veterinarian made a hook out of a coat hanger and, kind of like unlocking a car door from the outside, slipped the hook into the throat of the ostrich, snagged the padlock, and pulled it out."

Next door, in Perching Bird House, two new faces—newborn grey-headed kingfishers—made history as they were the first of their species to be hatched in captivity. Named Tittle and Tattle, the fledglings had to be hand-raised because their parents stopped feeding them. The Bird Department staff took to the task, regularly feeding the babies bits of meal, crickets, and tiny pieces of meat. "Looks like we have two more celebrities at Brookfield Zoo," commented curator of birds Dennis DeCourcey at the time.

Another incident involved a turkey vulture housed in Children's Zoo. Although wing-wounded, she was able to flap her primary feathers and coast a few feet. One day, she somehow caught a gust of wind and flew right out of Children's Zoo. Quite the event for her, except that she landed in the grizzly bear enclosure. Amazingly, the bird intimidated the mammoth grizzly bears! She flapped her wings, hissed, rushed at them, and carried on so tremendously that the bears didn't know what to do. Eventually, staff were able to entice the bears into their indoor enclosure and rescue the brave turkey vulture from the outside yard. It was certainly an unusual standoff.

Above: A 1978 birthday party was just like any other, except that the guest of honor was Mary, the 45-year-old black rhino.

Right: The zoo was the first to successfully breed grey-headed kingfishers. Keepers were forced to hand-raise the birds to save them.

Left: A turkey vulture from Children's Zoo made a surprise visit to some grizzly bears that were just that: surprised. Fortunately, the bird emerged from the incident unscathed.

A frightening episode took place in August 1978, when George and Mary Rabb noticed smoke billowing out of Seven Seas during their usual evening bicycle ride. The Brookfield Fire Department responded quickly, and it was soon discovered that a fire had originated in the building's kitchen due to a short circuit in a small fan used for ventilation. The fire was extinguished fairly easily, but the issue of greater concern was toxic smoke inhalation by the animals. Uncertain how much the dolphins would be affected, trainers carefully watched the animals, but they suffered no serious effects. In fact, the most serious damage was to staff nerves.

Some animal activities were more easily and regularly observed. On Baboon Island, originally the home of hundreds of rhesus monkeys and aoudad sheep, busy little meerkats joined the baboon troop, providing for even more activity and interaction among the animals. (Other cohabitants with the baboons over the years have included ibex, crocodiles, monitor lizards, and rock hyraxes.)

The nature of the animals that shared Children's Zoo had also changed by the late 1970s. At first an intriguing combination of domestic, farmyard, and exotic baby animals, it gradually changed from being an orphanage to housing only domestic and native species. Under the supervision of longtime Children's Zoo curator Gail Schneider, a large, heated exhibit barn had been built in 1972, thanks to Mrs. Clive Runnels and other donors. The original donors to Children's Zoo, the Seabury family, once again assisted by building an arena for "Animals in Action" shows featuring domestic animals.

As in Children's Zoo, the late 1970s were characterized by change, this time in the form of new staff, trustees, and animals. Corky Hamill spent his term as chairman strengthening the Board so it could tackle major projects and issues more effectively as the zoo moved ahead. Under new term-limit regulations set by the Board, he stepped down as chairman in 1981. His six-year term, though seemingly short in comparison to his predecessors', was a crucial one for the longevity of the institution. When he took the job, he inherited a huge operating deficit, an empty director's seat, inadequate annual tax income, an inflationary economy in which to work, and a shaky construction project called Tropic World.

By the end of Hamill's time as chairman of the Board, he had small annual operating surpluses, new docent and animal-adoption programs, a healthier tax situation, a more dynamic Board, a director steadily gaining confidence, and, still, a shaky construction project called Tropic World.

A HOST OF HORSES

This July 31, 1981, press release, entitled "The Clydesdales meet the Clydesdales at Brookfield Zoo," drew attention to popular Children's Zoo residents.

"The four Clydesdale draft horses of Brookfield Zoo's Children's Zoo will be meeting some well-known cousins on Monday, August 10. From 10 a.m. to 3 p.m. that day, the famous eight-horse Anheuser-Busch team and hitch will visit Brookfield Zoo.

"Starting when the zoo opens at 10 a.m., both teams will be tacked up with bridles, harnesses, etc.; this fascinating procedure will be done in public areas so visitors can watch. At about 11 a.m., the teams will move into the main zoo for their meeting. The horses, each of which weigh 2,000 to 2,500 pounds, will be paraded on the main circle around Brookfield Zoo's Roosevelt Fountain for the next two hours, then moved back to public areas for untacking."

1981 Corky Hamill steps down as Society chairman.
Penny Korhumel becomes the Society chair.

'82 The first Holiday Magic, County Fair Day, and National Pig Day are held.
The Gift Shop opens.
Tropic World: Africa opens.
The first Whirl is celebrated.
Two teeth are extracted from Babe the elephant.
Jane Goodall, Dian Fossey, Birute Galdikas, and Prince Philip all visit Tropic World.

'83 Tropic World: Asia opens.
Teddy Bear Picnic debuts.

'84 Tropic World: South America opens.
Discovery Center opens.
The zoo celebrates its 50th birthday.
A $12 million bond issuance for capital improvements is approved.

'85 Ground is broken for the new Seven Seas Panorama.
Clark the polar bear falls into his moat and dies.
The Conservation Biology Department is established.
The zoo helps found the Society for Conservation Biology.
Beta the gorilla undergoes dual hip replacements.
The steam train is shut down.

'86 The zoo takes over maintenance of a Metra train stop.
The first Zoo Run Run is held.

CHAPTER FOURTEEN

The People's Zoo

(1981-1986)

"A zoo has to be people-oriented. It has to do with the kinds of things that turn people on to it more and make people feel the zoo is important to them in providing the basics of life—pleasure."

"This zoo and these animals belong to the people of the entire Chicago area, and it is only through their involvement that Brookfield Zoo will continue to be one of the best and most innovative facilities of its kind in the world."

"The warm, fuzzy part of zookeeping is probably what I would take credit for bringing to Brookfield Zoo again. I think zoos are fun. I had a very strong feeling that there was a need to get people to think about the zoo in a much more fun and active way."

Penny Korhumel
Former Society Chair

Right: A child negotiates the stepping stones in Children's Zoo.

Penny Korhumel

Penny Korhumel

Pleasure. Recreation. Fun. If Corky Hamill broke the tradition of closely associated Society chairmen, new Board chair Penny Korhumel completely broke the mold. She originally became involved in the Society as a volunteer through her husband, Lee Korhumel, a trustee. Never one to sit on the sidelines, Penny jumped in as well, and her energy and enthusiasm soon won her a spot on the Board.

Her first major success was the Parents Program. Begun in 1977, it had by 1981 grossed over half a million dollars, garnering good public relations and a solid body of interested zoo "parents." Penny also cofounded the North Shore Association, the volunteer women's board. She was dynamic, bold, charismatic, a go-getter, and exceedingly people-oriented. Like the Board chairmen before her, Penny would leave her mark upon the Board and the zoo itself.

Penny's focus was people. In the constantly changing balancing act of the four elements of the zoo's mission—conservation, education, recreation, and research—recreation once again received more attention. The zoo began offering more programs for the public: parades, parties, concerts, and other enjoyable pastimes.

Left: Appropriately, Zoo Run Run is a time when kids can let loose and just run.

Below: A clown plants a puppet's kiss on a smiling visitor's cheek during County Fair Day.

PLAYTIME

At times, a zoo day can be all play and no work, as evidenced by a July 2, 1982, press release.

"At the end of your rope? The phrase will take on a very literal meaning for ten men and women and an African elephant on Saturday, July 10, at Brookfield Zoo. In the People vs. the Pachyderm, the teams of humans will be made up of winners of the Chicagoland Tug-of-War. At the other end of the rope will be Affie, Brookfield Zoo's eight-foot tall, three-ton female African elephant. The teams tugging against Affie will have won out over about 300 teams that first entered the Chicagoland Tug-of-War preliminaries, and over the 16 semi-finalist teams that will be competing at Brookfield Zoo on July 10. So they will have had some practice by the time they meet Affie. They will need it, too, according to the elephant's keepers, who often ask Affie to help clean up animal yards by moving logs, rocks, etc."

Right: Like everything else at the zoo during Holiday Magic, the Gift Shop is decked out in twinkling lights.

Affie the elephant's tug-of-war challenge, National Pig Day celebrations, County Fair Day, Holiday Magic, Teddy Bear Picnic, beer and wine sales, and a gift shop were all introduced in the early 1980s. They projected a lighthearted, friendlier image for the zoo in addition to their obvious marketing and financial goals. Some were more successful than others.

In 1982, when typical December attendance hovered around a few thousand, the first Holiday Magic helped attract 58,000 people. The free winter festival turned the zoo into a wonderland, with twinkling lights, carolers, storytellers, costumed characters, and special celebrity guests. As well, County Fair Day offered square dancing and craft demonstrations, luring 36,000 people to the zoo on an August day.

Also popular was National Pig Day, although it brought the academically oriented George Rabb some teasing from his colleagues. "Our pig Lassie celebrated National Pig Day with pictures in papers across the country," he jokingly lamented at the time. "In consequence, fellow zoo directors ask if I have no shame."

Another new endeavor, the Gift Shop, was motivated mainly by the need for additional income. Opened near the South Gate in July 1982, the shop was financed through bank loans (the first time the zoo constructed any facility through loans) and paid for itself in just a few years. It continues to be a source of steady revenue for the Society.

Above and left: Face painting and bear "veterinary" care are part of the enjoyment of participating in Teddy Bear Picnic.

Right: A hurdling pig entertains the crowds on National Pig Day.

Right: Tree decorating, a zoo aglow, and gibbons in motion are part of the Holiday Magic tradition.

PR PIG

Sometimes zoo staff had a little fun with special events. In February 1982, the Public Relations Department composed this creative letter, purely for fun, in honor of National Pig Day.

"Dear Miss Piggy,

"I have long been an admirer of you, and have tried to model myself after you in every way. My name is Lassie and I am a Poland China X Tamworth gilt (maiden pig), who lives at Brookfield Zoo's Children's Zoo. I am a star of the Animals in Action program in which I perform feats of grace and intelligence such as answering a phone, opening and closing doors, leaping over barrels, curtsying, retrieving and a variety of other behaviors. I also understand nine languages.

"I know none of this is a surprise to you as a fellow pig of the world. In any case, March 2 is National Pig Day and also my third birthday. Since my people are planning a party for me I wanted to extend an invitation to you as honored guest. I know it is short notice, but I hope you can come."

"Love, Lassie

"Star Pig, Brookfield Children's Zoo

"P.S. Please R.S.V.P. Kermie can come too."

Tropic World Finally Opens

Alongside the new people-oriented programs, a very significant event took place on May 8, 1982: the much-awaited opening of Tropic World—or at least a part of it. Begun under President Dickinson and Director Crowcroft and under construction for almost a decade, "Dickinson's folly" finally became "Dickinson's triumph." Tropic World: Africa was the first of three sections to open. With its thunderstorms, waterfalls, vibrant foliage, and lack of visual barriers between animals and visitors, the mixed-species exhibit was revolutionary for zoos. At the time, it was the largest zoo exhibit building in the world.

Tropic World was also unique in mixing species—among them pygmy hippopotamuses, colobus monkeys, mandrills, and a host of violet turacos, barbets, hornbills, and other birds—that normally lived together in the wild but were housed separately in captivity. "This building is as revolutionary to the zoological world as the space shuttle is to flight," commented curator of primates Ben Beck. The public found the African exhibit truly spectacular due to the western lowland gorillas. A gorilla family group, presided over by the magnificent Samson, climbed trees, played, ate, and threatened and groomed each other just a few unobstructed feet away from onlookers.

The exhibit drew visitors from around the world, including primate researchers Jane Goodall, Dian Fossey, and Birute Galdikas. His Royal Highness Prince Philip, Duke of Edinburgh, then president of World Wildlife Fund International, visited and declared it "a marvelous success and experience for people and animals alike."

Above: Former Society president Bill Dickinson and Forest Preserve District commisioner Jeanne Quinn cut the ceremonial garland at a Tropic World opening celebration.

FAVORABLE REVIEW

In 1995, in *Animal Keeper No. 2*, BBC television series *Zoo 2000* presenter Jeremy Cherfas explained why Tropic World is his favorite enclosure in any zoo, anywhere.

"Chicago is a huge urban conglomeration, and Tropic World allows the people of Chicago to experience something that is very like the wild. Once you've got them in that frame of mind, you've got people who are much more interested in preserving the wild, and that's what I think zoos should be all about: changing people's attitudes, educating them, making them think. Tropic World is truly remarkable in the way in which it does that: it does a better job than any other single exhibit that I have seen of changing the attitude of...people. And in doing something so radically different, they've altered the way in which zoos approach that changing of attitudes. It's a bringing up to date of Carl Hagenbeck, who in 1907, in his zoo in Hamburg, dispensed with bars and put animals behind concealed barriers for the first time."

Right: Prince Philip admires a hadada ibis during his visit to Tropic World: Africa.

Brookfield Zoo Tropic World

Left: The black-tie Tropic Whirl began an annual tradition that attracted a new audience to Brookfield Zoo.

Below: The periodic rainstorm in Tropic World provokes interesting and natural behaviors in the exhibit animals—and humans like it, too.

TROPIC WORLD FACTS

Building Dimensions: 475 feet long by 110 feet wide by 75 feet high, 55 feet above grade, 20 feet below grade

Concrete: 11,000 tons total, or 5,500 cubic yards

Structural Steel: 655 tons total

Skylights: 84 four-foot by 20-foot panels

Temperature: 70° to 80° Fahrenheit, 50% relative humidity

Ventilation: 400 tons of air-conditioning

Cost: Approximately $10 million

Special Effects: 40- and 50-foot trees, waterfalls, rivers, ponds, a stand of bamboo, a trickling stream, high cliffs, and a rainstorm complete with booming thunder

The opening of Tropic World also prompted the zoo to host its first black-tie gala, called Tropic Whirl. This provided a most unusual sight: women in ball gowns and men in tuxedos in the naturalistic setting of an African rain forest. Although the gala didn't raise any funds the first few years—in fact, it lost money at first—it attracted a new audience and provided unique opportunities for public relations. Eventually, the Whirl became one of the Society's most substantial annual fundraising efforts.

In 1982, the opening of Tropic World: Africa drove attendance up to 2,082,643—the first time the zoo had broken the two million mark in eight years. The remaining two sections of Tropic World, Asia and South America, opened in 1983 and 1984, respectively, as they were completed.

Discovery Center

A different type of facility opened in January 1984. Located near the North Gate, Discovery Center, Brookfield Zoo's first official education and orientation building, is today outfitted with sophisticated audio-visual equipment to provide visitors with an exciting multi-image preview of what the zoo offers.

Although the old director's cottage, long since torn down, had served as an education office for several years, Discovery Center marked the first time the zoo constructed a building to reflect its interest in education and orientation. The $1.5 million building was also the first facility to be financed entirely through private contributions, thanks to solicitations by trustees Lee Korhumel and Robert "Tad" Carr.

Early plans placed the orientation building adjacent to the South Gate, at the base of the mall, with glass walls providing a spectacular view of Roosevelt Fountain. They called for a three-story education building and a separate underground visitor center. Later, the plans were reworked to include one building housing a two-story auditorium, a family learning center, a bookstore, a gift shop, a reading library, a banquet hall and catering kitchen, an information and orientation lobby, restrooms, public lockers, and exhibits on zoos and conservation.

The southern location was considered ideal for the same reasons as Tropic World's location: by offering more indoor exhibits, it boosted the "year-round zoo" concept the Society was attempting to create in the southwest quadrant. However, reality intruded in the form of a $3 million price tag, and bit by bit the plans for the building first shrank and then moved to the less dense northern section of the zoo.

When finished, Discovery Center consisted of only a large auditorium, a holding theater, and a lobby with an information desk, washrooms, and drinking fountains. (A few years later, an addition provided several classrooms for school groups, meetings, and other assemblages.) Although the building was not as grand as first planned, it became hard to imagine life without it as lectures, conferences, and social events began to fill up the building's schedule months in advance.

A Milestone Passes

Indeed, 1984 was a busy year. In addition to the opening of Tropic World: South America and Discovery Center, the year marked Brookfield Zoo's 50th anniversary, and gala events were planned. A "Music at the Zoo" series, presenting concerts by the Osmond Family, the Beach Boys, and Johnny Cash and the Gatlin Brothers, attracted over 26,000 people. To commemorate the Sunday, July 1, anniversary, the Chicago Chamber Brass performed music from the 1930s, every 50th car entering the zoo received a prize, and a ceremony was held on one of the malls. Other festivities included a mountain of birthday cake and animals greeting visitors.

Forest Preserve District president George Dunne took a page out of Seymour Simon's 1964 anniversary speech. "If we emulate the heritage we have received," he said, "imagine what the zoo will be 50 years hence." Again, it was confirmation that the zoo always looked ahead to the next challenge and rarely paused to admire its accomplishments.

"WHERE ARE WE?"

The following comments were made by George Rabb on July 12, 1984, on the occasion of his annual report to governing members.

"Where are we fifty years later?

"We are in transition. Superficially, the basic facilities, as far as our public is concerned, have changed relatively little, with the exception of Tropic World and Seven Seas. The style of presentation, the simulation or at least suggestion of natural situations, has been transposed to many of the indoor exhibits. There are other changes, too, that have contributed to the present diversity of experiences available to the public—the transport system, the Indian Lake Trail, the nocturnal naturalistic exhibits at Australia House and in the Predator Ecology section, and the Children's Zoo.

"The physical plant was allowed to deteriorate in the middle course of the zoo's history and in many ways is inadequate to the fulfillment of needs in maintaining and displaying animals today. There is a basic shopping list of some $24,000,000 in exhibit projects.

"On the other hand, the zoo has grown greatly in the last 20 years in its capacity for maintenance and for service. For example, there are educational services of several kinds, bolstered by a superb volunteer corps and lately by the addition of a visitor orientation facility. The quality and quantity of medical and technical care for the animals is a light year ahead of what it was at the beginning of the zoo.

"Where are we in other respects and how are we looking to the future?

"In the first place, we are looking ahead and planning. We have staff capable of contributing to strategies and tactics for marketing, building, and managing for the future.

"However, there are some general matters that we should be clear about. One is that having a living animal collection is a much more complex and expensive proposition than it was at the beginning of the zoo. To maintain animal populations of the larger vertebrates is different from acquiring and disposing of individual animals. The former is the business we are in today for various reasons, including continuing degradation of natural environments, treaties and laws affecting trade in wild animals, and heightened public awareness of animal welfare.

"I close by emphasizing that we have accomplished a great deal, that we are very much one of the most beautiful zoological parks in the world, with several distinctive and unmatched exhibit features, that we have much to be proud of in our history, and a great challenge to be worthy of our heritage. I believe we are capable of meeting that challenge."

Above: The grounds bloomed in reflection of the zoo's 50th birthday.

A Second Bond Issuance

The year was busy for other reasons. The Forest Preserve District, ever mindful of Brookfield Zoo's ongoing financial battles, approved a $12 million bond issuance for capital improvements. However, unlike the earlier $15 million bond issuance granted during Peter Crowcroft's tenure, there was a catch: within a five-year period, the Society would have to match the bond issuance dollar for dollar. Unpracticed at fundraising, the Board rolled up its sleeves and, under Penny Korhumel's leadership, began raising $12 million.

The Board strategized, first by estimating it could raise about $4.5 million over five years through memberships, animal adoptions, and other development activities. Then, to get the campaign off the ground before going public, it decided to pursue a few large "cornerstone" gifts. As trustee Bill Lane stated, "We are looking for strategically planned gifts to make our unveiling.... That may take a year of special dinners in the middle of the lions' cage."

In fact, the task proved easier than first thought. Past chairman Corky Hamill and his wife, Joan, donated half a million dollars. Other trustees followed suit, none with quite so large a gift, but all generous on their own terms. The trustees also began soliciting foundations, corporations, and their friends and colleagues for donations. By mid-1985, they were already at the $2 million mark. The Forest Preserve District, seeing the Society well underway with its matching obligation, sold $6 million of bonds in 1985, providing the zoo with cash to begin its new programs.

The big-ticket item was a new Seven Seas Panorama. The zoo had outgrown the 1961 dolphinarium and needed a larger seating capacity, bigger pools, and more holding pools to effectively work with the animals. The old facility, so revolutionary when it was built, had suffered from two decades of saltwater and overuse. Small sections of the roof fell from time to time, floors crumbled, and tanks leaked. Much had been learned about inland marine-mammal facilities in the 20-plus years since the original Seven Seas had been built, and the trustees knew that only a new facility could maintain its animals and its visitorship.

Above: Ralph Graham's wonderful mural of animals of the world couldn't be saved during renovation on Safari Lodge.

The Board estimated the cost of a new facility—including a demonstration pool, holding pools, support facilities, public spaces, and neighboring pinniped pools for Olga the walrus, seals, and sea lions—at $12 million. With $6 million from the Forest Preserve District, another $2 million already pledged in the fundraising campaign, and income from memberships and animal adoptions, the trustees committed to the new exhibit. Ground was broken in fall 1985.

The effects of the new Seven Seas Panorama rippled. Anticipating that the facility would attract many more visitors to the zoo's northeast corner, the trustees decided to renovate Safari Lodge. Formerly a sit-down restaurant, it was remodeled to serve more visitors in a fast-food type of situation. Sadly, there was no way to save a wall on which Ralph Graham had painted, years earlier, a giant mural of the world's animals placed on their corresponding continents.

Below: Disembarking the local Metra train at the "Zoo Stop" is an unusual experience, thanks to rock work resembling that at the zoo a few blocks away.

Another change, part of the Seven Seas construction, was unpopular: the steam train was discontinued. The train tracks ran through the construction site, and rerouting proved impractical. Although zoo neighbors had been complaining for years about the train's frequent whistle, it became a bit of a legend once it no longer ran. The rubber-tired safari trams continued to provide transportation and tours around the zoo, but the experience wasn't quite the same. A decade later, people still inquire about the train, which apparently left its mark on many young minds.

With the loss of its train, the zoo adopted a different type of transportation experience. In 1986, the Society took over maintenance of a Metra train stop in Brookfield and rededicated it as the "Zoo Stop." The building structure was renovated and several lion sculptures were added to provide passengers with a reminder of the nearby animal adventure.

The Board, with help from staff, had devised a five-year plan for spending the Forest Preserve District's $12 million and the matching funds from the Society's efforts. At the top of the list was the new Seven Seas, followed by renovations to Lion House, a new African exhibit, and improvements in educational offerings.

The Board felt pride and accomplishment at the success of its fundraising campaign. By the end of 1986, pledges had reached $6.5 million, more than halfway to the goal. And this from a group of people for whom fundraising was a new and fairly frightening prospect. Much of the credit must go to Penny Korhumel, who pushed, prodded, and cheered through the whole process.

Korhumel was not without her own personal struggles at the time. In 1984, she announced that she and fellow trustee Lee Korhumel were divorcing and that she needed a compensating position to support herself. Her role as chairman of the Board was time-consuming and completely voluntary. Unwilling to lose its dynamic chairman, the Board decided to ask Korhumel to maintain her position and also serve as a special paid consultant on special events, philanthropy, and membership. It was a role that suited her well, and she accepted with pleasure. After all, in addition to the fundraising campaign, the popular Parents Program had been her brainchild.

Keeping the Veterinarians Busy

Animal happenings continued apace. The early 1980s were particularly busy for the veterinarians, with all kinds of unusual medical procedures: a rhinoceros pedicure of sorts, an elephant tooth extraction, emergency polar bear surgery, and dual hip replacements for a gorilla.

Brooke, a female black rhino, developed cracks in the toenails of both rear feet. If left unattended, such separations can lead to infection and lameness. Brooke was anesthetized and epoxy was laid in the cracks. The procedure had often been performed on horses but never before on a rhino. In the end, it was a relatively simple operation, lasting only about a half hour, and Brooke's problems were solved.

Babe the elephant's tooth extraction was more involved. Staff noticed that the 36-year-old pachyderm was losing weight—about 500 pounds, it turned out. The culprit, they discovered, was "malocclusion," in which upper and lower teeth don't meet correctly. If an elephant can't properly grind its food, it could starve.

Although tooth extractions had been performed on elephants before, this particular surgery "was a toughie," according to Dr. Dave Fagan, the animal dentist from the San Diego Zoo who performed the operation. On March 24, 1982, Fagan went to work.

Excerpts from docent Terry Dudas' eyewitness account, published in the zoo's *Docent Journal,* tell the story. "By 10:00 a.m....Babe was isolated and injected with a 6cc dose of M-99, a morphine derivative so powerful that a drop could kill a human being. In all, Babe received $8\frac{1}{2}$ ccs throughout the procedure. Next, Babe was assisted to her side by keepers who pulled on the stout ropes and the harness attached to her body. By 10:21 a.m., she was out like a light.

"The crew went into action transforming the elephant stall into an impromptu surgery. An IV was started in a vein behind Babe's right ear. Oxygen was administered through her trunk, and a monitor set up to track her heart rate. Babe's mouth was secured with ropes attached to both upper and lower jaws so that a good gape resulted." Fagan was able to extract the tooth by 11:25 a.m.

"Now the business of cleansing the wound was at hand," wrote Dudas. "Bucket after bucket of water was used to swab out the mouth and empty socket. It was close to noon when Dr.

Fagan finished the first portion of the operation. He changed his jumpsuit and returned to the job. After another in-mouth inspection, the dentist chose to remove only the crown of the lower tooth. Work began as before, and within 45 minutes the job was done."

Babe quickly rebounded from her surgery, happily gaining back the weight she had lost and probably not missing the six-pound, 12-ounce upper molar and one-pound, four-ounce crown.

Above: Brooke underwent surgery to fill in cracks in her feet. Her "pedicure" prevented lameness that usually strikes horses.

Left: Babe the elephant loses eight pounds of tooth as veterinarians remove a molar and a crown.

Clark the polar bear was not as lucky. In a bizarre incident in January 1985, the adult male bear oddly took a tumble into his moat, sustaining numerous injuries. Zoo staff scrambled to help. Welders built a special stretcher to accommodate the huge animal, and the veterinarians, keepers, and grounds crew managed to lift the unwieldy Clark out of the moat. X rays of the bear were seen by several consulting veterinarians.

Clark's condition deteriorated and he failed to respond to treatment, leading the veterinarians to conclude that his injuries were more extensive than first thought. They agreed that his condition was so bad that he wouldn't be able to undergo surgery. Reluctantly, the well-loved bear was euthanized. Autopsy results revealed a broken neck.

Female gorilla Beta fared better with her hip replacements. For this effort, veterinarians teamed up with specialists from Rush-Presbyterian-St. Luke's Hospital to replace the gorilla's painfully arthritic hip joints with stainless-steel implants. The radical procedure, a first with a great ape, gave Beta some relief. This was to be the second time Beta made zoological history because she was the world's first successfully artificially inseminated gorilla, which took place while she was on loan to the Memphis Zoo.

Veterinary science had come a long way since 1934—and even since the opening of Brookfield Zoo's hospital in 1952. The handiest of zoo medical equipment—the dart gun, used to immobilize animals—wasn't developed until the late 1950s. Zoological medicine wasn't formally taught at universities before 1968, and the American Association of Zoo Veterinarians wasn't formed until the 1960s as well. In 30 years, exotic animal care went from basic care to gorilla hip replacements and other such treatments.

After 15-year veterinarian Weaver Williamson left in 1969, the zoo hired a number of veterinarians, none staying more than a few years. Part of the problem was the hospital facility itself. Built in 1951, it was not equipped to handle more modern enterprises. A new hospital was added to the building wish list.

Left: Beta was the first gorilla to benefit from dual hip replacements, which gave her relief from arthritis.

Conservation Biology

On the surface, a zoo visit in 1985 wasn't all that different than a visit 50 years earlier. Many of the same buildings stood, the mall was still spectacular, a family could see lions, bears, and elephants, and children still begged for ice cream. Behind the scenes, though, caring for and learning about animals had changed.

In 1985, Brookfield Zoo established its Conservation Biology Department, a group of researchers concentrating on the behavior, ecology, and genetic health of populations of small animals. Population geneticist Dr. Robert Lacy soon joined the staff, as did behavioral researcher Dr. Jeanne Altmann and ecological specialist Dr. Pamela Parker—all sporting advanced scientific degrees from leading universities. It was a rebirth, in spectacular fashion, of the zoo's research program, which had dwindled due to lack of funds in the 1970s.

This new research was different than that conducted in the '50s and '60s. Instead of focusing on the biology of individual species, it was oriented more toward conservation. Goals centered around preserving biodiversity and managing small populations. In addition to studying baboon and dolphin behavior, newborn okapis and rhinos, and ecosystem management in South Australia, the new staff began long-term research on the effects of inbreeding in small populations.

Efforts to research the effects of inbreeding in small populations actually began with small animals. In 1985, Dr. Bruce Brewer returned to the zoo, having worked there for several years before leaving to earn his doctoral degree at Cornell. His thesis topic, in the field of population genetics, involved extensive research on inbreeding in large colonies of mice he had trapped in Texas and Florida. At the conclusion of his research, the colonies had grown to several hundred, and Brewer brought the mice to the zoo to continue his studies.

Transporting several hundred mice, however, is a bit tricky. His arrival at the zoo was a sight as he pulled up in a 20-foot truck filled with mice. Hundreds of these creatures in such a small space can generate considerable heat over a long journey, so Brewer had lined the walls of the truck with block ice to prevent the little animals from overheating. The mice were carefully transported to the basement of Tropic World and later moved to Lion House.

RECOLLECTIONS

My favorite story happened one afternoon when I was just sitting on a zoo bench. There was a family that had been there for some time. The little boy was fascinated with the elephants. His father finally said to him, "Come on, Bobby, we have to go."

"Oh, come on, Dad," said the kid.

The father replied, "We have to get home. Besides, you can see elephants on television. We even have a tape of elephants."

"Yeah, Dad, but it's not the same. I had no idea they were so big!"

You can't achieve on television what you can see in person. Until you appreciate it, you're not going to take an active interest in saving them.

Norris "Mike" Love
Current Trustee

Brewer eventually turned the project over to Lacy, and the zoo received a grant from the National Science Foundation to support this research and funds from the Institute of Museum Services to build a "mouse house" on zoo grounds specifically for the project.

In a 1989 article in *Bison* magazine called "How Many Pairs are Needed on the Ark?," Lacy discussed the importance of changes in thinking about the number of individuals within a species a zoo must maintain. "For ethical, legal, and economic reasons," he wrote, "zoos can no longer harvest from the wild to obtain most of the animals they wish to display. Within a few decades, zoos will probably be able to display to the public only those species which can be sustained by captive breeding.

"This shift in management, from being consumers to being producers of wildlife, requires that zoos provide more than just the care necessary to sustain each animal through a long, healthy life in captivity. Zoos must now also undertake population planning and propagation to assure breeding through decades or even centuries of stewardship.

"How many of each species must Brookfield, or collectively the world's zoos, keep to assure long-term survival in captivity? Certainly the pair of each species rescued by Noah would not suffice for a long-term breeding program: the next generation would all be brothers and sisters, and subsequent genetic problems caused by inbreeding would be severe. Moreover, with just one breeding pair, the next generation could easily be all males or all females—precluding any further reproduction. Disease or accident could readily eliminate such a tiny population. With more than one pair, there is more hope for long-term survival, but any small population faces the same genetic and demographic risks.

"At Brookfield, we are engaged in research designed to help us predict the severity of inbreeding depression for any species of concern and, by implication, the minimum numbers needed to sustain a genetically healthy population through many generations."

Shortly after forming its own Conservation Biology Department, the zoo helped establish the international Society for Conservation Biology, which brought together professional biologists in universities, zoos, wildlife agencies, and other organizations in hopes of sharing and compiling knowledge needed for effective conservation.

Above and left: The zoo conducts research involving mice as geneticists consider the effects of inbreeding in small populations.

The People Factor

Brookfield Zoo was simultaneously broadening the scope of its activities and the depth of its involvement in animal management. Professionals from a multitude of disciplines were working at the zoo, each one helping expand the body of knowledge in their field. By 1985, the zoo roster included professional horticulturists, zoologists, biologists, development officers, public relations personnel, editors, designers, educators, craftsmen, chefs, photographers, paramedics, and business administrators. The size of the staff had grown to 300 full-time and 350 seasonal workers.

As always, strange happenings were inevitable, such as the time welder Craig Tichelar fell into the lion moat. He was working on a project on a painter's plank directly over the moat when he lost his footing. His fall was broken by welding cables, and he came to a halt close to the bottom. He tried to climb the cables but was prevented from fully extracting himself because of a "lip" that hung over the top of the moat.

Several times Tichelar yelled to people he could hear above, "but I guess they just thought someone was fooling around," he later said. "I even tried taking my shirt off and putting it on the end of one of the steel bars. Nobody ever came. I was down there for several hours."

Finally, toward the end of the day, he heard some kids who were planning to hide from security staff and spend the night in the zoo. Tichelar yelled once again. Soon fire engines, ambulances, and police cars swarmed the walkway and he was helped to safety.

Working with animals is never routine. The keeper staff had their share of unusual happenings. "Normally, when we fed Susie the wolf [in her temporary cage at the animal hospital], we'd go in there with her," recalled Ron Zdrubecky. "One day, I went into the outside cage—it was winter, no jacket—and slowly the door slid and locked. There I was, locked in the cage with Susie. I said, 'Hi, Susie!' I didn't want to start screaming to someone. Finally I saw Mary Rabb walking by and I called, 'Mary, can you come and let me out? I locked myself in the cage!' I had been in there about five minutes and was starting to get nervous. It was scary."

In all such stories, people play a prominent role. Truly, a zoo is as much about people as it is about animals because it needs both equally to survive. Board chair Penny Korhumel was wise to recognize that as Director Rabb built up the staff's abilities and the institution's conservation involvements, equal focus was needed on the recreational aspect of the business. With new exhibits such as Tropic World, popular programs such as Holiday Magic, Zoo Run Run, and National Pig Day, the capabilities for zoo orientation in the new Discovery Center, and a new Seven Seas under construction, visitor satisfaction was greatly improved. Korhumel focused on the visitors while Rabb concentrated on the internal operations.

The combination struck a good balance, and the scope of operations grew tremendously, as did the budget. In 1935, operating costs had been less than $250,000. It took two decades, in 1956, before that number had grown to $1 million. And then it took off. In 1983, $10 million was spent on operating costs. That number would triple in the next decade as growth continued.

Left: During Zoo Run Run, young racers dash for the finish line with determination.

CHAPTER FIFTEEN

Extraordinary Change

(1987-1990)

Korhumel Departs

As the multifaceted, multimillion-dollar organization that was Brookfield Zoo moved into 1987, more changes were ahead.

Penny Korhumel left the organization in a manner similar to how she joined it: due to matters of the heart. After divorcing trustee Lee Korhumel, she married the zoo's marketing director, Ted Beattie, in 1985. Two years later, the Knoxville Zoo offered the Beatties a tempting package: they would hire Ted as executive director and Penny as community relations director. Although Brookfield Zoo's Board had discussed eliminating the six-year term limit on officers so Korhumel might remain chairman, the offer was too tempting to pass up. Despite the trustees' best efforts at persuasion, the Beatties moved to Tennessee.

LOVE AT THE ZOO

Penny and Ted Beattie have not been the zoo's only lovebirds. In fact, there have been several employee weddings in the park.

With marriage license already in hand, Carol and Vince Sodaro, both primate keepers, made a spur-of-the-moment decision on Valentine's Day in 1983 to get married on their break. Witnessed by fellow keepers, they were united in front of the orangutan cage by zoo employee Mike Kowalchek, a mail-order minister.

On their wedding day in July 1985, Bonnie and Bob Polis (below), a zoo tram driver and a security officer, respectively, had a tram take their wedding party around the zoo for official photos.

Aside from these occasions, the list of employees marrying fellow employees is long, a testimony to the shared interests that unite the work force.

Photo Courtesy Bonnie and Bob Polis

One of Korhumel's last duties was to preside over the seaweed-cutting ceremony for the June 6, 1987, opening of the $13 million Seven Seas Panorama. Moving the animals from the old facility to the new one proved to be a big undertaking. The dolphins were moved in the spring of 1987 with relatively few problems. After all, the zoo had managed to transport dolphins across the many miles between Florida and Chicago.

Olga the walrus was a little trickier. She hadn't been moved since she first arrived at the zoo, some 1,500 pounds and 25 years earlier. For several months, Olga's trainers acclimated her to the large dumpster in which she would eventually be transported. The pinniped area at the new Seven Seas wasn't completed until fall of 1987, by which time Olga was ready to move. To her keepers' relief, she cooperated. Her adoring public admired her in the larger, more naturalistic exhibit.

Unfortunately, there were glitches in the new facility. The dolphin pools leaked due to a problem with the liner. No repairs could be made with the animals in the exhibits, so in late 1987 the dolphins were temporarily moved back to the old Seven Seas while the pools were fixed. Again, all moves went smoothly, although the inconvenience was costly in terms of lost show revenue.

By the time the old Seven Seas closed in 1987, after more than 25 years, approximately 11.5 million people had enjoyed seeing the dolphins there.

Left: Moving Olga the walrus and the bottlenosed dolphins to the new Seven Seas was an elaborate process. The ado was finally worth it when state representative Jack Kubik, Illinois senator Judy Baar Topinka, and commissioner Harold Tyrrell cut the ribbon at the opening (photo, left).

Below and inset: Seven Seas Panorama has plenty more indoor and outdoor space for animals and humans.

The New Board Chair

Penny Korhumel Beattie's departure created a vacancy in the position of chairman of the Board. A relative newcomer—Philip W. K. Sweet, Jr., a former chief executive officer of the Northern Trust Company—was elected as her successor. Although only a two-year veteran of the zoo's Board, Sweet had been very effective in the fundraising campaign, and his fellow trustees agreed he would make a good chairman. After the originality of Chairman Korhumel, Chairman Sweet represented a return to the Society's roots in terms of his background at the Northern Trust Company.

Philip W. K. Sweet, Jr.

The Society's connection with Northern Trust was many years old—and quite strong. Solomon A. Smith, who had served as Society treasurer from 1931 until his death in 1963, was the son of the company's founder. Solomon's son, Edward Byron Smith, took over as zoo treasurer in 1963 and served in that capacity until 1976, when the mantle passed to fellow Northern Trust executive Lawrence Gougler. Early zoo trustees Charles Hutchinson, Martin Ryerson, Ezra Warner, John Pirie, and James Simpson had been Northern Trust employees as well. Throughout the zoo's history, numerous Northern Trust executives have served on the Society's Board, providing an unofficial corporate sponsorship. Philip Sweet, part of the tradition, was the first to ascend to the chairmanship.

By the time Sweet became chairman, the fundraising campaign had topped $11 million. The Board committed to a $3.5 million renovation of Lion House and continued planning for a new African exhibit at the site of Giraffe House.

Financially, by the late 1980s, the Society had turned the corner. Under the leadership of President George Dunne and General Superintendent Art Janura, the Forest Preserve District's steady support took the form of increased leeway in admission rates and other fees, additional tax revenue, and the second round of bond-issuance funds. By revitalizing and involving the entire Board, former chairman Corky Hamill was a major factor in ending the downward spiral. Penny Korhumel Beattie fostered the fundraising campaign that restored the Board's faith in itself and allowed for additional capital improvements. Finally, Director George Rabb, through careful administration of the operating budget and selective additions to the professional staff, helped steer the institution in a more stable direction.

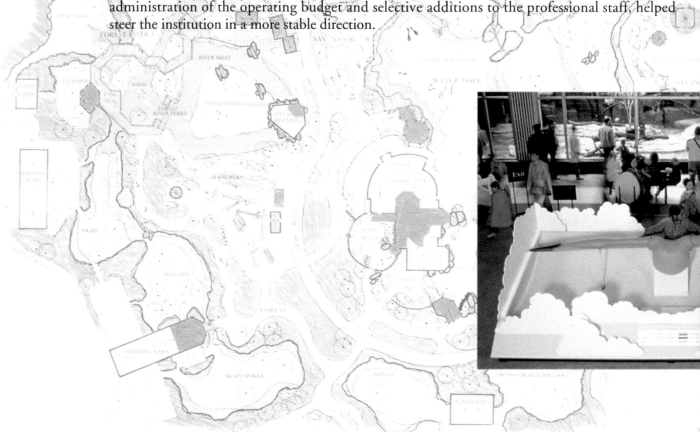

New Territories

As the zoo matured, it delved into unexplored territories. One was an educational outreach program called CONNECTIONS. Begun in 1987, the program was designed to use zoo visits to enhance classroom studies. Funded by a grant from the Joyce Foundation, CONNECTIONS provides materials to schools to supplement the state-mandated science curriculum. Materials include slides and other visual matter for students to view before their zoo visit, a teacher's guide, and postvisit activities. CONNECTIONS also incorporates a lecture by zoo personnel during the students' zoo visit.

The exhibits also began to take on a different flavor. The same year Seven Seas Panorama opened, an unusual exhibit took shape in Aquatic Bird House. The staff, aware that visitors were learning remarkably little about birds' physiology, behavior, and anatomy, created interactive displays designed to fill in the gaps. The "Be a Bird" displays, which were funded by the National Science Foundation and other sources, were unusual in that they didn't include live birds, but they were an immediate hit with the public. They included the "wing walk," a boardwalk with arm rails that helped people simulate the wing movement of a flying bird; a computer game that let people take on the challenges of bird life; and a docent center that allowed visitors to touch bird artifacts. Most popular was the "flying strength machine," an oversized set of wings people could try to manipulate as they learned about birds' incredible chest strength.

The zoo created these projects with the help of philanthropic foundations. At the same time, the capital-improvement program was moving ahead as Lion House and Giraffe House were renovated. However, funds were still desperately needed for repairs to roads, pipes, and other essentials. In 1989, thanks to efforts from Representative Jack Kubik and others, the state of Illinois came through with a $10 million "Build Illinois" grant to be spent on such projects during a three-year period. The zoo went ahead with badly needed behind-the-scenes repairs that had been unaddressed for years.

The campaign had met its $12 million goal, so fundraising took a back seat as the Board effected new ventures to set policies and direction. Phil Sweet, building on Corky Hamill's work, wanted the trustees more involved, so he decreased the annual number of full Board meetings from six to four and instead created more committees to direct various programs and interests.

The old Scientific and Educational Advisory Committee had been reconstituted as the SEACON Committee, with responsibility for reviewing conservation grants, so a new educational committee was needed. Also convened were committees to address marketing and government affairs. The trustees were asked to serve in groups that could benefit from their professional expertise.

Below left and right: Visitors learn the basics of bird flight in the "flying strength machine" and "wing walk" sections of Aquatic Bird House.

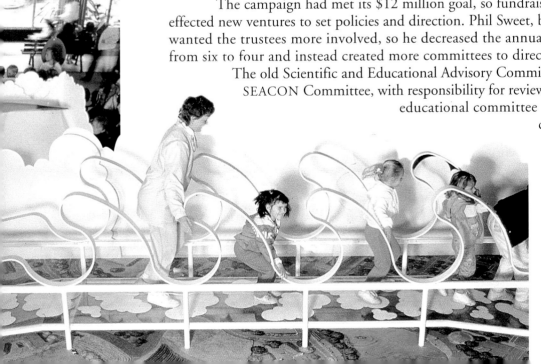

"Sad Songs for Olga"

There were some unfortunate changes in the animal collection. In 1988, the zoo lost two vital members of its family, much to the disappointment of keepers and visitors. Beloved Olga died in August as a result of age-induced kidney and heart ailments. At age 27, she was the oldest walrus in the country. The zoo received dozens of sympathy cards and children's artwork expressing sadness at her passing. The *Chicago Sun-Times* honored Olga with a front-page obituary, and the *Chicago Tribune* featured a "Voice of the People" tribute entitled "Loving, lovable, unforgettable Olga." Recognizing the need for a final good-bye to this individual who had touched so many, the zoo offered a memorial service and commissioned a life-size bronze statue (lower left) of the beloved walrus.

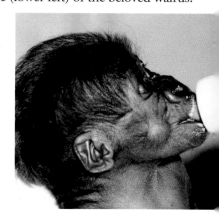

The other heartbreak came with the death of Samson the gorilla. He died in March of a brain tumor, robbing the gorilla world of a magnificent group leader and breeder. His passing created havoc in the gorilla group because the species depends on a rigid hierarchical social structure, with the silverback unquestionably at the top. With the loss of their leader, other group members fought for dominance. Adding to the confusion was the fact that mature females Alpha and Babs both gave birth to Samson's offspring within months of his death.

The newborns, Kwizera and Kwisha, whose Swahili names mean "to hope" and "the final one," respectively, were slightly injured as they were caught in the middle of the squabbling. Wary of the situation, staff decided to remove the two youngsters from the group so they could be hand-reared. The two were placed in an off-exhibit enclosure (complete with a playpen) from which they could see, but not interact with, the adult gorillas.

Brookfield Zoo avoids hand-rearing except when absolutely necessary because hand-raised animals are generally not as socially successful as those raised by their natural parents. Forced to hand-rear the two gorillas, the zoo decided to try an unorthodox approach to overcome the youngsters' fear of mature gorillas. One by one, keepers took turns entering their enclosure dressed in a gorilla suit and employing gorilla vocalizations and postures. "We weren't sure what they'd learn from all this," noted primate curator Ann Baker, "but we wanted them to get used to the idea of something very large, black, and hairy."

While perhaps unusual, the trick may have helped, for the two gorillas were eventually successfully reintroduced to the adult gorillas, although the participants are loathe to ascribe too much credit to the gorilla suit.

While keepers in Tropic World: Africa were jumping about in the gorilla suit, Tropic World: Asia keepers had their own difficulties. Orangutans Sam and Katie were diagnosed as mild diabetics, challenging the staff to figure out how to administer daily insulin to the powerful adult animals. Medication mixed into their food failed to do the trick, so keepers decided to try techniques learned through years of dolphin training.

TRIBUTE TO A PINNIPED

An editorial in the August 16, 1988, *Chicago Tribune* asked people to "sing no sad songs for Olga."

"Coming at you head-on, with her flippers at her sides, Olga looked like a shaggy mop with a 3,000 pound handle. But lovable, Lord she was lovable.

"Lolling around in her pool out at Brookfield Zoo, sometimes floating on her back, her tail stuck through an old black inner tube as she basked in the sun, her old buddy, Amy, the harbor seal, frolicking around her, Olga was a star.

"If you have to ask why, you probably won't understand. Just as you probably wouldn't be able to figure how a ton and a half of walrus that gobbled down 50 to 60 pounds of seafood a day at a cost of $15,000 [per year] could qualify high in the lovable sweepstakes.

"It's just that...well, stars are born, not made. There was Olga, taken in the wild waters off Norway in 1961, a bona fide star almost from her arrival at Brookfield in 1962. And from the time the zoo instituted its adopt-an-animal program, she was the most popular adoptee. More than 1,300 people donated $20 a year in her name. With an appetite like Olga's, that had to be comfort money. Small wonder she performed so merrily, blowing kisses—and only the occasional mouthful of water—at her fans.

"On Sunday, Olga, the oldest at 27 of the half dozen walruses in captivity in American zoos, died, apparently of advanced age. She'll be missed for sure. All 3,000 lovable pounds of her. But sing no sad songs for Olga. She went out as she came in—a star."

Above: Kwizera (photo, left) and Kwisha learned how to relate to adults of their species from a merely passable gorilla: a keeper in a gorilla suit (inset).

Above right: Step by step, orangutans Katie (photo, left) and Sam slowly learned to accept insulin injections to help manage their diabetes.

Peter Gorner's front-page *Chicago Tribune* article of April 23, 1989, described the process. "First the orangs were lured to the front of the cage for food. Then the handlers put two metal clips through the wires and taught the animals to touch them. Over time, they learned to position their arms properly. The keepers also mixed in enjoyable play behaviors, as they gradually accustomed the apes to letting their forearms be touched, then to be pinched, then pinched with increasing amounts of pressure. Getting them used to the alcohol wipe came next, followed by the hypodermic. The keepers also taught the orangs to urinate in their holding cage so that the urine may be collected and analyzed for sugar."

The painstaking training—14 sessions a week for nearly a year—paid off. Sam and Katie gradually learned to accept the insulin injections and their diabetes was brought under control.

Looking Back

The next year, during the zoo's annual meeting, George Rabb looked back on the previous 10 years, stating that the institution had "concluded a decade of extraordinary change unmatched since the beginning of the zoo."

Truly, it is a bit overwhelming to consider what made up the decade. New exhibits included the massive Tropic World and a new Seven Seas, and planning and construction was underway on two innovative projects: The Fragile Kingdom on the site of Lion House and *Habitat Africa!* in place of the old Giraffe House. Educational efforts included Discovery Center, Be a Bird, and the CONNECTIONS program. In terms of public programs, the list is long and included Holiday Magic, Zoo Run Run, Teddy Bear Picnic, Boo! at the Zoo, National Pig Day, and the Easter parade. Roads and other infrastructure around the zoo had received much-needed repairs.

Fundraising had reached an all-time high. Financially, the zoo was more stable and able to quit the borrowing pattern it had adopted for many years. The Society was regularly funding conservation projects around the world in addition to conducting significant research in-house through the Conservation Biology Department. And the Board and the staff were much more professional and much more involved in all aspects of zoo business.

Extraordinary change indeed. One wonders what Edith Rockefeller McCormick would think about the busy organization she helped to create.

The Evolution of the Zoo

If John McCutcheon miraculously could have visited the zoo in the 1980s, he would have been struck by the tremendous changes. McCutcheon's Brookfield Zoo of the 1930s was characterized by collecting trips, the popular pandas, high animal-mortality rates, competition between zoos for the largest or most diverse collection, polar bears strutting for marshmallows, visitors' delight in seeing real animals they had seen only in photographs, and a scope of operations limited practically to animal display—with a smattering of refreshments and souvenirs thrown in. How drastically the zoo had changed. How drastically many of the world's zoos had changed.

Comparing these aspects of 1930s zoo management to the same in the 1980s shows how the zoo business and Brookfield Zoo in particular were, so to speak, very different creatures.

Below: George Rabb's model on the evolution of zoos characterizes how the institutions today build on past missions to practice conservation concepts, work with each other to help endangered species, and inspire people by bringing them into the picture, among other goals.

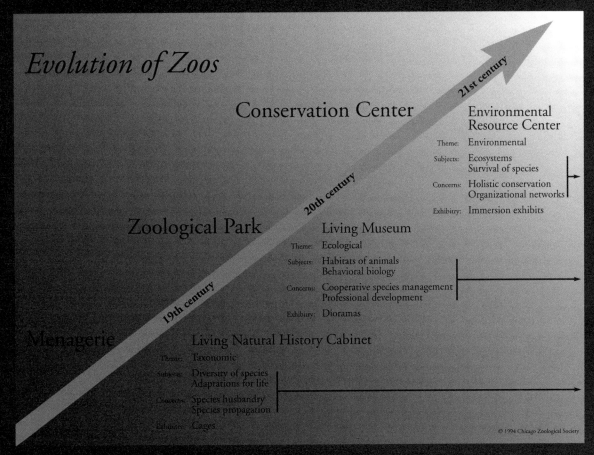

Evolution of Zoos

21st century
20th century
19th century

Conservation Center

Environmental Resource Center
Theme: Environmental
Subjects: Ecosystems
Survival of species
Concerns: Holistic conservation
Organizational networks
Exhibitry: Immersion exhibits

Zoological Park

Living Museum
Theme: Ecological
Subjects: Habitats of animals
Behavioral biology
Concerns: Cooperative species management
Professional development
Exhibitry: Dioramas

Menagerie

Living Natural History Cabinet
Theme: Taxonomic
Subjects: Diversity of species
Adaptations for life
Concerns: Species husbandry
Species propagation
Exhibitry: Cages

© 1994 Chicago Zoological Society

COLLECTING TRIPS

In the 1980s, almost all animals in zoos were born in captivity. Animals born in zoos accounted for well over 90% of the mammals and 70% of the birds in Brookfield Zoo's collection. Animals were collected from the wild only when fresh genetic material was needed to ensure the long-term health of a species or to start breeding programs for species newly endangered.

THE GIANT PANDAS

Concern over this endangered species led zoos and conservation groups to call a halt to short-term exhibit-only loans of giant pandas and to encourage breeding by consolidating the world's remaining small populations. Brookfield Zoo has not had a giant panda since Mei-lan died in 1953, and it will not have one in the near future, despite the considerable economic benefit such a popular exhibit would provide.

In a 1989 issue of *Town & Country* magazine, mammal curator Bruce Brewer addressed the issue of why particular species are—and are not—kept at the zoo.

"Here at Brookfield, we are the moralists of the zoo world," he said. "We are interested in the ethical questions raised by zoo-keeping. We are not in a popularity contest. We will not exhibit a pair of koalas merely because they are crowd-pleasers. Until we can make a serious contribution to the propagation and conservation of koalas, we don't want any here. Basically, we refuse to get into the rent-a-panda business."

ANIMAL-MORTALITY RATES

In the early days, a zoo's goal was to display as large and diverse an animal collection as possible. Not much was known about how to care for the animals as keepers learned through trial and error. Zoos shared information only occasionally, and little effort was made to gather information on exotic animals. As a result, mortality rates were high. When an animal died, another representative of the species was taken from the wild to replenish the exhibit.

Today, much more is known about caring for animals. In fact, caring for endangered species has become a major part of the zoo business. When an animal from an endangered species dies, it is a blow to the whole population, so every care is taken to ensure a long, healthy life.

Page 216 and above right: Brookfield Zoo participates in Species Survival Plans for golden lion tamarins (page 216), Asian small-clawed otters, cotton-top tamarins, Grevy's zebras, and Humboldt penguins (above, left to right).

COMPETITION BETWEEN ZOOS

In the 1970s and '80s, zoos began cooperating on behalf of endangered species. A national organization now called the American Zoo and Aquarium Association (formerly the American Association of Zoological Parks and Aquariums) inaugurated Species Survival Plans, which are pro-

Species Survival Plan

grams determining which individuals within a species should be bred to maintain a healthy population. SSPs are now in place for over 70 species, and loans between zoos are commonplace as animals are exchanged for breeding purposes. (Brookfield Zoo's Design Department created the SSP logo.)

In 1974, the International Species Information System (ISIS), a database of information on individual captive animals from around the world, was set up. ISIS is a further effort to responsibly manage animal populations through planned breeding. (George Rabb was instrumental in getting the program going. He served as head of its Policy Advisory Group from 1974 to 1989 and as its board chairman from 1989 through 1992.)

The degree of cooperation between zoos is exemplified by the relationship between Lincoln Park Zoo and Brookfield Zoo, which is much advanced since the rivalrous days of Marlin Perkins and Robert Bean. In fact, Rabb and Dr. Lester Fisher, who served as Lincoln Park Zoo's director for many years, have been good friends for a long time. Before he was appointed Lincoln Park Zoo's director, Fisher, a veterinarian by trade, often assisted Brookfield Zoo, and he and Rabb became quite close. The two still meet regularly for breakfast at Brookfield Zoo. Fisher agrees to drive out to the suburbs as long as Rabb cooks up a spectacular breakfast. The relationship has strengthened both men—and both zoos.

POLAR BEARS STRUTTING FOR MARSHMALLOWS

In the mid-1980s, not only had Brookfield Zoo abandoned the lucrative marshmallow business, it also hired a Ph.D.-trained nutritionist, specializing in exotic animals, to formulate diets for its entire animal collection. One of the few zoos in the country with this capacity, Brookfield Zoo often advises other zoos on nutrition. In addition to concern about the animals' health, the halt of marshmallow sales signaled a desire on behalf of zoo management to encourage the animals' natural behaviors.

VISITORS' DELIGHT IN SEEING EXOTIC ANIMALS

Certainly the role of zoos in educating the public had changed. With television, dramatic scenes of wild animals in their natural habitats became accessible to most households. People no longer had to leave their living rooms to view an elephant or a lion.

On the other hand, these improved vehicles for communication boosted the nation's awareness of conservation issues. In the 1970s and '80s, "Save the Whales," "Give a Hoot, Don't Pollute," and other environmental catchphrases became part of the collective vocabulary. Sensitized to the fragility of the existence of giant pandas, mountain gorillas, tigers, and even majestic American eagles, the public began to take a different interest in zoo animals.

Zoos played their part in heightening awareness through greater naturalism in exhibits, not only where the animals were, but also in the public spaces. Walk-through aviaries were an early means of achieving environmental immersion, but in the 1970s and '80s, whole buildings, including Tropic World, were built with this idea. Tropic World was a pioneer in mixed-species tropical-forest

A LIMITED SCOPE OF OPERATIONS

The scope of operations had expanded to include education, research, and international conservation efforts, as well as special promotional events at the zoo. The Chicago Zoological Society had grown to include enterprises such as the Australian conservation park, Discovery Center, the Gift Shop, travel programs, membership programs, special events such as Holiday Magic and Teddy Bear Picnic, radio and television programs, visitor studies, and participation in worldwide conservation programs. It was the same zoo that Ed Bean had directed in the 1930s, but it wasn't the same business.

'90 | '91

A genetics lab is built.
The Society helps found the Declining Amphibian Populations Task Force.

The Fragile Kingdom opens.
Brookfield Conservation Park inspires Murray-Sunset National Park.
The Society purchases The Dolphin Connection.
A zoo experiment involving mice sends a message about small populations.
The Board of Trustees meets to modernize the Society's mission.
A totem pole is constructed at Seven Seas.
An Imagenetics AKSII gene analyzer is donated to the genetics lab.

'92

The Women's Board is created.

'93

Habitat Africa! opens.
Paul Magut builds a traditional Nandi home on zoo grounds.
The Chicagoland Environmental Network is founded.
A new animal hospital opens.
The World Zoo Conservation Strategy is published.
An additional 600,000 acres is set aside for conservation in Australia.
The first golden lion tamarins are released at Indian Lake.
A joint zoo pathology program is begun.
A $16 million bond issuance kicks off a 10-year capital development plan.
Philip W. K. Sweet, Jr. is succeeded as Society chairman by Clyde W. Reighard.
Hand-reared Sophie the orangutan successfully takes care of her daughter, Kutai.
The Behavioral Enrichment Group is created.

'94

The Zoo Nutrition Network is founded.
Chicory the gorilla undergoes history-making brain surgery.
Animal Athletes is started.
The zoo begins to help teach conservation biology to international wildlife managers.
The Regenstein Foundation donates $2.5 million for The Swamp.

'95

The Daniel F. and Ada L. Rice Conservation Biology and Research Center opens.
Tropic World's interpretive plan is updated.
The zoo helps rescue two brown bear cubs in Alaska.
The Zoo Adventure Passport program is founded.
Office space is constructed around the South Gate.

CHAPTER SIXTEEN

Inspiring Others

(1990-1995)

The Mission Is Refocused

Very much in the news in the early 1990s was the fact that the mighty London Zoo, one of the first public zoos in the world, was struggling to stay afloat. Apprehension rippled throughout zoos all over, for if that one could fall apart, so could any. It raised the question of whether zoos were still relevant. With the availability of television and commercial flight, seeing exotic animals was no longer the novelty it had been earlier in the century. Perhaps the time for zoos had already come and gone.

If nothing else, it became increasingly obvious that the role of zoos in society had changed considerably as the natural world steadily deteriorated and the public became more aware of conservation issues. Visitors no longer were impressed with zoos that showed animals in small, barren cages, no matter how great the collection's diversity. The public demanded much more of zoos than it had in the past.

In November 1991, the Board of Trustees held a retreat to talk about the long-term goals and direction of the Society. It had been clear for several years that the mission of the institution did not do justice to the Society's enterprises.

Above: The zoo works to ensure the future of the natural world by inspiring all generations to become more environmentally responsible.

"Our basic mission statement has remained the same: research, entertainment of the public, education, conservation. These things still continue in our new mission statement. But we've now realized that a very important part of it is a harmonious relationship between people and animals, ecosystems; the idea that we are all interrelated and have to live together. Many of the new exhibits are going to be using that theme.... So after people come to the zoo, they go away with a message.... I think it's a very important one."

Philip W. K. Sweet, Jr.
Former Society Chairman

The mission, as originally set forth in 1921, was "the foundation, maintenance and control of Zoological Parks and Gardens and other collections; the promotion of Zoology and kindred subjects; the instruction and recreation of the people; the collection, holding and expenditure of funds for zoological research and publication; the protection of wild life; and kindred purposes." It had been reworded in 1986 to read "the mission of the Chicago Zoological Society is to enhance appreciation of the earth's biological heritage by providing for the recreation and education of the people, the conservation of wildlife, and the discovery of biological knowledge."

In 1991, it seemed time to move past merely "enhancing appreciation." The retreat was meant to outline a new role Brookfield Zoo could play in the community, not just as a place to practice the elements of its mission, but to truly inspire the public toward actions on behalf of conservation.

During the meeting, some Board members expressed concern that this new vision would endanger the one thing that made the zoo popular: recreation. They argued that people come to the zoo to have fun, not be lectured. Supporters of this new idea countered that recreation and motivation were not mutually exclusive.

Throughout the meeting, it was shy George Rabb's voice that was heard the loudest, and eventually even those with hesitations bowed to his expertise. The subsequently reworded mission statement retained the four original elements of the business but directed them at a more ambitious end: "The mission of the Chicago Zoological Society is to help people develop a sustainable and harmonious relationship with nature. In so doing, the Society shall provide for the recreation and education of the people, the conservation of wildlife, and the discovery of biological knowledge."

"I think that over the last 10 years, perhaps the most significant change that has taken place is that the mission of the zoo has been more sharply defined as we move from primarily an entertainment vehicle into one of really focusing on our conservation message: our attempt to make our audience understand that we all have a very vital role in this ecological society in which we live, and that we have the capacity to make a significant impact."

Clyde Reighard
Current Society Chairman

Becoming a Conservation Center

The new mission spurred many discussions about what the changes meant. The Board knew it wanted to turn the zoo into a "conservation center" by helping people "develop a sustainable and harmonious relationship with nature," but that was such a broad goal that many people had difficulty understanding the implications. The confused staff wanted to know how the new mission affected day-to-day operations, what it meant for the zoo's place in the community, and how the visitor experience would change.

Rabb recognized the confusion, as well as a possible reluctance by staff to go along with the changes, especially when the end results were so unclear. He formed a special team of employees whose charge was to ensure that everyone understood the new mission and possessed the necessary tools, including education about customer service and cultural diversity, to fulfill their role within the mission.

To many, the phrase "conservation center" was particularly vague. After much discussion, staff finally took the matter in hand by breaking the idea into four distinct ways the zoo could become a true conservation center.

• As a **model citizen**, the zoo had to conduct its business in the most environmentally efficient and sustainable manner possible. This meant recycling more, designing new facilities with conservation in mind, and maximizing the efficiency of existing facilities.

• The zoo was already working as a **wildlife, habitat, and ecosystem conservationist** by researching animals' biology and natural history, as well as by participating in breeding programs for endangered species and projects such as Australian land management.

• Being a **mentor** and trainer meant teaching others to become involved in conservation of nature, a responsibility the zoo took very seriously by educating promising young conservation scientists and inviting visitors to join in conservation efforts.

• The zoo needed to become a **community resource and motivator**. In this regard, exhibit planners and the Education Department began to focus their attention on designing exhibits and signs to inspire the public to live in a more environmentally friendly manner.

Below: At The Fragile Kingdom, a window with a remarkable view into the outdoor snow leopard enclosure allows for some nose-to-nose contemplation.

The Role of Humans

Newer exhibits such as The Fragile Kingdom and the soon-to-be-opened *Habitat Africa!* helped support the zoo's initiative to become a community resource and motivator. Earlier exhibits such as Tropic World had tried to mimic natural conditions by recreating entire habitats, complete with the mixed species, plants, and weather conditions found in a part of the world. What they hadn't addressed well was how humans lived in or affected a particular habitat. Tropic World did subliminally address humans' roles in the rain forest by exhibiting jeep tracks in Africa, a guard post between exhibits, and rice paddies in the forests of Asia, but no great effort was made to point out these violations of the forest or to explain what they really mean.

While changes that reflected the new mission were ahead, the zoo had already made a step in that direction with the opening of The Fragile Kingdom. The first exhibit to manifest a human presence along with displays of animals, this Lion House renovation, undertaken with bond-issuance money, was completed in 1991. The exhibit illustrates how a variety of Asian and African life-forms depend on their environment and upon each other for survival. The Fragile Desert at one end of the building and its opposite, The Fragile Rain Forest at the other, highlight the challenges animals face in their daily lives, as well as long-term threats by human activities. Woven throughout the exhibit are suggestions for how humans can reduce the impact they have on these and other threatened habitats.

Above and right: In Lion House, the big cats were displayed in uniform cages in a grouping typical of taxonomic displays of the time it was built. The Fragile Kingdom features naturalistic settings for African crested porcupines and black-backed jackals.

THE FRAGILE KINGDOM

Just a week before The Fragile Kingdom opened to the public in 1991, Peter Kendall reported on the exhibit's mission in a *Chicago Tribune* article entitled "New zoo exhibit has more than animals."

"Unlike most zoo exhibits, the Fragile Kingdom, which opens to the public on May 18, is not organized around types of animals, but around the complex webs of life of a desert and a rain forest. And unlike any other exhibit at Brookfield or Lincoln Park Zoo in Chicago, the Fragile Kingdom displays are tied together with a narrative thread. Planners hope that this loose narrative, a kind of story, will help make the zoo into a place where visitors don't just gawk at the animals but learn of their struggle for survival amid hostile environments and man-made problems.

"In the Fragile Desert, a desert nomad has hung scarves along a path, marking spots where information can be found about the difficulties of survival in the parching sun and heat. In the Fragile Rain Forest, a researcher has left field guides and notebooks behind, offering a naturalist's observations about the wildlife.

"The exhibits, including new outdoor quarters for large cats, reflect the changing mission of zoos, which have evolved from the little-understood menageries housed in severe quarters of Victorian times. Now zoos are increasingly important laboratories for research, and zoo husbandry offers the only hope for survival for an increasing number of species."

The opening of the exhibit prompted hopeful words in *Bison* magazine. "The Fragile Kingdom seeks to generate understanding, commitment, and a sense of adventure in the visitor. Brookfield Zoo's educators hope that visitors will develop both a greater appreciation of the animals of Asia and Africa and a clearer understanding of the role humans play in the destruction and preservation of these fragile worlds. Most importantly, visitors will leave knowing that they can take action to promote the long-term survival of these environments."

The renovation of Giraffe House into the first phase of a multiphase project called *Habitat Africa!* was another step down this path. The five-acre recreation of an east African savannah includes a large waterhole and a "kopje," a rocky outcropping sheltering a variety of animals. The subtitle of the exhibit, which focuses on how animals cope with water, shelter, food, and other dwindling vital resources, is "Caring for Resources that Give Life." In addition to addressing resource conservation issues, the exhibit introduces complex conservation topics such as ecotourism, disease management among wild populations, and population control.

"The goal of *Habitat Africa!*," explained a zoo educator, "is to impart to the visitor the idea that habitats such as the kopje and waterhole—as well as habitats closer to home—are worthy of our attention, respect, and most of all, action. If *Habitat Africa!* motivates people to take positive steps on behalf of the natural world, even on a small scale, the most important goal of this ambitious project will have been realized."

Above: Concurrent with the 1993 opening of *Habitat Africa!*, Kenyan Paul Magut (right, with former staff member Steve Stratakos) was invited to the zoo to construct a typical "Nandi home," made entirely of natural materials. Magut talked to visitors about the structure and life in Kenya—another opportunity to emphasize how native peoples interact with their environment.

Above: The new giraffe yard at *Habitat Africa!* allows them to stretch in a setting more closely resembling their natural habitat.

Left and below: *Habitat Africa!* is a striking example of how much exhibit design has changed. African wild dogs (photo, left), klipspringers (below), and red bishops (bottom inset) benefit from the naturalistic exhibits.

HABITAT
AFRICA!
BROOKFIELD ZOO

With these exhibit openings, Brookfield Zoo demonstrated its evolution as an institution. When first built, Lion House was a typical indoor exhibit, with barren cages lined up side by side. While zoo planner Edwin Clark had designed spacious outdoor exhibits, the indoor ones were lacking in space and naturalism. After the renovation, the exhibit not only reconstructs complete desert and rain-forest habitats displaying a wide variety of animals, it also conveys a very distinct conservation message. Similarly, the metamorphosis of Giraffe House into phase one of *Habitat Africa!* demonstrates the movement from strictly functional indoor exhibits to the display of a complete habitat for the sake of illustrating a conservation message.

The 1995 renovation of Tropic World is perhaps the best example of how rapidly exhibit philosophy can change. Open for barely a decade, Tropic World was already considered outdated by the early 1990s. Its aging skylights, faulty rain systems, and deteriorating handrails required attention, but most of its needs were educational in nature. Designed as an "immersion" exhibit,

with no signs to distract visitors, it was not living up to its potential. Thanks to a grant from the National Science Foundation, the zoo was able to develop interpretive materials that help visitors understand the concept that primates, including humans, make choices every day that affect their environment.

As planning for the renovation began, focus groups were assembled to explore the public's feelings and knowledge about primates. The results revealed that only 60% of the participants thought humans were primates—an idea central to the exhibit's new interpretive scheme. Some were even insulted by the idea, a finding that led to a more sensitive approach in dealing with the topic.

After prototypes of signs were in place, visitors were observed, timed, and interviewed about the messages they were learning. Based on the results, the signs were modified in size, shape, placement, and language and content. The testing continued throughout the planning process until each sign and interactive device had been honed to maximum effectiveness. After the renovation, final evaluations offered clues about whether the signs communicated the appropriate message—and whether they supported the zoo's mission of teaching people about the natural world.

The renamed Tropic World: A Primate's Journey now focuses on the relationships among primates, their environment, and people, reinforcing how important human choices are to the future of the natural world.

The World Zoo Conservation Strategy

The Role of the Zoos and Aquaria of the World in Global Conservation

IUDZG—The World Zoo Organization
and
The Captive Breeding Specialist Group of IUCN/SSC

Instructing Others

As part of its metamorphosis into a conservation center, the zoo augmented its function as mentor by offering its leadership in conservation and research to other zoos and organizations. In 1993, under George Rabb's prodding, *The World Zoo Conservation Strategy* (right) was published jointly by three entities: the Chicago Zoological Society, IUDZG—The World Zoo Organization, and the Captive Breeding Specialist Group of the Species Survival Commission, of which Rabb was chairman. This impressive document, which communicated to hundreds of zoos worldwide a new charge, included Rabb's "Evolution of Zoos," which clarified the role of zoos in the past and, more importantly, in the future.

"[The book] is a very important contribution to the whole concept of partnership between zoos and conservation organizations in the task of conserving nature and the natural environment," commented Prince Philip, HRH The Duke of Edinburgh, in the Foreword. "Zoos serve some 600 million visitors annually and their potential for making people of all ages aware of the threats to the global ecology is unlimited. I hope that *The World Zoo Conservation Strategy* will bring about the cooperation and partnership between zoos all over the world that is so vital to the conservation of nature, and so help them to realize that potential."

The book's audience was zoos large and small. In fact, Brookfield Zoo has a history of helping conservation efforts at smaller, regional zoos all over the world through its annual Presidential Award. (Many major zoos had conservation programs.) The award had been established in the mid-1980s when Rabb repeatedly refused a raise and insisted that the money instead be used to support and recognize others. By 1996, the award had grown to $25,000.

Opposite above: Exhibit planners let prototypes guide them in designing the new interpretive signs and games in Tropic World.

Above and left: Interactive signs in the renamed Tropic World: A Primate's Journey let people see, touch, and do.

Another opportunity to offer aid to others worldwide came in 1994, when the zoo, along with the Field Museum and the University of Illinois at Chicago, founded a program to teach young professionals from some of the world's most biologically rich countries the most modern, comprehensive techniques for sustainably managing and conserving their resources. The program, funded by the John D. and Catherine T. MacArthur Foundation, trains young but established scientists and wildlife managers from tropical countries in the principles of conservation biology, such as management of small populations, analyzing biological diversity, and pure ecological research. Every year, participants come to Chicago from as far away as Vietnam, Kenya, India, Indonesia, Venezuela, and Brazil.

"All of Chicago, including the three institutions involved in this program, benefit from the efforts of conservationists working at local levels to save the phenomenal biota of the world," explained Joel S. Brown, an associate professor of biological sciences at UIC. "This is one way for us to give thanks, to give something back."

Another type of training, the Mentor Program, was begun in the early 1990s to encourage minority and female high-school students to pursue careers in science. Once a student is selected, he or she engages in a multiyear partnership with a staff member from an area related to animal care or conservation biology to develop a research project and learn about the zoo business.

To serve and inform the public on a broader scale, the Chicagoland Environmental Network was founded in 1993. Funded by the U.S. Environmental Protection Agency and the Illinois EPA, with additional support from the Chicago Zoological Society, CEN was created to improve cooperation and sharing of information among some 200 local conservation organizations and to promote the public's understanding of, and participation in, conservation issues and actions. People who find CEN useful include schoolchildren interested in starting a recycling program, college students preparing for a career in conservation, people seeking volunteer opportunities, citizen groups needing guidance in planning local cleanup projects, reporters searching for information or news sources, and employees and volunteers of member organizations wishing to share information about their activities.

CEN is located, with easy access by the public, in the zoo's original animal hospital. Since its construction in the early 1950s, the facility had gradually become outdated, and a new, $4.5 million hospital became operational in 1993. Funds for the new hospital in the southwest corner were made available through the Forest Preserve District, the state's "Build Illinois" fund, and a $2 million fundraising effort led by trustees Dennis Keller and Fred Krehbiel.

A veterinarian's dream, the facility houses a surgical suite, an intensive-care unit, a quarantine area, and 44 individualized holding areas. State-of-the-art laboratory facilities include an X-ray machine large enough for a 2,000-pound Clydesdale horse, yet sensitive enough for a 33-gram blue-crowned hanging parrot; a surgical table that can be lowered, loaded with a heavy animal, then raised to the proper height; a culture incubator for checking the water in animal pools for bacteria; and lights encased in concrete to prevent damage by curious primates. With these capacities, the hospital staff can provide the animals with the best care possible and contribute to the growing body of information about exotic animals.

Above and right: The construction of a state-of-the-art animal hospital in 1993 (above) left the original hospital empty and ripe for conversion into the Daniel F. and Ada L. Rice Conservation Biology and Research Center (right), providing much-needed space for the zoo's conservation and research departments.

Left: Young participants in the Mentor Program are encouraged to pursue careers in science and areas related to the work of zoos.

Right: On August 19, 1992, Marina Danilevsky was the 100 millionth person to enter Brookfield Zoo.

Two years later, the old animal hospital, which had been refurbished the year before, was reopened as the Daniel F. and Ada L. Rice Conservation Biology and Research Center, named in honor of the foundation that provided $1 million for the project. In addition to CEN, the Rice Center now houses the Conservation Biology Department and provides lab and office space for the zoo's genetics, behavioral, and nutrition researchers.

Another department located in the Rice Center is the Communications Research Department, which uses surveys, interviews, observations, and focus groups to provide information about the level of knowledge, attitude, and behavior of the zoo's various audiences. The department helps shape the zoo's policies in effectively communicating with visitors and in fact proved critical when the messages provided to the public inside Tropic World were updated in 1995.

While the Tropic World renovation and exhibits like The Fragile Kingdom and *Habitat Africa!* reflect the 1991 changes to the zoo's mission statement, the refocusing of the ideas behind what drives the zoo has been a big step for the institution. Along with inspiring people to action, the new mission acknowledges the incredible amount of research and conservation the Society has been involved in. These two areas have taken staff members to far corners of the world—and to new territories in their own backyard.

1990

A genetics lab is built.
The Society helps found the Declining Amphibian Populations Task Force.

'91

The Fragile Kingdom opens.
Brookfield Conservation Park inspires Murray-Sunset National Park.
The Society purchases The Dolphin Connection.
A zoo experiment involving mice sends a message about small populations.
The Board of Trustees meets to modernize the Society's mission.
A totem pole is constructed at Seven Seas.
An Imagenetics AKSII gene analyzer is donated to the genetics lab.

'92

The Women's Board is created.

'93

Habitat Africa! opens.
Paul Magut builds a traditional Nandi home on zoo grounds.
The Chicagoland Environmental Network is founded.
A new animal hospital opens.
The World Zoo Conservation Strategy is published.
An additional 600,000 acres is set aside for conservation in Australia.
The first golden lion tamarins are released at Indian Lake.
A joint zoo pathology program is begun.
A $16 million bond issuance kicks off a 10-year capital development plan.
Philip W. K. Sweet, Jr. is succeeded as Society chairman by Clyde W. Reighard.
Hand-reared Sophie the orangutan successfully takes care of her daughter, Kutai.
The Behavioral Enrichment Group is created.

'94

The Zoo Nutrition Network is founded.
Chicory the gorilla undergoes history-making brain surgery.
Animal Athletes is started.
The zoo begins to help teach conservation biology to international wildlife managers.
The Regenstein Foundation donates $2.5 million for The Swamp.

'95

The Daniel F. and Ada L. Rice Conservation Biology and Research Center opens.
Tropic World's interpretive plan is updated.
The zoo helps rescue two brown bear cubs in Alaska.
The Zoo Adventure Passport program is founded.
Office space is constructed around the South Gate.

CHAPTER SEVENTEEN

Hands-on Conservation

(1990-1995)

Worldwide Conservation

By the early 1990s, the Society was involved in conservation projects around the world. While the most significant change in the zoo's mission was in conservation education, there was also a focus on hands-on conservation. For decades, an emphasis on this type of conservation badly lagged behind the other three mission elements.

The Society's initial foray into international conservation, the 1971 purchase of the 16,000-acre Brookfield Conservation Park in Australia, paid big dividends in 1991. When the Society first had purchased the South Australia property two decades earlier, the land was badly depleted. Years of drought and overgrazing by sheep and rabbits had exhausted its resources. Over the years, Society researchers helped local conservationists manage the reserve, allowing it to recover. Records of rainfall, systematic photos of established sites, wildlife counts, and other long-term data documented a spectacular recovery by vegetation and wildlife.

Early in the decade, the Land Conservation Council, a land-management advisory board in Victoria, was struggling to figure out what to do with a large patch of land known as the Sunset Country, made up of dry country much like the zoo's land in neighboring South Australia. Inspired by the zoo's inexpensive and incontestable success, the Land Conservation Council arranged for the Sunset Country to be managed similarly—as a national park—by June 1991. The 16,000 acres of Brookfield Conservation Park inspired roughly 1.6 million acres of Murray-Sunset National Park.

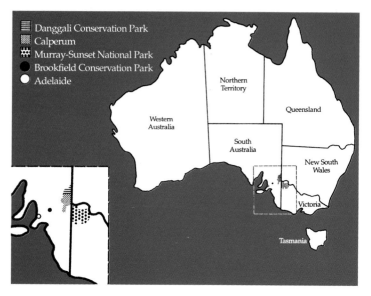

Danggali Conservation Park
Calperum
Murray-Sunset National Park
Brookfield Conservation Park
Adelaide

Northern Territory

Queensland

Western Australia

South Australia

New South Wales

Victoria

Tasmania

Left: By 1993, over two million acres of Australian land had been converted into preserves, the result of the zoo's early success with restoring the 16,000 acres of Brookfield Conservation Park.

Opposite: Research on populations of bottlenosed dolphins off the coast of Florida has complemented observations by zoo staff in the more controlled environment of Seven Seas.

In 1993, thanks to philanthropists William Rutherford (once again) and Brooks McCormick, an additional 600,000 acres were purchased by the Society and the Australian government. It was a huge return on the original conservation investment by the Society and Rutherford's Forest Park Foundation.

The Society also became involved in dolphin conservation and research in 1991 with its purchase of The Dolphin Connection in the Florida Keys. Under the direction of Society staff, the ocean-front facility served as a location for studying bottlenosed dolphins' needs, educating people about marine environments, and breeding a population of bottlenosed dolphins.

Like long-term comparative studies of baboons taking place simultaneously at the zoo and in Kenya, the data from Florida complemented the zoo's research on dolphins' habits and behavior. (In fact, for many years it had been assumed but never proved that bottlenosed dolphins receive

AN ILLUMINATING MOMENT

Conservation biologist Pam Parker once had what she calls a "bolt-of-lighting moment." In Australia, where she does most of her research, she was in charge of a camp of students and other researchers and so had responsibilities that ate into her research time.

One day, she was behind in her research and was trying to transect her study area when a truck pulled up. Driving it was a local named Freddy who had ongoing problems with wombats eating the same grass as his sheep. Busy as Parker was, Freddy had chosen that moment to talk about the animals.

"Freddy was struggling with land management, and we had had a number of desultory discussions about wombats and their right to live," said Parker. "Just then I was thinking, 'The sun's going to go down and I'm not going to get these data.' He said, 'I've really been thinking about these wombats. They were here before I was.'

"Here's a guy whose land-management practices and attitudes about wombats not only pertain to his own land, but the whole social scene at the [local] bar and hotel. If I said, 'Gee, sorry, Freddy, maybe later, I've got to do my transect,' I'd lose him and the potential of the interaction. Because it's not about content, it's about relationships, feelings, and values.

"At that moment, I realized that my job was to talk to Freddy. Am I a scientist or a conservationist? Basically, I stopped being a scientist at that point, other than to use science as a legitimizing tool for policy and cultural issues about how to value land and wildlife and how to see the wealth of the future, whether it includes noneconomic, cultural intangibles that are part of the wealth of a community and its relationship with its environment."

sonar signals through their lower jaws. In the mid-1980s, the zoo's training supervisor, Randy Brill, with Nemo the dolphin's assistance, conducted a study that proved the theory. Loyola University awarded both Brill and Nemo doctorates for their study—another Brookfield Zoo first.) The Society withdrew from The Dolphin Connection project in 1996 due to lack of interest and support from other institutions. Other dolphin work continues, including Society researcher Randy Wells' 25-year study of a dolphin population in Sarasota Bay and Amy Samuels' studies on the intricate behavioral relations among dolphins.

Other off-site conservation research has been conducted at trustee William Lane III's Bell Ranch in New Mexico. In the mid-1980s, the zoo established a collaborative management and breeding program there for addax and Przewalski's horses to determine if these two endangered species could, with minimal intervention, successfully maintain themselves and reproduce in an environment similar to their native habitat. The addax have fared remarkably well. A population of two was gradually supplemented and bred successfully until, by 1996, 17 individuals were in the group, 14 of which were born at Bell Ranch.

The Przewalski's horses didn't manage as well. The ranch was intended as a holding area for bachelor groups of the species, and four stallions were transported there in late 1987. They proved enterprising, jumping fences and attacking ranch workers on horseback. The workers never knew where the horses might turn up, and they feared that the stallions would find the domestic mares. Eventually, all of the Przewalski's horses were removed from the ranch. They were healthy, but the fencing was simply inadequate to maintain them. Zoo and ranch staff continue to consider alternatives for breeding and maintaining other endangered species at Bell Ranch.

On the Hawaiian islands, the Society is now part of a joint conservation effort with four other zoos, the state of Hawaii, and the U.S. Fish and Wildlife Service to develop techniques for bird management. Native birds there are severely endangered due to the introduction of nonnative birds and other animals, and the trend shows no sign of stopping. Of 71 species found on the island of Hawaii (and nowhere else on earth) in 1788, at least 23 species, and possibly a dozen more, are extinct. State and federal wildlife biologists are restoring habitat, removing predators, studying diseases from and competition by other species, and planning captive breeding programs for unstable populations. But so little is known about the husbandry and breeding of these small Hawaiian songbirds that "surrogate" species, ones closely related to the endangered birds, are being studied first.

Brookfield Zoo is helping to develop techniques for capturing, acclimating to captivity, caring for, and breeding surrogate species. These techniques will then be applied to endangered birds at state and federal facilities in Hawaii. Along with representatives from other zoos, Bird Department staff have collected surrogate species on the island and brought them back to Illinois. In the zoo's Avian Propagation Environment, in back of Perching Bird House, they are carefully monitored and maintained with the hope that establishing breeding colonies will lead to insights into their species and those of endangered Hawaiian songbirds as well.

"BABOONS IN TWO WORLDS"

Jeanne Altmann (above), curator of research in the Conservation Biology Department, contributed the following commentary to a 1989 *Bison* article called "Baboons in Two Worlds."

"As the 64 baboons on Baboon Island return their attention from the antics of visitors to the rhythm of baboon life, researchers from the Conservation Biology Department leave their computers to unobtrusively observe and record the intricacies of baboon society....

"At the same time, halfway around the world, another group of baboons and several other Chicago Zoological Society biologists are stirring in the chill of pre-dawn in Kenya's Amboseli National Park. Before the rising sun briefly bathes Mt. Kilimanjaro's snow in a pink glow, the researchers will have breakfasted by candlelight and readied vehicles and equipment. Then it's off to the field for a ten-hour day of following one of the baboon study groups until the animals settle again for the night in one of their scattered tree-top refuges. On this day, the researchers hope to locate Alto's Group, a group of almost 70 baboons that has been the object of continuous studies since 1971.

"In the years since Stuart Altmann and I began the Amboseli studies, researchers from Kenya, the United States, and other countries have conducted studies in Amboseli and helped maintain the continuity that is so vital to a project such as this. These have included studies of competition among juveniles...and grooming behavior.... During the past ten years, two other baboon groups in Amboseli have been added to the study, and starting in 1985, Amy Samuels and I began a comparison of the group living on Baboon Island at Brookfield Zoo. Through detailed daily records on births, deaths, infant care, play, fighting among foes, and grooming among friends and family members, an understanding of the full lifecourse of female baboons is emerging."

Below and inset: Captive breeding of Przewalski's horses in zoos has saved the species from extinction, but management of the horses at Bell Ranch has proved difficult.

Bottom: The zoo manages and studies "surrogate" species like this amakihi to learn how to save Hawaiian birds that are facing extinction.

Ongoing research projects coordinated through the Conservation Biology Department have continued, some at the zoo, others around the world. In addition to research in Florida, Kenya, Hawaii, and Australia, studies have been conducted on the behavior of newborn rhinos, okapis, and giraffes.

In some studies, the most valuable research is that conducted right at the zoo. For example, it's nearly impossible to tell the difference between sexes in many types of birds, among other animals—a tricky problem in breeding endangered species. In these instances, the only way to determine gender is by decoding genetic information.

In 1990, Brookfield Zoo built a genetics lab to help in species management. The following year, the donation of an Imagenetics AKSII gene analyzer made the zoo the only one in the world with a computerized chromosome-analysis system. As such, the genetics team responds each year to several hundred requests from other zoos for genetic decoding.

Population geneticist Robert Lacy is a world expert on the genetics of small populations. In 1989, he developed VORTEX, a computer program designed to predict the fate of populations of highly endangered animals such as black-footed ferrets and Florida panthers. This program combines genetic, demographic, and environmental variables to assess the likelihood of extinction, sometimes from inbreeding, of small populations. By 1996, scientists around the world had used VORTEX to determine the extinction risks of many wild endangered populations, including black rhinos in Africa, pumas, and Hawaiian birds.

In 1991, as reported in *Science* magazine, an interesting experiment drew attention to the zoo's research on inbreeding. Nearly 800 inbred and genetically healthy mice, descended from mice captured in Brookfield's wooded areas, were released into the same woods. The inbred mice died faster—and were 50 percent likelier to die—than the other mice. Researchers believe that inbreeding made the mice weaker, slower, and less capable of seeing and smelling predators. The experiment sent a warning signal to conservationists intent on capturing the last few survivors of endangered species for the purpose of breeding them in captivity.

"There are two very important messages here," said Lacy. "In the future, we should never wait until a species gets down to the last few dozen before we take heroic measures to save them. We should be doing that when there are still thousands. And when we breed in captivity, we should be taking every precaution we can to avoid inbreeding."

Above: Brookfield Zoo has a long history of breeding black rhinos, one of the most endangered of the five rhino species.

Right: Indian researcher Sanjay Molur (left), a participant in the MacArthur Advanced Training Program in Biological Diversity, and researcher Sandy Manne observe newborn giraffes to add to the catalog of knowledge about the species.

Above right: Population geneticist Bob Lacy plugs information into his VORTEX computer program. VORTEX (inset) is an important tool for helping scientists determine the chances of survival of many small populations of endangered species.

Far right: A golden lion tamarin, restricted only by a radio collar, learns the fundamentals of survival at Indian Lake. The zoo is helping to replenish populations of the endangered monkeys in the Brazilian rain forest.

For some endangered species, inbreeding is not the problem. In the 1970s, the near disappearance of golden lion tamarins from their natural habitat in Brazil prompted zoos into action. Led by Dr. Devra Kleiman, the National Zoo's assistant director for research (who started her zoo career as a Brookfield Zoo intern), zoos began cooperating in breeding the primates, conducting behavioral studies, and reintroducing individuals to the wild. It became clear that captive-bred monkeys released into Brazil's rain forests didn't always have the necessary survival skills, so a multizoo program in which the monkeys are "trained" for survival on zoo grounds was founded. Brookfield Zoo's tamarins, accustomed to climbing trees and living with other species in Tropic World's South American rain forest, were a step ahead of those from other zoos.

In 1993, for the first time, the zoo released a pair of tamarins onto the grounds by Indian Lake so they could learn additional skills, such as navigation and foraging. There were no fences or boundaries, and except for radio collars, the animals were free. Tamarins that have passed such training at Brookfield Zoo and at other zoos are now being introduced to the rain forest in Brazil so that one day the habitat may be repopulated with the small, enchanting primates.

Mental, Physical Health

In captivity, the mental health of animals is considered as important as their genetic health, so in 1993, animal training coordinator Marty Sevenich created the Behavioral Enrichment Group at Brookfield Zoo. This group of employees from many different areas devises mechanisms and activities that encourage natural behaviors in the animals. Hidden food items, special toys, and training sessions keep the animals as active as they would be in the wild and allow keepers to learn more about their natural behaviors.

Recently, training has become vital in ensuring that some animals receive special attention, as it did for Katie and Sam, the diabetic orangutans who were taught to offer their body parts for insulin injections—saving their lives. Training paid off for orangutans again in 1993, when Sophie was taught to care for Kutai, her baby. Because she had been hand-reared, Sophie never learned maternal skills.

Another aspect of conservation the zoo has shouldered is nutrition. In the early days of zoos, little was known about the dietary needs of animals. Cataloging a wild animal's diet and figuring out the nutritional content of its food is not easy, so animal nutrition was poorly understood for many years.

As the only zoo in the world with a comprehensive program devoted to animal nutrition, Brookfield Zoo is now a leader in this area. Its Nutrition Department formulates diets, trains other nutritionists through a residency program, and advances the science. The Zoo Nutrition Network, founded in 1994 by Nutrition Department head Dr. Sue Crissey, offers nutritional assistance to zoos around the country. This important program provides better care to animals at Brookfield Zoo and at other zoos, and it also contributes to the rapidly growing data on animal nutrition.

ZOO PATHOLOGY

Brookfield Zoo delved into zoo pathology (the study of animal diseases) in the 1950s and '60s and has been conducting necropsies for many years. But there has never been a formal program at the zoo until recently.

In 1993, Brookfield Zoo joined with Lincoln Park Zoo, the Shedd Aquarium, the University of Illinois College of Veterinary Medicine, Loyola University, and the Edward Hines, Jr. Veteran Affairs Hospital to more thoroughly research zoo pathology and train residents in the topic. The program also provides diagnostic services to the three zoological institutions.

Because few qualified pathologists specializing in exotic animals are available to zoos, this type of training has helped meet one of the most critical needs in zoo medicine.

Getting Involved

While some researchers have concentrated on specific areas of animal management, others turn their energies to animal groups. Important contributions have been made by staff members' participation in international conservation programs. They have served as coordinators of several Species Survival Plans (multizoo breeding programs for endangered species), participated in over 20 other SSPs, and maintained various international studbooks. (A studbook is the record of all individuals within a species in captivity.) Curators and others regularly attend national and international conferences concerning animal conservation and management.

George Rabb has led these efforts. From 1989 to 1996, he held the post of chairman of the Species Survival Commission (SSC) of IUCN—The World Conservation Union. The SSC, an international assemblage of some 7,000 people from 179 countries, serves as a volunteer advisor to governments and conservation groups worldwide. Divided into 110 Specialist Groups that focus on particular animal and plant groups, the SSC determines the status of endangered species and outlines action plans for conserving them. The Commission's impact has been powerful, and as head of the organization, Rabb shaped environmental policy and elevated Brookfield Zoo's status to an international one.

The effectiveness of the marriage of the Chicago Zoological Society to the Species Survival Commission is illustrated by the Declining Amphibian Populations Task Force. Concerned with the dramatic decrease in amphibian populations worldwide, the SSC established the DAPTF in 1990 with money provided in part by the Society's SEACON Fund. Rabb, a trained herpetologist, played an instrumental role in the process.

The SEACON Fund, begun in 1979, has continued to allocate small grants to conservation efforts all over the world. The variety of projects supported by the Fund and their geographic range are notable. Research programs on collared peccaries in Costa Rica, black-necked cranes in Tibet, red howlers and capuchin monkeys in Trinidad, black-faced impalas in Namibia, and neotropical migrant birds in Michigan, among many others, have been helped along by the small grants, which are mostly a few thousand dollars each.

Ten years after the SEACON Fund was started, trustee Jerry Manne initiated a similar granting body, the Chicago Board of Trade Endangered Species Fund, administered through the Society. He has tenaciously—and successfully—solicited his fellow traders for donations to help support conservation projects. By 1996, the CBOT Fund, which uses zoo staff as advisors, had amassed over $325,000. Through his efforts, Manne has made possible dozens of conservation research projects.

All of these programs mirror the shift in priorities subsequent to the November 1991 meeting of Brookfield Zoo's Board of Trustees, in which the zoo's mission statement was changed to balance the four main elements: recreation, education, conservation, and research. In fact, as exhibits and programs have begun to be designed to inspire people through education and recreation, conservation and its cousin, research, have found their place as well. All four elements have became a cohesive whole for the first time in the zoo's history.

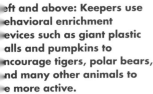

Left and above: Keepers use behavioral enrichment devices such as giant plastic balls and pumpkins to encourage tigers, polar bears, and many other animals to be more active.

Right: The SEACON Fund has supported a research project in Trinidad's capuchin monkeys, among many species throughout the world.

1995
The Daniel F. and Ada L. Rice Conservation Biology and Research Center opens.
Tropic World's interpretive plan is updated.
The zoo helps rescue two brown bear cubs in Alaska.
The Zoo Adventure Passport program is founded.
Office space is constructed around the South Gate.

96
The Society withdraws its support from The Dolphin Connection.
George Rabb steps down as chair of the Species Survival Commission.
Binti Jua the gorilla rescues a boy who falls into the gorilla enclosure.
The Swamp opens.
Peter Crowcroft dies.
Encil Rains dies.

97
The Living Coast opens.

CHAPTER EIGHTEEN

A Flurry of Activity

(1995-Present)

Meanwhile...

International collaborations, Australian land management, and genetic research aside, what was happening on a daily basis? Penny Korhumel Beattie's lesson—that Brookfield Zoo is about people—was more fully realized as the zoo tried to motivate people in addition to educating and entertaining them. More programs were developed to attract people to the zoo and inspire them with the conservation message. And more people were attracted. No one knows if the new programs, new exhibits, popular animals, or bright, sunny days brought them, but in 1996 attendance topped two million.

Beattie would be proud to learn that in 1996, over 95,000 visitors attended Holiday Magic, more than 37,000 people took part in Boo! at the Zoo, Zoo Run Run attracted some 2,500 local runners, Teddy Bear Picnic provided "veterinary" care for too-often-cuddled teddies, and National Pig Day continued to be a big hit. The CONNECTIONS program served over 23,170 students, and more than 216,600 school-group participants visited the zoo. A new event called Animal Athletes, begun two years before, encouraged children to measure their athletic abilities against those of animals, jumping like a kangaroo and balancing like a flamingo.

Above: Participants in Animal Athletes get to race, jump, and test their strength as if they were exotic animals.

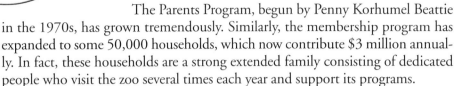

The Parents Program, begun by Penny Korhumel Beattie in the 1970s, has grown tremendously. Similarly, the membership program has expanded to some 50,000 households, which now contribute $3 million annually. In fact, these households are a strong extended family consisting of dedicated people who visit the zoo several times each year and support its programs.

To serve audiences unfamiliar with the zoo, an educational outreach endeavor called Zoo Adventure Passport, or ZAP, was created in 1995. Twice a month, zoo staff and volunteers visit three branches of the Chicago Public Library on Chicago's west side to deliver programs that increase awareness of the zoo and its programs.

Because of another new enterprise, many more women have become involved in the zoo's leadership. Although the Society's history has included numerous remarkable women—among them Edith Rockefeller McCormick, Grace Olive Wiley, Ellen Thorne Smith, and Penny Korhumel Beattie, as well as Edie Duckworth and Pris Meyers on the Board of Trustees—the female sex has been underrepresented at that level. In 1991, the new director of development, Mena Boulanger, puzzled over how to raise more support for the zoo. She realized that many energetic, well-connected women in the Chicago area were not involved in the Society. In October 1992, she worked with trustees Beverly Blettner and Meyers to create the 75-person Women's Board in order to extend the Society's presence in new areas and secure additional financial resources.

In just a few years, the Women's Board has been tremendously successful. It took over the reins of the black-tie Whirl, increasing the party's revenues from just over $100,000 to $330,000 in 1996. Each year, on the day following the event, Women's Board members take advantage of the huge tent put up for the Whirl to put on a special program for the Boys and Girls Club. They've sponsored inner-city schools to attend the Education Department's Zoo Camp and made it possible for family-service shelters to enjoy Holiday Magic. Also, they've been adept at community outreach by attracting new audiences from distant neighborhoods.

Above: During Members' Nights, members get a few summer evenings for themselves to see the animals behind the scenes and participate in other activities, such as face painting.

Above: The original Women's Board and George Rabb (left) gather in *Habitat Africa!*, then under construction, to celebrate the new group's first meeting. Carter Brooksher (third from right, first row) was the Women's Board's first president.

Responding to the Extraordinary

In the zoo's unpredictable environment, staff members are prepared to respond to many different situations. Often these situations test the abilities and the resourcefulness of the people involved.

For instance, in 1995, the zoo received a phone call from the Alaska Fish and Game Department, which said that two six-month-old brown bear cubs needed a home. Living on Admiralty Island in Alaska, the siblings had wandered the wilderness for two weeks after their mother was killed by a reprobate. The zoo dispatched 35-year veteran keeper Jim Rowell, who was attending an annual bear conference in Fairbanks, Alaska, at the time, to help rescue and transport the bears. Working with the Alaska Fish and Game Department and island residents, Rowell helped catch the cubs and escorted them back to Brookfield, where they were made at home in Bear Grottos.

Craftspeople, too, are continually challenged to be creative. Occasionally, artists are brought in to work on special projects, such as a life-size bronze statue honoring Samson and new murals in Tropic World, but mostly the work is done in-house.

Above: Brown bear cubs Angoon-Axhi (left) and Kootznoowoo-Jim have adapted well to their home in Brookfield after being rescued from a risky existence in the wilds of Alaska's Admiralty Island. The bears were named in honor of keepers Axhi Dardovski and Jim Rowell (inset).

Right: To commemorate famed silverback gorilla Samson, sculptor Edwin Bogucki crafted a life-size likeness in bronze. The statue stands at the entrance to the queue leading to Tropic World.

In 1991, one exhibit designer was called upon to fabricate a totem pole for the sea lion and walrus underwater viewing area. At the same time, a welder "built" an anchor that was placed in front of Seven Seas Dolphinarium. (The anchor is actually hollow and very light.) For the 1995 renovation of Tropic World, one of the zoo's exhibit developers designed a hot-air balloon basket that looks to be made of woven materials but is strong enough to handle wheelchairs and heavy foot traffic. And the design of the new fence around Roosevelt Fountain is elegantly simple, incorporating images of animals, somewhat like the North Gate.

For its part, the Security Department routinely handles many different situations. Brookfield Zoo is the only one in the country with a fully trained security staff. (Every other zoo relies on police from local parks or a similar system.) Over the years they've saved choking babies and adults, rescued heart-attack victims, administered first aid for all kinds of minor injuries, found lost children, jump-started hundreds of cars, changed thousands of flat tires, and handled crowd control on summer days. Most often they're unnoticed, but they maintain a sense of calm and safety throughout the park.

Above: The new fence surrounding Roosevelt Fountain, elegant and functional, incorporates the Chicago Zoological Society's logo showing running bison.

Right: The totem pole he created to highlight the Pacific Northwest theme at one of Seven Seas' underwater viewing areas towers over exhibit designer Rick Cortes.

What is perhaps the most publicized situation in the zoo's history involved the Security Department, but the focus of the event was not a staff member. In August 1996, a three-year-old boy climbed the planter-fence surrounding the gorilla exhibit in Tropic World and fell about 20 feet to the bottom of the enclosure. Binti Jua, an eight-year-old western lowland gorilla who was carrying her 17-month-old daughter on her back, rushed to the rescue, scooping up the youngster and carrying him to the keepers' access door, where staff were waiting.

The episode transpired in only a few minutes, but the initial media frenzy lasted weeks. A visitor had caught the rescue on videotape, and the footage of the gorilla cradling the human boy was so touching, it drew attention from as far away as Australia, Iceland, and Moscow.

Reporters descended upon the zoo. Stories appeared on *Good Morning America*, *CBS This Morning*, *The Today Show*, *Larry King Live*, *Dateline NBC*; in publications such as *USA Today* and *People* magazine; and in hundreds of newspapers around the world. Binti Jua was named *Newsweek*'s Hero of the Year and was one of *People*'s 25 Most Intriguing People of the Year. *The Tonight Show*'s Jay Leno featured Binti Jua skits for several consecutive nights, and a song about the gorilla took to the airwaves. Even Hillary Rodham Clinton mentioned Binti Jua in her speech at the Democratic National Convention, held in Chicago later in the year.

The story propelled the zoo's behavioral training program into the spotlight. Binti had received maternal training prior to the birth of her daughter, Koola, because she herself was hand-raised and there was concern that she wouldn't know how to be a parent. The maternal training, which included skills such as cradling, breast-feeding, and, perhaps most importantly, handing a youngster to keepers, may have helped save the boy.

"One friend suggested that I appear here tonight with Binti, the child-saving gorilla from the Brookfield Zoo. You know, as this friend explained, Binti is a typical Chicagoan, tough on the outside but with a heart of gold underneath."

Hillary Rodham Clinton
Current First Lady

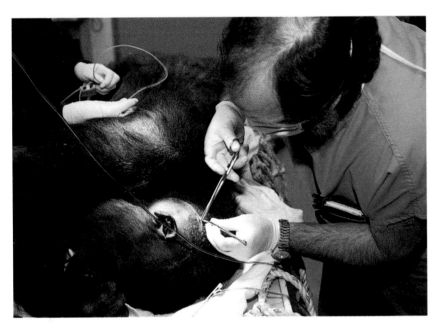

Above: Veterinarian Dr. Tom Meehan carries out a follow-up procedure after zoo and Loyola doctors performed groundbreaking brain surgery on Chicory, saving the gorilla's life.

Left: Binti Jua, here with daughter Koola, was catapulted to international fame in 1996 when she assisted to safety an unconscious young boy who had fallen into the gorilla enclosure in Tropic World.

The incident followed a few years behind another one concerning a gorilla, this one less publicized but quite important. Alarmed by seizures that Chicory, a nine-year-old male gorilla, suffered throughout 1994, the Primate Department decided to have him undergo a magnetic resonance imaging test, which revealed a life-threatening, lemon-size tumor in his brain. Certain that the growing tumor would kill Chicory if left unchecked, the zoo committed to saving his life.

A few days later, neurologists Dr. Doug Anderson and Dr. Andrew Zelby of Loyola University Medical Center, assisted by the zoo's veterinarians and primate keepers, attempted to remove the tumor—the first time brain surgery had ever been performed on a gorilla. After 14 hours, several of which were spent cutting through the primate's tremendously thick skull, the tumor was successfully removed. Chicory was returned to the zoo's animal hospital, where he recovered for several days before being transported back to Tropic World. Shortly after he rejoined his troop, the reigning silverback, Abe, died of old age, making Chicory the highest-ranking male. As the silverback, he would eventually maintain peace within the group and play a role in the zoo's program for breeding endangered gorillas, as Samson had years earlier. The surgeons remarked that the brain surgery was an opportunity for medical science to repay the debt it owes for years of research on animals that has provided valuable information on human health.

Planning for the Future

Besides dealing with the immediacy of these situations, the zoo is busy planning for the future. A $16 million bond issuance by the Forest Preserve District in 1993 effected a 10-year capital development plan. The bond issuance has allowed for $6 million in annual renovations, to be used over a three-year period, and $10 million toward exhibit developments such as the new animal hospital, Phase I of *Habitat Africa!*, and two new exhibits, The Swamp and The Living Coast.

The Society agreed to raise $20 million in matching funds against the $10 million for exhibit developments plus an additional $10 million promised down the road. The Society also pledged to raise, on top of the $20 million, an additional $5 million for the zoo's endowment fund. Part of this fundraising effort was the single biggest gift the zoo has ever received: a $2.5 million donation from the Regenstein Foundation to help create The Swamp.

The $2.5 million gift is appropriate because the new 10-year plan is the largest renovation effort undertaken by the zoo throughout its history. The plan identifies eight exhibit developments, five major interpretive programs, four major visitor-service developments, two support facilities, programs for audience and staff development, and a repair and improvement schedule.

The number of projects underscores the fact that despite new exhibits and improvements in fundraising, there are still many areas of the zoo that need attention. Priority has been given to the exhibits most in need of repair or renovation, such as the old Primate House. Other, less prominent exhibits, such as Small Mammal House, have languished at the bottom of the wish list, awaiting the day when enough funds are available to address their shortcomings.

As part of the 10-year plan, teams have been mobilized to develop ideas for quadrants within the zoo; new exhibits such as The Swamp, The Living Coast, Phase II of *Habitat Africa!*, and a revamped Children's Zoo; and new signs for Tropic World and Indian Lake, among other exhibits. Other groups address the visitor experience on entering the zoo, basic visitor needs within the zoo, and the need for office space and a new library.

Each team—comprised of a mix of animal keepers, educators, designers, administrators, groundskeepers, craftspeople, visitor-services personnel, and others—is given a timetable, a budget, and a set of objectives that meets the zoo's mission. Under guidance by the zoo's trustees, a committee of three senior staff members—Patty McGill, curator of birds; Ralph Piland, manager of buildings and grounds; and Cynthia Vernon, director of education—has been assembled to oversee all of these projects.

Team members are encouraged to visit other museums and zoos to gather ideas. Brainstorming sessions are commonplace, as are visits by architects from around the country and by experts from other companies and institutions, including Walt Disney World and McDonald's. All efforts are made to ensure that new exhibits are groundbreaking and, above all, effective in communicating the zoo's vision. (It is worth noting that the more than 100 staff members who are involved in these teams assume these additional responsibilities without relief from their old.)

As part of the plan, new buildings for additional office space were completed at the South Gate in 1995. For years, new employees kept taking up diminishing space, and everyone was stuffed into shared offices and odd nooks. The situation was untenable from the point of view of members, who had to navigate confusing corridors to hunt down Membership Services in the Administration Building; docents and volunteers, who had to climb a steep set of stairs; and the Development Department, which couldn't properly court potential donors in its cramped quarters. The cheapest solution was trailers, but so many lined the south service road that it resembled a trailer park.

Money from undesignated bequests allowed the zoo to add office space on both sides of the South Gate. In 1995, the Membership, Education, and Development departments moved in, as did others, such as the Travel Department and first-aid personnel. While the zoo was always reluctant to invest in employee amenities when improvements for animals and visitors were more necessary, in this case it was a wise investment.

The Board of Trustees has been much involved in the planning activities. In addition to its $20 million fundraising campaign, it has inspired the staff to create new exhibits that in turn inspire the public to take positive conservation actions. They are led in these endeavors by current Board president Clyde W. Reighard, who succeeded fellow Northern Trust executive Philip Sweet in 1993. Reighard had become involved with the zoo in 1982 when he offered his assistance to Society treasurer Larry Gougler. A life-long zoo aficionado, Reighard officially joined the Board in 1984.

Recently retired from his post as head of international affairs at the Northern Trust Company, Reighard is fortunately able to commit much of his time to the zoo. He works closely with Rabb, who recently celebrated his 20th year as director. For his part, Rabb was recently honored with the American Zoo and Aquarium Association's Marlin Perkins Award for his longtime leadership in the zoo business. (Sadly, Rabb's predecessor, Peter Crowcroft, died in 1996, as did Encil Rains.)

"THE ULTIMATE TEAM"

In a 1996 *Bison* magazine article entitled "Team Players: Brookfield Zoo's Approach to Creating New Exhibits," director of education Cynthia Vernon detailed the benefits of relying on a variety of staff members in the process of developing exhibits.

"...the team approach to exhibit development has been embraced at Brookfield Zoo, in part because it exemplifies and fosters the values zoo staff have identified as most important to the organization: cooperation, responsibility, involvement, and recognition. We believe that involving staff from all areas and levels in the organization not only makes for a better exhibit, but also strengthens commitment to the overall mission of the zoo. And that's the ultimate team."

Clyde W. Reighard

"In my business life, I've traveled all the world over, and I've seen zoos everywhere. I am fully persuaded that right here at home we have in Brookfield Zoo one of the finest places of its kind, one that is making a difference for all of us."

Clyde W. Reighard
Current Society Chairman

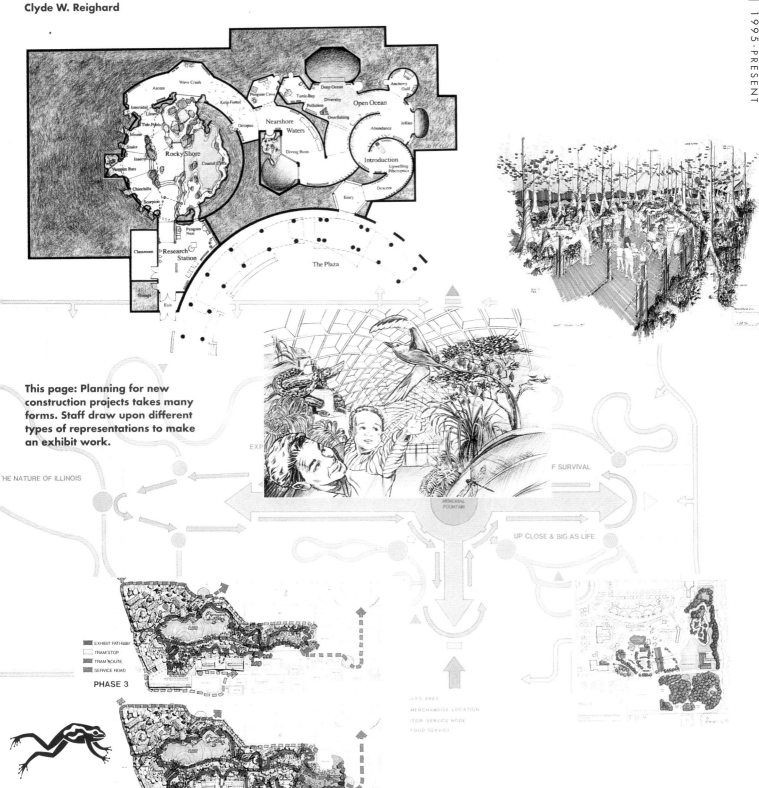

This page: Planning for new construction projects takes many forms. Staff draw upon different types of representations to make an exhibit work.

A Day in the Life

The last few years have been the busiest time Brookfield Zoo has seen. Never before has the Society had its fingers in so many different pies—and with the extensive planning efforts underway, chances are good that the number of undertakings will only continue to grow.

In 1996, the zoo's budget stood at close to $38 million—quite a change from the anticipated budget of $50,000 in 1926—and the staff had multiplied to 400 full- and part-time employees, with an additional 600 seasonal workers in the summer. Along with 300 volunteers, nearly 300 docents communicated the zoo's messages by serving as park greeters and exhibit guides, manning special "touch carts" with interesting animal materials, teaching classes, and, perhaps most importantly, engaging visitors throughout the zoo.

Even discounting the invaluable help of 1,200 seasonal workers and volunteers, the variety of activities undertaken by the 400 regular employees during one recent day is remarkable. Really, operating Brookfield Zoo is akin to running a town, with businesses, residences, and schools.

"WHOEVER IS BORROWING FRAN CROWLEY'S CHAIR..."

Random excerpts from the minutes of a staff meeting held in 1995 illustrate the variety of ideas, projects, and daily operations underway at the zoo at the time.

- G. Rabb met with Dr. Murnane regarding continuation of the joint pathology program.
- Discussion of the programmatic dimensions of the 1996 budget have begun.
- The Women's Board presented Chairman Reighard with a $318,000 check representing the net proceeds of the Whirl.
- The Zoological Committee of the Forest Preserve District meets Tuesday.
- The young male okapi has gained ten pounds in one week and continues to do well.
- Kali dolphin is practicing her fish-whacking behavior on the kayak with the trainer inside the boat.
- Basilla walrus is off-exhibit, recovering from removal of a small stone from between her teeth.
- Steel is in for alligator holding in The Swamp. Plaster and exhibits work begins this week.
- Whoever is borrowing Fran Crowley's chair is asked to please return it promptly.
- Membership figures are at goal for the year. Members' nights are June 17 and June 24-25.
- Trustee McKeever will celebrate his birthday at a surprise party at BZ on Thursday.
- C. Vernon met with representatives from other Chicago cultural institutions regarding use of sophisticated networking opportunities available through the Internet.
- Over 11,500 people attended the Columbia HealthCare picnic.
- Over 7,500 people used Motor Safari on Saturday—a new record for a single day.
- A review of the Wage and Salary program is underway.
- DDB Needham will be in on Tuesday to review the television advertising campaign.
- Promotions for Animal Athletes begin this week for two weeks.
- The Feast with the Beasts press briefing generated several media contacts.
- Seven Seas interpretive graphics installation continues, with projected completion in two weeks.
- The Society's Planning and Facilities Committee will meet on June 22.
- Representative Kubik visits the zoo Monday afternoon.
- Speaker of the House Newt Gingrich's visit to the zoo continues to generate news coverage.

On that day, security staff were trained to give first aid, control gang activity, and manage crowds. Artists designed T-shirts, banners, signs, and brochures. Carpenters built interpretive signs, repaired buildings, and engineered enclosures for the animals. Photographers and videographers documented animal births and other notable events. A "special populations" coordinator helped physically impaired visitors around the zoo and took the zoo's messages to those in the community who weren't mobile.

On that day, cooks whipped up a gourmet meal for a dinner honoring donors, as well as chicken sandwiches and hot dogs for visitors. Other service personnel poured drinks, sold stuffed animals and hamburgers, and drove Motor Safari trams.

On that day, public relations staff wrote press releases and ushered reporters. The Finance Department worried over accounts payable, the payroll, and cash flow. The Development Department planned a fundraiser, wrote grant applications, and helped Board members identify potential donors.

On that day, the people who care for the animals not only ministered to their charges but carried out conservation and research projects as well.

On that day, painters and roofers, editors and educators, secretaries and librarians—each made their contribution to the goals and activities of Brookfield Zoo.

And on that day, another visitor walked through the gates to experience the wonders of the natural world in the unique context of a zoo that had found a mission in its long, remarkable evolution.

Left and above: Every day, more than the animals are tended. Carpenters, grounds staff, and painters—among many others—work hard to ensure a positive visitor experience.

" Upon behalf of the Chicago Zoological Society, I welcome you here today to share with us a dedication ceremony to which the Society has been looking forward for a long time…. As new methods of display are developed, there will be changes and additions as there may be freshness and novelty."

Strangely, although John McCutcheon's words were written for an opening day more than 60 years ago, so much of his speech has rung true for recent exhibit openings. They have come one on top of another: the newly interpreted Tropic World in May 1995; The Swamp the following March, to much public interest; The South American Marketplace at The Living Coast later, in fall 1996; and in May 1997, The Living Coast itself.

As visitors flow through the new exhibits and the animals become acclimated to their surroundings, the planning continues. A *Habitat Africa!* team now wrestles with the issues involved in recreating a segment of the Ituri Forest. The exhibit is to feature okapis, an animal with which the zoo has had so much breeding and management success. The team is also examining how to best demonstrate how the forest people live compatibly with their natural resources.

Another team, meanwhile, considers issues of early childhood education as it plans to renovate Children's Zoo and Small Mammal House. So much has been discovered lately about how children learn. The question is, how can the zoo best use that information to help children learn to care about the environment? Experts are called in and discussions begin.

Still another team works on renovating the north entrance experience. An Indian Lake team designs a wetland and considers additional interpretation. Another group considers what food and merchandise outlets are needed in each area. And, yes, the Development Department, together with the trustees, works hard to raise funds for all of these incredible dreams.

Moreover, the zoo and its governing Society truly believe in these dreams and the worth of the enterprise that is Brookfield Zoo. Solid evidence is a set of 1996 projects financed through $10 million in bonds that the zoo will repay. These projects include improvements to the north entrance, a gas-powered electricity-generation facility to safeguard the electrical supply and save money, a new tram fleet that is more accessible for handicapped people, and The South American Marketplace to complement The Living Coast.

Right: Within The Living Coast, people see animals living as they would along South America's western coastline, but they also learn how land and sea creatures depend on each other and their environment for survival—and how those interactions in turn affect life in Chicago and the Midwest.

Epilogue

The evolution continues. As Seymour Simon pointed out in 1964 and George Dunne reiterated in 1984, Brookfield Zoo is a forward-looking institution. Despite its many successes in animal husbandry and exhibit design, the zoo is constantly driven to move ahead, not resting on its laurels. This impatience is inextricably linked to its conservation vision—an outgrowth of the need to educate society about the severity of the environmental crisis before time runs out.

Or perhaps John McCutcheon cast a magical spell upon the park on that opening day.

The zoo has gone through tremendous changes in its 60-plus years, not all of them easy transitions. But it has grown into its maturity, and that has its own power, and its own charm.

"A new zoo is like everything else that is new. It takes some time to get it running smoothly. A new house is not really charming until it has been lived in and the newness softened by love and occupancy."

Afterword

By George B. Rabb

This history is the work of one person: Andrea Friederici Ross. At the same time, it is also the work of many other wonderful people from the very inception of the idea that came to be Brookfield Zoo.

As with many histories, the events recounted in these pages generally reflect changes or circumstances that are out of the ordinary. There simply is not room in a single book to record the myriad efforts of all who contributed routinely through the years by their diligence in caring for animals, and people, and the place itself. Yet the love in their labor shows through, as does willingness to learn from mistakes and successes.

Looking ahead, it is gratifying that trustees, employees, and dedicated volunteers—the Brookfield Zoo team—are committed to a challenging vision of the zoo's multifold mission. What is the significance of this commitment? Chicago has been extraordinarily fortunate to have had visionary business, professional, and social leaders who have given us exceptional cultural institutions: the major universities, The Art Institute of Chicago, the Field Museum, Chicago Symphony, and Lyric Opera. Our institutions devoted to the living world—Morton Arboretum, Chicago Botanic Garden, Shedd Aquarium, Lincoln Park Zoo, and Brookfield Zoo—are on the threshold of recognition as part of this distinguished array. We need to promote ourselves in this vein for all we offer, primarily because we have key relevance to the sustainable and harmonious relationship our species must achieve with the rest of the living world and the environment we share.

An important illustration of our value locally is that our institutions joined in 1996 with 30 other institutions, conservation organizations, and governmental agencies to start the Chicago Wilderness initiative. This collective effort is intended to help manage the surprisingly rich biological diversity of the metropolitan area on a sustainable basis. It has the direct involvement of thousands of citizens working as volunteers in environmental restoration.

What gives me optimism in this instance is the remarkable evolution that Brookfield Zoo has manifested, as so well reflected in this history. In this sense, it is a living organism. An organism important as an exemplar for its species—zoos and aquariums everywhere—because it is committed to evolving further as a conservation center. May it forever prosper and progress in this vital role for human society while demonstrating the utmost concern for the welfare of its animal ambassadors and the well-being of their species. And finally, may it never lose its joyfulness in inspiring all to care for the marvelous variety of life!

"When we can make scientific deductions of 1923
the actions and reactions of animals we will find ourselves
in a position to reach the human being.
We must get nearer animals to reach the human soul."
Edith Rockefeller McCormick

1922

"We miss half the joy of life if we do
not know nature, and this Zoological Garden
will help our people to that knowledge."

Charles Wacker

1927

"It is only a matter of a few
years until all animals will
have to be reared in captivity if we are to preserve the
various species for scientific
and educational purposes.... It is my purpose, with
the approval and cooperation of the members of the
Society, to make our animal
collection an educational
factor of considerable
importance to Chicago and
suburbs. It should take its
place in this respect along
with art institutes, museums
and similar institutions."

Edward Bean

"Fundamentally...the object of a zoological garden is 1922
first of all to preserve the wild life of this country....
In America nearly every form of wild life can be
found, but nearly every species has already been so
desperately ravaged that some have lost the struggle and surely many others are going to. The little
that is left must be saved, must be saved soon, and
can best be saved in the American zoological park."

Edward Bean

1954

"I think we can count
on human nature
as our ally. Human
nature will not
change, at least not
in its fundamentals,
and we know from
experience that
securely planted within the human breast
is a deep abiding
interest in animals....
The love of children
for animal stories is
something inherited
at birth and passed
down through countless generations."

John McCutcheon

" It will be the purpose of
the Chicago Zoological
Society in the years to come
to maintain a beautiful,
distinguished, and interesting zoological park where
old and young may gain
health, pleasure, knowledge and understanding,
and where, in connection
with our great collection
of birds and beasts
humanely maintained, we
may accumulate scientific
data of value to all."

Clay Judson

1934

1956

"It does not now seem so important to aspire to maintain a great catalog of animals as it does to exhibit them with feeling and with the expression of providing the whole story of their mode of living and place in nature."

Robert Bean

1965

"People that understand animals are sympathetic to their needs and will make efforts to preserve them. Zoos are in an advantageous position to present this education.... In addition, we must take positive actions towards propagating these endangered forms.... The day is gone when all we needed to consider was whether the price was right. Now we must consider whether or not we have the moral right."

Ron Blakely

"It has become increasingly apparent through the last few years that sooner or later zoos are going to be making spectacular and far-reaching strides in [education].... We have, not only in every zoo, but in every cage in every zoo, a story to tell, and this story is vital to our public. For the sake of us all, even urban man has to realize that he is, and must function as, a cog in the wheel of nature."

George Rabb and Ron Blakely

1965

1968

"I aim to help to establish Brookfield Zoo as a great cultural institution...an educational institution in the broadest sense. The great zoo of the future will not be the zoo that breeds the most bongos, or sells the most hot dogs. Its glory will not be measured in terms of the size of its budget, the number of species, the height of its elephant, or the age of its chimpanzee. It will be measured by the extent to which it changes the attitudes of its visitors, and through them, affects the culture of the nation."

Peter Crowcroft

1981

"A zoo has to be people-oriented. It has to do with the kinds of things that turn people on to it more and make people feel the zoo is important to them in providing the basics of life—pleasure."

Penny Korhumel

1995

"Our basic mission statement has remained the same: research, entertainment of the public, education, conservation. These things still continue in our new mission statement. But we've now realized that a very important part of it is a harmonious relationship between people and animals, ecosystems; the idea that we are all interrelated and have to live together.... So after people come to the zoo, they go away with a message.... I think it's a very important one."

Philip W. K. Sweet, Jr.

Forest Preserve District, Society, and Zoo Leaders (1919-1997)

Year	Forest Preserve District Presidents	Forest Preserve District General Superintendents	Chicago Zoological Society Board Presidents*	Brookfield Zoo Directors
1919	Peter Reinberg			
1920				
1921	Daniel Ryan		John T. McCutcheon	
1922	Anton Cermak			
1923				George F. Morse, Jr.
1924				
1925				
1926				
1927		M. S. Szymczak		Edward Bean
1928				
1929		Charles G. Sauers		
1930				
1931	Emmett Whealan			
1932				
1933				
1934	Clayton Smith			
1935				
1936				
1937				
1938				
1939				
1940				
1941				
1942				
1943				
1944				
1945				Robert Bean (Acting Director)
1946	William Erickson			
1947				Robert Bean
1948				
1949			Clay Judson	
1950				
1951				
1952				
1953				
1954	Daniel Ryan			
1955				
1956				
1957				
1958			William R. Dickinson, Jr.	
1959				
1960				
1961	John Duffy			
1962	Seymour Simon			
1963				
1964		Arthur L. Janura		Ron Blakely, Encil Rains
1965				
1966	Richard Ogilvie			
1967				
1968				Peter Crowcroft
1969	George Dunne			
1970				
1971				
1972				
1973				
1974				
1975			Corwith Hamill	
1976				George B. Rabb
1977				
1978				
1979				
1980				
1981			Penny Korhumel	
1982				
1983				
1984				
1985				
1986				
1987			Philip W. K. Sweet, Jr.	
1988				
1989				
1990	Richard Phelan			
1991		Joseph N. Nevius		
1992				
1993			Clyde W. Reighard	
1994	John Stroger, Jr.			
1995				
1996				
1997				

* Title changed to chairman in 1974

1934	1,292,720
1935	1,528,772
1936	1,573,661
1937	1,762,457
1938	2,089,223
1939	1,590,861
1940	1,395,531
1941	1,516,111
1942	1,027,768
1943	669,769
1944	848,259
1945	985,912
1946	1,319,030
1947	1,426,480
1948	1,471,630
1949	1,439,212
1950	1,565,290
1951	1,566,826
1952	1,501,920
1953	1,745,810
1954	1,745,810
1955	1,553,856
1956	1,517,863
1957	1,642,346
1958	1,643,837
1959	1,436,568
1960	1,601,568
1961	2,015,000
1962	2,018,495
1963	2,280,292
1964	2,088,258
1965	1,907,327
1966	1,763,687
1967	1,873,419
1968	1,917,461
1969	1,905,298
1970	2,146,714
1971	2,209,052
1972	1,964,382
1973	2,038,413
1974	2,022,597
1975	1,986,680
1976	1,886,158
1977	1,435,549
1978	1,458,751
1979	1,522,204
1980	1,696,836
1981	1,788,067
1982	2,082,643
1983	1,759,688
1984	1,917,809
1985	1,804,368
1986	1,838,954
1987	1,944,870
1988	1,991,541
1989	1,914,610
1990	1,942,628
1991	2,000,448
1992	1,924,242
1993	1,984,050
1994	2,113,329
1995	1,868,442
1996	2,076,519
TOTAL	108,547,871

Recorded Attendance (1934-1996)*

Methods for calculating attendance have varied over the years. These numbers reflect the zoo's best estimate for each year.

Sources

During research on this book, hundreds of sources were used, including newspaper articles, interviews, Brookfield Zoo and Forest Preserve District of Cook County documents, zoo publications, original historical correspondence, meeting minutes, and publications not specific to the zoo. This is as complete a list as possible.

Chicago Zoological Society Publications:
50-year Anniversary History by Corwith Hamill and John McCutcheon; yearbooks from 1927 to 1933; *20-year Anniversary Book* by Christopher Holabird; guidebooks; *Ziggy Fund Newsletter; Bison;* annual reports; *Bridge; Brookfield Briefs; Bandar-log;* and *Docent Journal.*

Graham, Ralph. *Rhino! Rhino!* Chicago: Chicago Zoological Society, 1949.

Chicago Zoological Society Documents and Materials:
Trustee meeting minutes; original correspondence; Edward Bean's daily reminder; John McCutcheon's papers; recent meeting minutes; press releases; fundraising materials; Institute of Museum Services grant applications; *Zoo World* tapes; and old films and audiotapes.

Nonzoo Publications:
"Baby Boom hits Chicago's Brookfield Zoo," *Life,* Vol. 11, No. 18, 1941, pp 38-39.

Bean, Edward H. "Zoological Gardens," *Parks & Recreation,* September/October 1922, pp 59-66.

Bentley, Richard; Ryerson, Alice Judson; and Smith, Ellen Thorne. *Clay Judson 1892-1960 as seen by Richard Bentley, Alice Judson Ryerson, Ellen Thorne Smith.* From a program in memory of Clay Judson, January 23, 1961.

Birmingham, Stephen. *The grandes dames.* New York: Simon and Schuster, 1982.

Bishop, Glenn A. *Chicago's Accomplishments and Leaders.* Chicago: Bishop, 1932.

Brady, Erika. "First U.S. panda, shanghaied in China, stirred up a ruckus," *Smithsonian,* Vol. 14, No. 9, December 1983, pp 145-164.

Brookfield History Book Committee. *Brookfield, Illinois A History.* Brookfield, 1994.

Cherfas, Jeremy. *Zoo 2000.* London: British Broadcasting Corp., 1984.

Crowcroft, Peter. *The Zoo.* Australia: Mathews/Hutchinson, 1978.

Derks, Scott. *The value of a dollar: prices and incomes in the United States, 1860-1989.* Detroit: Gale, 1994.

Dunn, Betty. "An elephant spends thirty years in solitude," *Life,* Vol. 71, No. 17, 1971, pp 79-80.

"Fecundity in the Chicago Zoo," *Life,* Vol. 17, No. 15, 1944, pp 41-42.

Hahn, Emily. *Animal Gardens.* New York: Doubleday & Co., Inc., 1967.

Harkness, Ruth. *The Lady and the Panda.* New York: Carrick & Evans, 1938.

Harris, Leon. "New Life at the American Zoo," *Town & Country,* March 1989, p 163.

Judson, Sylvia Shaw. *For Gardens and Other Places.* Chicago: Henry Regnery, n.d. (1967?).

Keysor, Charles W. "Pioneering at Chicago's Zoo," *Nature Magazine,* May 1947, pp 258-260, 276.

Koebner, Linda. *Zoo Book.* New York: Doherty Associates, 1994.

Lewis, George. *I Loved Rogues: The Life of an Elephant Tramp.* Seattle: Superior, 1978.

Luoma, Jon R. "Brave New Zoo," *Chicago,* May 1989, pp 133-135, 166-167.

McCutcheon, John T. *Drawn From Memory.* Indianapolis: Bobbs-Merrill, 1950.

McCutcheon, John T. *John McCutcheon's Book.* Chicago: Caxton Club, 1948.

Pawley, Ray. "Perspective: To Catch a Wild Bird," *Animal Kingdom,* August/September 1980, pp 22-23.

Rabb, George B. "The Changing Roles of Zoological Parks in Conserving Biological Diversity," *American Zoologist,* Vol. 34, 1994, pp 159-164.

Rabb, George B. "Education and Zoos," *The American Biology Teacher,* April 1968, pp 291-296.

Rabb, George B. "Facing Up to Conservation Education," AAZPA Conference, September 1985.

Rabb, George B. "The Unicorn Experiment," *Curator,* Vol. 12, 1969, pp 257-262.

Raven, Harry C. "Further Adventures of Meshie," *Natural History,* Vol. 33, 1933.

Raven, Harry C. "Meshie: The Child of a Chimpanzee," *Natural History,* Vol. 32, 1932.

Speidel, George. Personal letter to Loren Osman. July 1, 1990.

Tuson, John. "The ideal zoo," *Animal Keeper,* No. 2, 1995, pp 40-42.

van Reken, Donald L. *Getz Farm, Lakewood: The Farm that Was a Zoo.* Michigan, 1983.

Who's Who in Chicago. Chicago: A.N. Marquis Co., 1945.

Newspaper Articles:
Associated Press reports, *Brookfield News, Chicago Daily Journal, Chicago Daily News, Chicago Daily Times,* the *Chicago Tribune, The Evening Bulletin* (Philadelphia), *The Grand Rapids Herald, Grossdale Gazette, International Herald Tribune, Riverside News, Suburban Magnet,* United Press International.

Other Sources:
Oral histories, letters and notes from individuals, and Forest Preserve District meeting minutes and records.

Acknowledgments

Of tremendous help throughout the research involved in this book was Dr. V. Jon Bentz, who interviewed dozens of individuals. Thanks, too, to those who agreed to be interviewed: Robert Bean, Penny Korhumel Beattie, Ted Beattie, Edward McCormick Blair, Jr., Ron Blakely, Herman Buttron, Peter Crowcroft, Bob Cruse, Edie Duckworth, Frank Farwell, Lester Fisher, Larry Gougler, Corky Hamill, Mae Rose Jana, Bob Johnson, Larry Kozerski, Mike Love, John T. McCutcheon, Jr., Terrie McLean, Frank Michalek, Gail Nachel, Mari Paget, Pamela Parker, Ray Pawley, Pete Price, George Rabb, Mary Rabb, Clyde Reighard, Jim Riley, Jim Rowell, Bill Rutherford, Lillian Ryzenga, Louis Schauer, Ralph Small, Carol Sodaro, Vince Sodaro, George Speidel, Ed Steiner, Pat Stout, Phil Sweet, Craig Tichelar, Ed Vondra, Leroy Woodruff, Jr., and Ron Zdrubecky. Joyce Greening and several other transcriptionists helped type out the hundreds of hours of interviews—an invaluable aid.

Many thanks to my reviewers, including Karin Nelson, Chris Howes, Jill Allread, Joyce Barloga, Pamela Freese, Peter Friederici, Sarah Myers, Craig Pugh, Carol Saunders and Greg Melaik. Without their perspective, honesty, and insight, this project would have been impossible.

Thanks to Lou Schauer and Peter Freeman for their expert legal advice.

Many local residents and staff members submitted their stories in writing, helping round out the zoo experience. Thanks for the memories!

Thanks to memorabilia collectors Bob Salika, Carol and Vince Sodaro, and Ron Zdrubecky for sharing their impressive collections.

Thanks must go to staff members at the Forest Preserve District of Cook County, the Brookfield Historical Society, the Chicago Historical Society, the Lake County Historical Society, the Oak Park Historical Society, the State Historical Society of Wisconsin, the American Museum of Natural History, the Library of Congress, Newberry Library, the Illinois State Historical Library, Hull House Association, Quaker Oats, Shedd Aquarium, the *Chicago Tribune*, and numerous libraries around the Chicago area (Berkeley, Elmhurst, Brookfield, Skokie, Northwestern University, and Oak Park, among others) who helped dig up old newspapers, WPA information, photographs, speeches, and other helpful materials.

Sincere thanks to the John D. and Catherine T. MacArthur Foundation, which provided funding for moving this history from manuscript to publication.

So many zoo staff members helped, in particular Nancy Pajeau, Jim Schulz, Howie Greenblatt, Nancy Bent, Lucy Greer, Helene Fitzsimmons, Nancy Watson, Mena Boulanger, Linda Rucins, Gloria Mezera, and Davida Kalina.

Thanks to my friend April Arnold for her expert advice and much-appreciated support.

Many thanks to editor Chris Howes for holding me to a painfully high standard of quality, always aiming for perfection. He embodies the Brookfield Zoo mentality.

Many thanks to zoo designer Krista Mozdzierz-Skach for lending her design eye to this project and coordinating the creative end. She came through with flying colors.

Bob Faust and Tanya Quick, of Quick+Faust, did an incredible job on design and layout. Their use of the zoo's layout as the grid, their ideas for "barless" sidebars, their dramatic chapter heads, and so many beautiful little touches add another layer of complexity that zoo folks are certain to appreciate.

Thanks to Jim and precious Gregory, and my wonderful friends and family—all great cheerleaders!

And finally, thanks go to George Rabb, for the opportunity, the faith, and the friendship.

Photographs

PHOTO CREDITS: All photos are property of the Chicago Zoological Society unless indicated. Thanks to Ed Steiner for allowing us to use photographs from his collection. And a tip of the hat to the incredible photographers the zoo has employed over the years, among them Ralph Graham, Leland LaFrance, Rick Search, Mike Greer, and Jim Schulz. Their pictures speak volumes.

ABOUT THE AUTHOR: Andrea Friederici Ross is an employee of Brookfield Zoo. She is a special assistant to the director, working on odd projects as assigned, including staff training, exhibit development, and the occasional history book.